Structured Commodity Finance

Techniques and Applications for Successful Financing Arrangements

Structured Commodity Finance

Techniques and Applications for Successful Financing Arrangements

Emmanuelle Moors

Published by Euromoney Books

in association with

United Nations Conference on Trade and Development

Published by
Euromoney Books
Nestor House, Playhouse Yard
London EC4V 5EX
United Kingdom

Tel: +44 (0) 20 7779 8999 or USA +1 800 437 9997
Fax: +44 (0) 20 7779 8300
www.euromoneybooks.com
E-mail:hotline@euromoneyplc.com

ISBN 1 84374 063 X

Printed in England by Alden.

Contents

About the author

Emmanuelle Moors is a senior financial engineer with Technip Italy SpA, which is part of Technip, a global engineering and construction company of about 18,000 employees worldwide, serving primarily the energy sector.

In 1990 Emmanuelle obtained an MBA (Honors) in Finance and International Business from the Leonard N. Stern School of Business at New York University, where she also worked as a fellow for the L. Glucksman Institute for Research in Securities Markets and as a research assistant in the accounting department. In 1986 she received her undergraduate degree in economics and finance from the Université Paris-IX Dauphine in Paris.

Emmanuelle started her banking career in 1987, gaining experience in both the front and back offices of the New York office of Crédit Commercial de France. After graduating with her MBA, she moved to the City of London, where she joined the Africa group at Bankers Trust Company, widely recognised as one of the pioneers in structured commodity finance. In 1994 she moved to the Structured Commodity Finance group of Standard Bank London. Prior to joining Technip Italy, Emmanuelle was also briefly involved as a finance consultant in developing a B2B market-place for the food commodity sector in Russia.

Over the past decade Emmanuelle has also worked as a consultant and expert for UNCTAD, preparing various research papers and participating in several conferences in the fields of price risk management and structured finance for the commodity sector. Between 1997 and 1999, Emmanuelle also served as contributing editor to *African Business* (IC Publications), Africa's leading English language business magazine, writing the monthly finance section.

She lives in Rome with her partner and her two children.

Acknowledgements

I wish to thank the Commodities Branch of the United Nations Conference on Trade and Development (UNCTAD) for having commissioned the research paper that formed the basis of this book. More particularly, I would like to commend Lamon Rutten, Chief Finance and Energy, for his relentless and excellent work in putting together research papers, expert meetings, conferences and practical workshops, which produced in just a few years what is probably today the most comprehensive body of knowledge in the field of structured finance and price risk management for the commodity sector. Within UNCTAD, I'm also grateful to Friday Youssef for having shared with me her clear and thorough understanding of trade payment instruments and for having designed the supporting exhibits.

I'm also grateful to the following people for their valuable comments and corrections: Nicholas Budd, Stephen Kemp, Alan Linger and Laure Reboul. I shall of course retain full responsibility for all omissions and errors still present in the book.

Emmanuelle Moors
November 2003

Foreword

Nicholas Budd
Senior Partner, Commodity Trade & Finance Group, Denton Wilde Sapte, London

Market practices in the area of international commodity finance have undergone a substantial evolution during the past 20 years, driven by several related factors. Prior to the mid-1980s most financing of physical commodities was provided to commodity producers in origin countries by large international trading companies such as Philipp Brothers, André and Continental Grain (none of which exists today). The trading companies in turn obtained financing at very competitive rates in the form of unsecured short-term financing lines from money-centre banks. Similarly, the international banking community included a number of substantial banks such as Chemical Bank, Irving Trust and Midland Bank (none of which exists today) that knew and understood physical commodity trading, and were able to provide necessary funding with minimum involvement in deal structuring. The world of physical commodity financing was a happy, contented and mutually prosperous place with few unpleasant surprises.

There were some surprises, however, and suddenly they seemed to occur at a compounded and accelerated rate: Tino d'Angelis and the Great Salad Oil Swindle; Billy Sol Estes and the drilling pipe scandal; the Sasetru grain collapse in Argentina; the Mexican and Brazilian debt moratoria; the sudden collapse of Beresfords, Woodhouse, Drake & Carey, Kaines and Hofflinghaus; the mergers and absorption of old-line Dutch trade banks such as Slavensburgs and Helvering; and the withdrawal of many New York banks from physical commodity finance activities. The days of inexpensive and unlimited financing lines to commodity trading companies were brought to an end by these developments. From the mid-1980s, the banks that stayed in the business wanted to be involved in the underlying transaction, ensure that the transaction was well-structured and documented, and that their loans were secured by physical commodities and the proceeds of sale as far as possible. Lawyers were brought in to a degree unheard of in the heyday of the big trading companies, and professional collateral managers were not far behind. No longer were multimillion-dollar trade-finance deals documented by an exchange of telexes between traders.

In the meantime, the fall of the Berlin Wall in 1989 brought with it enormous new demands for working capital finance by the huge Soviet-era metals and oil companies, which were previously financed through Foreign Trade Organisations (FTOs) and Soviet central bank guarantees. Virtually overnight some of the world's largest aluminium and other metals smelters and oil companies were starved for foreign exchange to import spare parts and equipment. These industrial groups were on doubtful footing in terms of ownership, had no reliable financial statements or indeed financial management, operated in a country where the commercial laws and courts were badly in need of updating and refinement, and employed hundreds of thousands of workers. They were also the main source of foreign exchange in the newly privatised economies and financing had to be mobilised very quickly to continue to operate. These companies turned to their western customers, the commodity trading companies and end-users, and the customers turned to their banks. There was no security available for the hundreds of millions of dollars of working capital finance required apart from the physical commodities and export sales proceeds. Structured commodity financing, as we know it 15 years later, to a large extent rose out of the ashes of collapsed commodity trading houses and defunct command economies.

Emmanuelle Moors's book defines and examines the elements of this fast-changing field of international physical commodity financing on a very current basis. She describes the techniques used by bankers to obtain reliable security in circumstances where the local laws are as yet underdeveloped or judicial remedies are slow or unreliable. She describes the use of ancillary products such as casualty and political risk insurance to mitigate risks without distorting the economics of the transaction. She describes the new interest of bank regulators who have decided to reward the banks that follow the best practices as described in the 'specialised lending' treatment in Basle II, and to punish those banks that are casual in their handling of security and commodity price risk management. She has described the role of investment banks and securitisation in the trillion-dollar international commodity trade and related financing and hedging sectors, and she has illustrated these issues with examples and commentary from well-known practitioners.

I believe this book will find a comfortable place not only on the bookshelves of bankers and practitioners, but also in the reading lists of courses offered to young bankers and finance managers. Ms Moors has touched on virtually every important theme within this broad and multidisciplinary area, and provides a good starting point for further investigation on particular topics.

Preface

This book was born out of a research paper entitled *The Role of Collateralised Finance in Funding the Commodity Sector*, the first draft of which I presented in May 1998 at an Expert Meeting organised by the United Nations Conference on Trade and Development (UNCTAD).

Back in the 1990s, anyone marketing structured commodity finance still needed a quasi-religious zeal. Just consider that sections dedicated to 'loans secured by inventory' and 'loans secured by sales receivables' together filled a mere two pages in the 924-page corporate finance book (*Principles of Corporate Finance* by Brealey and Myers) that was on my desk when I joined Bankers Trust in 1991. I was then fortunate enough to work on the first structured commodity finance deal for the Ghana Cocoa Board and this gave me an interest in structured commodity finance that has not abated since. At that time, banks' credit committees were rather sceptical of the ability of these techniques to mitigate the risks of doing business in emerging markets, while borrowers in those markets simply suspected that the banks' hidden agenda was to control their commercial operations. Although tremendous progress had already been made in applying sophisticated risk management techniques to the field of finance, these techniques were largely restricted to corporate finance transactions. With a few notable exceptions, innovations had bypassed the field of commodity finance.

I was therefore surprised when UNCTAD approached me a few months ago and told me that there was interest in the market for a commercial publication of my former research paper. However, as I started to conduct more research for this new edition, I realised that structured trade and commodity finance had become the name of the game. Its principles had even pervaded other finance areas. The emerging markets crises of the late 1990s had finally focused the minds of market players on the tremendous opportunities offered by structured finance to raise funds for the commodity sector despite difficult environments. In recent years structured commodity finance transactions have flourished, while its techniques and applications have evolved continuously in line with changing emerging market environments. Unfortunately, the body of knowledge gathered by market players has remained the privilege of a few.

I believe there is ample scope for structured commodity finance to expand further, serving more financing needs, and reaching more countries and commodities. As a tribute to the pioneers who developed the first structured commodity finance transactions, I wrote this book hoping to contribute to the understanding and diffusion of these innovative techniques.

Emmanuelle Moors
November 2003

Introduction

Finding attractive financing solutions to fund the commodity sector has become crucial because the production and trading of commodities is now largely deregulated, and more competitive and volatile than ever. Without the proper financing, a commodity producer may not be able to expand its facilities; a trading company may think twice before buying from a high-risk country; and an importer may simply go out of business.

Producers, exporters, local merchants, international trading companies, importers, processing companies and other intermediaries – in effect all 'players' in the commodity business – need financing at some time or another, and in particular hard-currency financing. While traders need hard currency to pay for commodity imports, producers do so to pay for a portion of their production costs – for example to import fertiliser or machinery. Likewise, partners in crude oil production joint ventures often need to pay for cash calls in hard currency. Any party hedging its commodity price risk would generally have to pay hard currency for the related cash outlays (premiums, margin requirements and settlement amounts). Provided that foreign exchange risk can be adequately mitigated, hard-currency loans become attractive for a wide range of purposes.

Evolution of commodity financing

The 1980s: financing trading companies on a corporate basis

After the 1982 world debt crisis, it became increasingly difficult for both private and sovereign borrowers in emerging countries to obtain loans from commercial banks. This difficulty was further exacerbated for the commodity sector by worsening terms of trade and increased commodity price volatility. The debt crisis also reduced the availability of trade finance to countries where governments still controlled domestic and international trade, and had previously relied on balance-of-payments support to fund their commodity sector.

By the mid-1980s commodity financing was provided primarily through simple corporate loans to commodity trading companies, which would in turn finance the trading of commodities on their own balance sheet, often on the back of red-clause letters of credit. Typically, trading companies would be prepaying commodity exporters and extending favourable payment terms to commodity importers. Banks would not scrutinise the terms and conditions of the transaction between the trading company and the commodity producer or importer based in emerging countries. At the most, they would require that the purpose of the financing be disclosed and that the trading company receive its payment at an account with the bank. These corporate loans were typically big-volume, low-margin transactions.

Towards the end of the decade, however, as more private capital was starting to flow to the 'best' emerging markets, commercial banks began to resume their direct involvement in the commodity sector of emerging countries, albeit on a different basis.

The 1990s: financing producers and importers on a structured basis

With the sudden demise of several trading companies in the 1980s and the resumption of bank loans to emerging countries, the situation later tilted back in favour of directly financing producers and importers. This forced banks to properly assess the risk of underlying commercial transactions, as they were less knowledgeable about the financial situation of borrowers. In higher-risk countries, commodity sector borrowers were generally unable to raise funds solely on the back of their balance sheet, while government guarantees not only had proved to be unreliable in the past, but also were fast disappearing.

Banks now required collateral when making new loans to the commodity sector of emerging countries. However, sovereign risk was not effectively mitigated until banks insisted that borrowers establish foreign exchange escrow accounts based outside the country. In the late 1980s and early 1990s, a few innovative banks, notably Bankers Trust Company and UBS, turned to Organisation for Economic Cooperation and Development (OECD)-based commodity buyers to effect payments to such offshore escrow accounts. This enabled these banks to resume business with the high-risk countries of Africa and marked the birth of structured commodity finance. In these early days, borrowers were exclusively central banks, commodity boards or state-owned companies.

Meanwhile, banks that continued to provide financing to those international trading companies that had not gone bankrupt did so in a more secured and structured way, with greater scrutiny of, and recourse to, the underlying commercial transaction, with full or limited recourse to trading companies. The analysis of both commodity producers and end-users became an inherent part of the risk assessment process. From then on, risks had to be properly identified, quantified, mitigated and remunerated.

Spurred on by the fall of the former Soviet Union, the liberalisation and deregulation of the commodity sector in most emerging countries again changed the rules of the game, and created an even greater need for structured finance. This new environment encouraged the development of new companies that had neither the size, the government support (or guarantees), the track record and even less the comfort of a monopoly situation that were necessary to support unsecured or unstructured loans. There was also a massive demand for commodity finance from CIS borrowers. Finally, the greater competition for private sector funds put banks in a better position to ask for tighter security requirements, often trespassing on the commercial territory of clients by selecting satisfactory commodity buyers to support the proposed structured commodity financing.

In the second half of the 1990s the sudden financial crises in South-East Asia and Russia for a short period reduced the availability of unsecured commercial loans to even the best emerging countries. However, by the late 1990s Russia had already returned to the banking markets thanks to new loans arranged on a structured commodity finance basis. In fact, throughout the decade the techniques of structured commodity finance evolved by taking lessons from successive emerging market crises and the idiosyncratic weaknesses of a few structured deals.

Today: extending the applications of structured commodity finance

With the development of more sophisticated structured finance techniques, the range of alternatives available to finance the commodity sector is wider than ever. Most structured transactions continue to be designed on an ad hoc basis, relying on available assets and flows provided

Exhibit A

Introduction

The funding of large-scale projects in capital-intensive industries (such as mining, oil and gas, petrochemicals, steel manufacturing, large real-estate developments, power generation, telecommunications and transportation) is usually beyond the means of a single company in terms of both risk-taking and financial support (equity and debt capacity).

This has led to the development of project finance, a term used when the project is separated from its sponsors and funding is based on the assumption that the project will generate a sufficient surplus cash flow after operating costs to enable debt servicing and to provide a return to the sponsor(s) and other investors. In practice, pure project-supported finance is now rare, and complex structures are put together to provide limited recourse to sponsors and other parties. At the same time, even smaller projects, or expansions of existing projects, now often rely on project finance to minimise the exposure of the parent company.

A fairly standard approach to structuring a project financing is for the sponsor(s) to establish a special purpose vehicle (SPV) in which they are principal shareholders and through which funding will be routed. Once the SPV has been established, the financing of the project must be 'engineered'. The financial design process must take into account the risks involved, the various prospective sources of financing, accounting and tax regulations, the possibility of recourse to the various parties, and many other considerations. A central function in project finance is to identify and quantify the various categories of risks, and then structure the deal to allocate these risks acceptably among the various participants. Clearly, it is possible for the cost of arranging a project finance transaction to become prohibitively expensive.

Besides tapping traditional sources of funds (multilateral banks, commercial banks, ECAs and so on), sponsors can also raise financing for a new project in the commodity sector on the back of part or all of their existing assets or receivables, in effect using the techniques of structured commodity finance to fund new projects. There are notable differences in the techniques and implications of structured commodity finance versus project finance, as illustrated in the following table:[1]

Project finance	Structured commodity finance
Need to find equity investors	No need to find equity investors
Intervention of constructors	Assets already constructed
Due diligence on new project	Due diligence on existing facilities
Analysis of estimated future cash flows	Analysis of identified existing cash flows
Market risk not always mitigated	Market risk easily mitigated by contracts with buyers
Supports long-term financing	Provides up to medium-term financing
Initially, security can be obtained only on fixed assets	Security can be obtained on existing short-term assets (inventory, operating contract or receivables)
Risks are bigger and more complex to evaluate	Risks are smaller and easier to evaluate
Off-balance sheet financing for sponsors	Possibly off-balance sheet financing
Without recourse financing	Possibly without recourse financing

by the commodity owner. Thanks to innovative techniques and good performance track records, structured commodity finance deals have also pushed tenors well into the medium term.

It does not matter whether, from a strictly technical point of view, financing is provided to the trading company, commodity end-buyer, producer, exporter, processor or importer. What sets structured finance apart from traditional trade, export and commodity finance is its ability to provide attractive financing solutions that build on and facilitate the underlying commercial transactions.

Nevertheless, structured commodity finance is not the solution to all financing problems and is not applicable in all circumstances. For instance, this financing product is more attractive when commodity prices are low, and in an environment of high political and financial instability. In fact, since the beginning of the worldwide economic slowdown in 2001, with depressed levels of international trade flows and direct foreign investment, structured commodity finance deals are taking a larger share of a smaller volume of financing business.

What is structured commodity finance?

By 'structured commodity finance' we simply mean structured finance for the commodity sector. Banks include various products under this umbrella. A French commercial banker once defined it as 'the sum of banking operations pertaining to an import or export of commodities which are not plain vanilla'. Others define structured commodity finance more narrowly, such as the Austrian banker who includes only transactions that 'provide working capital in difficult environments by mitigating the risk through mortgaging an export flow.' Although this definition rightly stresses the ability of structured commodity finance techniques to mitigate risk in difficult environments, it covers only a portion of what this book defines as structured commodity finance, excluding, for instance, structured inventory financing. Likewise, it is commonly acknowledged that 'structured trade finance' is the same thing as 'structured commodity finance' when the goods traded can be classified as commodities. However, this perspective now seems outdated, since the techniques of structured commodity finance have evolved to provide medium-term financing for general purposes or capital investment.

In practice, structured commodity finance is increasingly disconnected from traditional trade and commodity finance, and its offering is now often combined with that of structured export and trade finance. Some banks even put structured commodity finance and project finance under the same business division. In effect, in the commodity sector, structured finance can be an attractive financing alternative to project finance. Some projects are even financed on the back of hybrid structures, taking elements of both techniques.[2] However, as explained in Exhibit A, there are fundamental differences between the two financing solutions. Finally, outside the field of commodities, in the area of corporate finance and investment banking, structured finance typically relates to complex products such as leveraged and management buy-outs, asset-based financing, and structured leases.

To open the discussion, this simple definition of structured commodity finance is proposed: 'Financing transactions whereby an inventory and/or flow of commodities can be isolated from its owner and used as collateral for security and repayment'.

Scope

As will be shown in this book, structured commodity finance has been developing in all directions, overcoming conventional commodity financing habits linked to particular commodities, geographical areas or financing needs.

Applicable commodities

Many traditional financing techniques are being used overwhelmingly for a limited range of commodities – for example, tolling in the case of sugar, wool or aluminium. At the same time some structured finance techniques have also been confined to specific types of commodities, such as metals and crude oil in the case of asset-backed securitisation. Yet the basic techniques presented in this book are applicable to both the extractive (natural resources) sector, which is characterised by a depleting resource base and high development costs, and the agricultural sector, which involves smaller-scale production and perishable commodities. The discussion will not exclude *a priori* any commodity but, where relevant, will mention the type of commodities typically covered by a particular financing technique or instrument.

Geographical focus

In the same way that the discussion will not exclude any particular commodity, it will not be restricted to specific regions. Since its emergence in sub-Saharan Africa, the techniques of structured commodity finance have spread to every corner of the world. Nevertheless, the book will focus on the financing needs of borrowers located in emerging countries, as opposed to OECD-based borrowers.

Financing needs

This book will not cover micro-credit and rural credit, although some of the underlying concepts of structured commodity finance are also applicable to this specific finance area.[3] The discussion here will largely be restricted to medium and large financing needs.

One core tenet of structured commodity finance is its flexibility. This book will therefore cover most types of financing needs potentially present in the commodity sector, including trade financing at various stages of the marketing cycle, general purpose financing (for example, to pay for operating expenses), specific purpose lines of credit (for example, to pay for hedging costs) and medium-term financing (for example, for new projects).

Outline

This book will discuss the techniques and applications of structured commodity finance within the range of financing alternatives available to the commodity sector. In particular, it will endeavour to put discipline into a subject that has been extensively discussed by banking, insurance, capital markets and legal professionals, yet often with their own professional bias.

Before the discussion of the various forms in which structured commodity finance can present itself, there is a review of the building blocks of trade finance. Understanding the role of more complex forms of letters of credit, forfaiting and factoring in financing trade is also essential. These issues are covered in Part I of this book. The techniques of structured commodity finance are presented in Part II. They include both inventory financing and pre-export financing, the latter being further split between export receivables financing and prepayments. This is followed by other forms of structured finance applicable to the commodity sector, such as countertrade, and more complex structures. As techniques are evolving in the direction of using more third-party credit enhancement, Part III is dedicated to the insurance and guarantees that are now increasingly supporting structured commodity finance deals. Part IV of the book presents the applications of structured commodity finance within the range of financing alternatives available to the commodity sector, ranging from concessional lending to Islamic banking.

[1] Source: Presentation by Denis Child, head of trade and commodity finance, Société Générale, entitled Structured Commodity Finance Versus Project Finance, at the IBC Conference on 'Structured Trade and Commodity Finance', London, 1995.

[2] This was notably the case with a financing arranged in July 2001 jointly by Standard Bank London and Glencore to fund a new capital investment by Russia's Severnaya Neft (Nord Oil).

[3] See the report entitled *Inventory Credit: An Approach to Development Agricultural Markets* by the Food and Agriculture Organisation (FAO) and the Natural Resources Institute, FAO Agricultural Services Bulletin No.120, Rome, 1995.

Part I

Traditional trade finance

Introduction to Part I

Trade finance is the oldest business of banks. Banks have played a vital intermediary role in supporting trade by circumventing information costs, effecting payment from buyers to sellers and extending credit to trading parties.

Structured finance emerged first as a technique to finance commodity trade. Therefore, it is essential to first understand the building blocks of trade payment and financing techniques (bills of exchange, letters of credit and so on). More complex forms of letters of credit are then presented, followed by an update on the role of forfaiting and factoring in financing trade.

What should eventually become apparent is that structured commodity finance did not emerge suddenly as a fully fledged financial technique, but rather developed as an extension of the field of application of ancestral trade finance techniques combined with a new 'can do' philosophy.

Chapter 1

Building blocks of trade finance

This chapter presents the principal means of payment used for cross-border sales, followed by an overview of the traditional instruments used by exporters and importers for raising pre-shipment and post-shipment financing.

Principal payment methods

There are four principal payment mechanisms for settling international trade transactions:

- open account;
- advance payment;
- documentary collections; and
- documentary credits.

Importers (buyers) and exporters (sellers) have divergent interests in the selection of the payment mechanism because the level of security and risk that these mechanisms provide to the buyer and seller varies subsequently, as shown in Exhibit 1.1. The same goes for the level of banks' involvement and the respective cost of these payment mechanisms. The main characteristics of each of these payment mechanisms are described in the following subsections.

Open account

Open account is the most secure payment method for importers, but also the most risky for exporters. The exporter ships the commodities and payment is made at some specific date in the future by the importer without any negotiable instrument evidencing the importer's contractual obligations. Open account is probably the cheapest payment method for international trade, but it places the onus on exporters for both the credit risk and the cost of financing.

There is no bank contribution to the transaction because the importer pays the exporter directly, generally via cheque or money transfer. The role of banks is limited to moving the payment due from the account of the importer to that of the exporter. As a result, there is no protection for exporters in the event of non-payment. As will be discussed later in this chapter, and in Part III, there are various ways that exporters can manage these risks.

Open account trade is typically used when an exporter has a well-established commercial relationship with a creditworthy importer and when the importing country experiences little or no political or economic instability. It is also a valid trade payment mechanism when an exporter is shipping goods to a parent company or a subsidiary, or when the repercussions for the exporter of a total loss on the goods are minimal. Otherwise, exporters will only want to sell on open account when they are faced with excessive inventory or when market demand for their commodity is weak.

Exhibit 1.1

Risk profile of trade payment methods

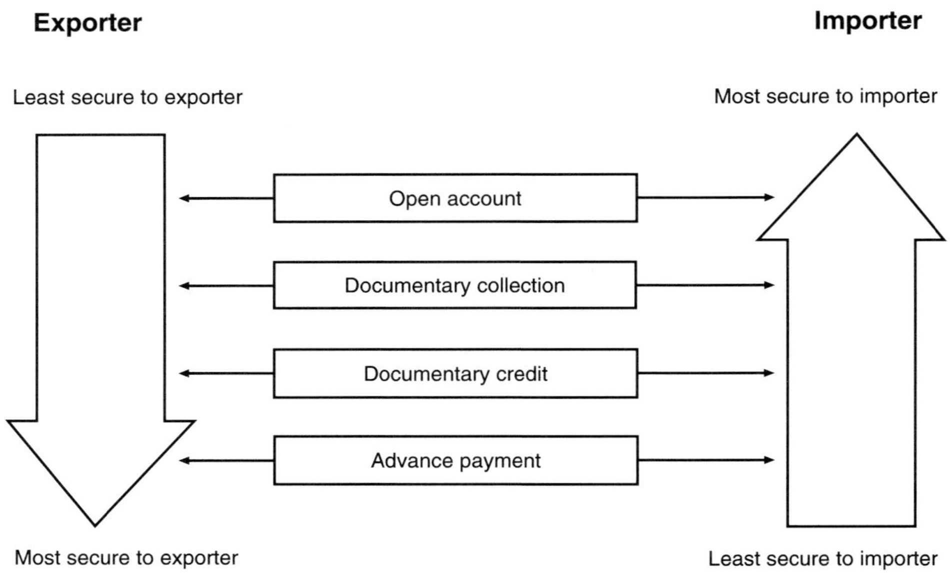

Trade can also take place on a consignment basis, which adds yet another hurdle before the exporter can be paid. The goods are shipped by the exporter, but the importer, acting as agent for the exporter, will pay the exporter only after the goods have been successfully re-marketed locally or regionally (net of the agent's fees). The exporter therefore must bear all market risks and the exporter may even have to take unsold goods back (and pay for related transport costs).

Advance payment

In contrast to open account, advance payment (also called 'cash in advance' or 'payment in advance') is the most secure payment method for exporters, but also the most risky for importers, since the commodities are not shipped until payment is received in full. Under this payment method all risks are placed on the importer, who must pay for the commodities prior to shipment. There is no guarantee that the commodities will be delivered as and when agreed. With advance payment, the exporter retains total control over the transaction. Again, bank involvement is limited to effecting payment.

Cash in advance can be used when the importer's credit status is doubtful and/or when political or economic conditions in the importer's country are unstable. Cash in advance for the full value of the shipment is used mainly for small purchases. This payment method can be expensive for the exporter because importers who are forced to pay in advance may ask for a discount. In practice, importers generally will not accept a condition to effect full payment before shipment, and will make only partial payment in advance and try to negotiate other means of payment for the balance, such as a letter of credit (see the 'Documentary credit' section below). Moreover, in some countries advance payments may be illegal due to foreign currency controls prohibiting foreign payments prior to shipment, or may simply be too onerous for tax reasons.

Documentary collection

Documentary collection is a method of payment by which an international sale transaction is settled through an exchange of documents. The importer's bank (the collecting or presenting bank) acts as collecting agent for the importer by effecting payment to the exporter's bank (the remitting bank) for the benefit of the exporter once the stipulated set of documents has been received. This payment method is supported by a draft[1] plus related documents, including:

- shipping documents (such as a bill of lading);
- insurance documents;
- commercial invoice;
- packing list; and
- certificate of origin.

Documentary collection offers some protection to both importers and exporters. Each party retains a certain element of control: the importer is not required to pay the exporter before the goods are shipped and the exporter is able to retain title to the goods until the importer either pays the draft upon presentation (sight draft, or documents against payment) or accepts the draft (term draft, or documents against acceptance). In the latter case the exporter will release the documents only once the importer has accepted the accompanying draft, thereby incurring an obligation to pay the exporter as per an agreed schedule, usually expressed in terms of numbers of days after acceptance of documents (sight) or after the bill of lading (B/L) date, as agreed between the exporter and the importer. For instance, payment of the draft could be 20 per cent sight, 30 per cent at B/L plus 60 days and 50 per cent at B/L plus 90 days.

The remitting bank transmits the exporter's instructions and documents to the collecting bank in the importer's country. The collecting bank will seek payment from the importer and will not release documents until the importer has effected payment or accepted the drafts (as the case may be). For its part, the remitting bank does not assume any risk, nor does it make any undertaking to pay the exporter.

Under a documentary collection, banks control the flow and transfer of documents, and regulate the timing of payments. They must ensure the safety of the documents in their possession, but are not responsible for their validity and accuracy, as they do not have any legal obligation to verify the documents. In practice, however, the remitting bank will at least undertake a superficial examination of the documents and advise the exporter in case of any major error in the documents or any conflicting instructions. The flow of documents and payments under documentary collection is presented in Exhibit 1.2.

By using documentary collection, an exporter reduces the risk of non-payment compared with open account trade. However, this risk is not completely eliminated because, after delivery of the goods, the importer may be either unable or unwilling to pay. In case of non-payment, the exporter would have a choice between paying for the return of the goods or selling the goods at a reduced price. The risk faced by the exporter is even higher with a time draft,

Exhibit 1.2

Documentary collection

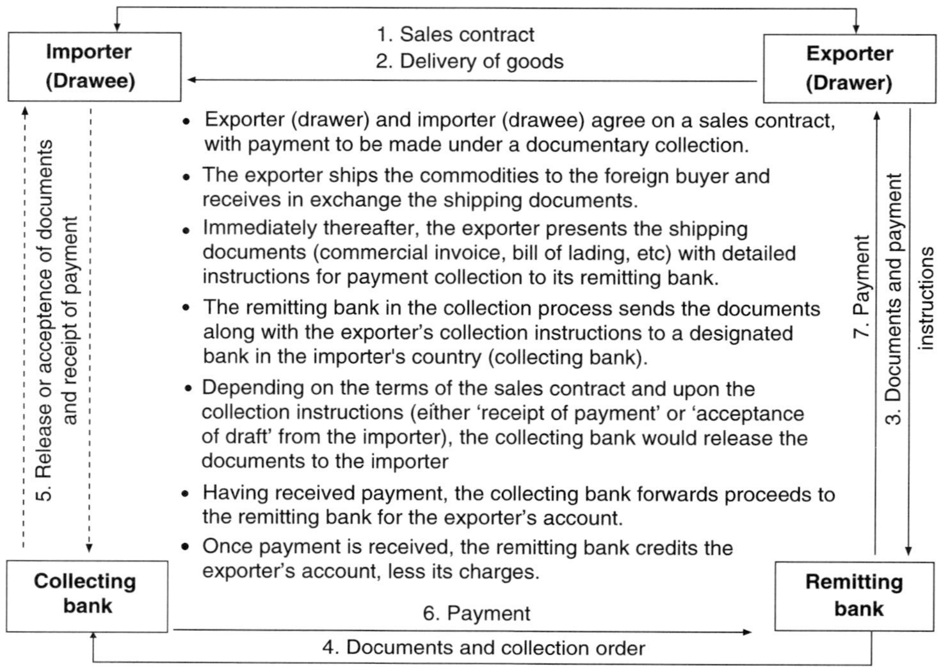

given the time lag between delivery of the goods and the payment due date. Collecting payment in the country of the foreign buyer may be difficult. Exporters can reduce this risk by requesting a bank to accept the time draft in exchange for an immediate cash payment (bankers' acceptances are discussed later in this chapter).

Because banks take less risk and responsibility in documentary collections than in documentary credits, fees for handling documents and collecting payments are also much lower.

Documentary collections are typically used when exporters have well-established relationships with importers, when they face little or no threat of total loss, when the political and economic situation is stable, and when letters of credit are either too expensive or not allowed.

The basic responsibilities of the parties to a documentary collection arrangement are set out in the guidelines of the Uniform Rules for Collection (URC) drafted by the International Chamber of Commerce (ICC) based in Paris. In case of dispute, there is legal recourse under trade-related rules, regulations and case law such as the Uniform Customs and Practice of the ICC, as well as under bills of exchange regulations.

Documentary credit

For exporters, documentary credits (that is, letters of credit) represent the next best payment mechanism after advance payment. Compared to other payment forms, the role of banks in documentary credits is substantial: they provide additional security to both the importer and the exporter.

A documentary letter of credit (L/C) consists of a written undertaking from the importer's bank (the issuing or opening bank) to pay at sight or at a future date up to an agreed sum to the seller/exporter (the beneficiary) on behalf of the buyer/importer (the applicant) provided that the exporter presents certain documents to the issuing bank, in compliance with the terms and conditions of the L/C. Payment is made to the exporter by its bank acting as advising bank.

Banks play a larger role in documentary credits than in other trade payment methods. They give comfort to exporters that they will duly receive payment if the required shipping and related documents are presented to the issuing bank in compliance with the terms of the L/C; and to importers that payment will be made on their behalf only if proper documents have been presented.

The advising bank must verify that the L/C duly originates from the issuing bank. This authentication may be effected electronically through test keys or Swift[2] messages, or may involve the actual verification of issuing bank signatures as they appear on a paper-based L/C against signature books that banks maintain for such purposes.

In general the negotiating bank is also the advising bank. See Exhibit 1.3 for an overview of the different forms of settlement available under documentary credits. The exporter should seek a bank that offers a 'true' negotiation, meaning a bank that pays the exporter upon acceptance of documents instead of waiting until funds have been received from the issuing bank.

In a documentary credit the issuing bank has an obligation to pay the exporter regardless of whether or not it has been or will be reimbursed by the importer. However, if the exporter is uncomfortable with the credit risk of the issuing bank, or the political or economic situation in the importer's country, the exporter can request that the L/C be confirmed. L/C confirmation is generally made by a first-class international bank, usually the advising bank (now the confirming bank) and, less frequently, by a third-party bank. What the confirming bank undertakes is to pay the exporter even in the absence of payment by the issuing bank.

In international trade, the norm is for a letter of credit to be irrevocable, meaning that its terms cannot be amended without the consent of the issuing bank, the confirming bank (if any) and the beneficiary. In contrast, a revocable letter of credit may be amended or cancelled at any time by the issuing bank. Revocable L/Cs are sometimes used between parent companies and their subsidiaries operating in other countries. The revocable L/C was not uncommon in the 1970s and earlier when dealing with developed countries, but it is rarely seen these days in international trade.

Documents are key to documentary L/Cs. Banks decide on the basis of documents alone whether payment, negotiation or acceptance is to be effected. If proper documents are presented, banks will make payment whether or not the actual goods shipped comply with the sales contract. Thus, special attention must be paid to the preparation of shipping documents because a slight omission or discrepancy between required and actual documents may cause additional cost, delays and extra work for both the importer and the exporter. When instructions or documents presented to the negotiating bank do not exactly conform to the terms of the original L/C, discrepancies have to be corrected, the documents possibly resubmitted and any amendment approved by all parties. This can result in an exporter not being paid or even in the seizure of the exporter's goods by national or foreign customs services.[3] A discrepancy may arise due to late shipment of the merchandise or because of a simple typographical error in the description of the goods. It is estimated that 60–70 per cent of letters of credit worldwide (up to 90 per cent on first presentation) are discrepant in

Exhibit 1.3

Settlement methods

According to UCP 500 (Article 10), payment under documentary credit may be available under four terms (in each case assuming that the documents presented comply with the terms and conditions of the credit):

a. By sight payment

Payment is made to the seller by the issuing or confirming bank immediately upon presentation and examination of the documents.

b. By deferred payment

Payment is made to the seller at a specified future date, for example 60 days after presentation of the documents or after the date of shipment.

c. By acceptance

This type of credit requires the seller to draw a usance draft (bill of exchange) on either the issuing or confirming bank. The draft is accepted by the bank for payment at a future fixed date, for example 90 days after presentation of the documents.

d. By negotiation

A credit payable at sight or at usance can be negotiated, either with a freely chosen bank or with a bank specifically nominated by the issuing bank. Under negotiation, three payment options may occur:

i. The negotiating bank would pay the beneficiary only when it receives payment from the issuing bank. The seller would present the documents to the advising/negotiating bank for payment. The negotiating bank would in turn forward the documents to the issuing bank and claim payment, and would pay the seller on receipt of payment by the issuing bank. Payment is made by the issuing bank on receipt of proper documents.

ii. The negotiating bank would negotiate the documents by 'giving value' to the documents and paying the beneficiary the value of the documents less a charge (ie, discounting the documents), while awaiting reimbursement from the issuing bank. When the negotiating bank 'gives value' to the documents, it does not receive immediate payment itself; therefore it will deduct interest to cover the period between paying and receiving payment from the issuing bank. The bank may agree to advance payment 'without recourse', which means that the bank will not have the right to reimbursement from the beneficiary if payment is not received from the issuing bank as expected. In that case the negotiating bank is advancing the payment at its own risk.

iii. The negotiating bank would offer to give value if it is prepared to accept the payment risk of the issuing bank. The bank may agree to advance payment 'with recourse' to the seller for reimbursement.

Note: Deferred and acceptance credits (ie, term credits) are considered to be financing instruments for the buyer because during deferred payment the buyer can often sell the goods and pay the amount due with the proceeds.
Source: Documentary Risk in Commodity Trade, UNCTAD, 1998.

some way, but discrepancies can only present a problem when either party uses them to avoid concluding the transaction.

Each instruction to open, advise or confirm a documentary letter of credit must clearly list the documents to be presented. The set of documents supporting documentary L/Cs is generally similar to that supporting documentary collections. Documents conforming to the

Exhibit 1.4

Documentary letters of credit

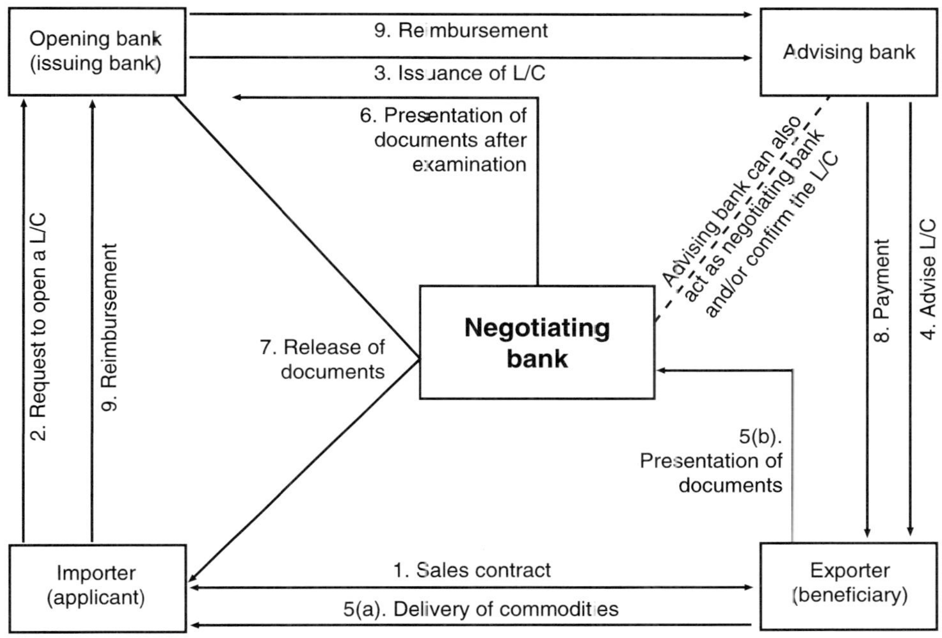

L/C terms and conditions must be presented by the beneficiary to the negotiating bank. As in documentary collections, payment is made either at 'sight', that is once documents have been accepted, or 'term', as per an agreed schedule. The flow of documents and payments under letters of credit is presented in Exhibit 1.4.

L/Cs are typically issued and advised or confirmed via tested telex. L/C charges are split between the applicant (issuing fees) and the beneficiary (negotiating fees and advising or confirmation fees). Negotiating fees are generally in the range of 0.10–0.15 per cent flat of each payment. Advising fees are negligible and are often expressed as a flat figure per L/C (such as €500). Confirming fees represent the bulk of L/C fees payable by the beneficiary, and are expressed as a percentage of the confirmed and unused L/C amount. Confirmation fees are generally payable quarterly in advance and depend mainly on the confirming bank's assessment of the credit risk of the issuing bank.

Exporters generally request importers to open L/Cs when the commercial relationship is new or the political or economic situation in the importer's country is unstable.

The success of L/Cs testifies to their usefulness and versatility. Documentary L/Cs can be straightforward or detailed and highly complex. More complex forms of L/Cs have emerged to better adapt this instrument to the conditions of the underlying commercial contract and to support pre-shipment financing to the exporter. The use of deferred payments provides relatively cheap and simple bank financing to the importer. (How letters of credit can provide financing to both parties is examined in the next section.)

L/Cs can nevertheless be expensive to issue, not only in terms of issuance fees but also because importers with a poor credit rating may have to maintain cash collateral with the issuing bank. Moreover, importers may not be able to open an L/C with an issuing bank acceptable to the L/C confirming bank chosen by the exporter. Also, L/Cs do not entirely remove payment risk and they only guarantee payment to the exporter to the extent that the documents are in compliance. This means that an importer can avoid payment by simply refusing to sign the commercial invoice. Last but not least, confirmation fees may be very expensive – often even more expensive than issuing fees.

In fact, letter of credits now represent a decreasing percentage of the growing international trade finance market. Somehow, L/Cs seem to have become too expensive for importers and exporters as a means of payment and, at the same time, not sufficiently profitable for banks: 'As the demand for L/Cs shrinks, the market power of large, technologically advanced institutions that have entered this arena has created unprecedented pricing pressure. In addition, the cost of technology associated with L/C issuance has steadily and prohibitively increased'.[4]

L/Cs are governed by the Uniform Customs and Practice (UCP) for documentary credits established by the International Chamber of Commerce (ICC).[5]

Basic trade financing instruments

This section explains how importers and exporters can obtain finance on the back of a simple trade transaction, with or without the intervention of a letter of credit. Financing the period prior to shipment is referred to as pre-shipment financing and that for the period following shipment is called post-shipment financing.

Post-shipment financing based on L/Cs

As already mentioned, L/Cs are primarily a tool to ensure safe payment, but they can also provide financing to either (or both) the applicant (the importer) and the beneficiary (the exporter). With a letter of credit an exporter is usually paid at the time the advising or confirming bank receives the funds from the issuing bank. Let us assume, however, that the exporter wants to be paid upon acceptance of documents and that the importer is unable to do so. Banks involved in the L/C could intervene in two basic ways to provide post-shipment financing.

1. The issuing bank could refinance the payment due from the importer under the L/C, for instance through a conventional short-term loan or an overdraft in favour of the importer. The issuing bank could, in turn, pay the advising bank at sight or ask the advising/confirming bank for a similar extension of payment terms in its favour. This method is a simple way for importers to obtain short-term financing (say for a maximum of 360 days), for instance until the marketing cycle is complete.
2. The exporter can agree to grant deferred payments under the L/C and draw a term draft on the issuing or advising bank (that is, a bankers' acceptance) to evidence the fact that the importer's liability is extended up to the draft's maturity (for example B/L plus 30 days, and so on). The exporter may, in turn, negotiate (sell in the secondary markets) or discount (sell for less than the face value) this bankers' acceptance to obtain an immediate payment. The importer would pay for the goods on the agreed deferred payment date(s). The exporter may of course build into the price of the goods a premium covering the cost of

discounting the draft. Documentary credits available by term drafts drawn on the issuing or advising bank are also known as documentary acceptance credits.

Trade paper

The exporter can grant extended payment terms to the importer even in the absence of a letter of credit, for instance if the export sale takes place on an open account or documentary collection basis. Actually, in much of world trade, sellers provide post-shipment financing to their buyers through deferred payments. The importer's debt is generally (but not always) acknowledged through some form of 'trade paper', most of which is 'negotiable' (that is, transferable from the exporter to a third party). There are three major types of such trade paper that can be used as a credit instrument: bills of exchange, promissory notes and bankers' acceptances.

Exporters for their part can obtain post-shipment financing by discounting or negotiating this trade paper. In other words, rather than providing credit to importers out of their own financial resources, exporters can transfer the financing obligation to banks or other third parties.

Bills of exchange and promissory notes

One way of achieving this is for the exporter to issue term drafts or bills of exchange addressed to, and accepted by, the importer (drawee) who commits to pay on demand, or at a fixed or determinable future time, a certain sum to the exporter (drawer and, generally, payee). A bill of exchange is a trade bill drawn by one commercial party on another. A bill of exchange is similar to an invoice in that it is a demand for payment.

The claim of the exporter on the importer may also be supported by promissory notes issued directly by the importer, usually with a guarantee or 'aval' from the importer's bank. Such a guarantee is generally essential for making the promissory notes negotiable.

However, to avoid a potential charge to stamp duty, the importer may ask the exporter for deferred payment terms without the support of bills of exchange or promissory notes, in which case the financing is less regulated and thus more risky for the exporter (consider recent court cases concerning discounting credits without negotiable instruments).

Once a bill of exchange has been accepted or endorsed by the importer, or once the exporter has accepted a promissory note issued by an importer, it becomes a trade acceptance. Acceptances delay the payment of the underlying obligation by the importer, thus providing short-term financing to the importer. As already mentioned, acceptances can be negotiated or discounted by the exporter against cash, thus providing financing to the exporter. In short, an acceptance is simply a commitment to pay the face value of a draft to a bona fide holder at the agreed time.

To qualify as a negotiable instrument, trade paper must meet at least three conditions.

1. The obligation of the importer to repay the debt to the exporter should be absolute, meaning that it should not depend on the performance of the underlying commercial transaction by the exporter. Nevertheless, the buyer of the trade paper will generally seek assurance that the exporter will meet or has met (as relevant) its obligations, and will generally disburse funds only after shipment.
2. The trade paper must be endorsed as 'non-recourse' by each successive holder, meaning that the obligor remains the importer and that neither the exporter nor the previous holder(s)

of the debt is (are) responsible for effecting repayment at maturity. However, this is not the case in the United Kingdom, where any endorsement creates liability and cannot be negated by a 'without recourse' annotation.

3. If the importer is not widely accepted as a highly creditworthy counterparty, then a guarantee must be provided by a third party, usually a solid bank with a record in international trade.

Bankers' acceptances

When an exporter asks its bank to provide its 'aval' or guarantee to the trade paper, it becomes a bankers' acceptance (B/A). Again, the exporter can obtain an immediate payment by discounting or negotiating the bankers' acceptance. By discounting the bankers' acceptance, the exporter receives an amount equal to the face value of the trade paper, less discount charges, which are fixed until maturity (as a function of interest rates) and calculated on a discount-to-yield or simple interest basis, plus fees. Unlike other trade paper, bankers' acceptances can be with recourse to the exporter, which must repay the debt obligation at maturity or roll it over.

The market for B/As is highly liquid. Sterling B/As are governed by the Bank of England and US dollar B/As are governed by the Federal Reserve of the United States. US dollar B/As are theoretically eligible for discounting if they (i) are accepted by eligible banks, (ii) have a maximum tenor of six months, (iii) ultimately relate to a trade transaction and (iv) are self-liquidating. In practice, however, eligibility criteria are not always fully respected.

For the exporter, financing based on the discounting of B/As is attractive because the interest rate is fixed and the all-in financing cost is often lower than for alternative sources of financing. Although the market is restricted to eligible banks, these banks will tend to invite other banks on a risk participation basis if large amounts are involved. On the minus side, the financing that an exporter can raise against identified export receivables is for less than six months. Also, B/As always require an underlying trade transaction, as theoretically they cannot be used to obtain general purpose financing. B/A financing can also be used for imports.

Pre-shipment financing for importers

An importer can request pre-shipment credit lines from its bank to cover either miscellaneous expenses or specific import contracts. A loan would typically be granted to an importer by its local bank in either local currency or hard currency. In the latter case, the local bank would in turn obtain an equivalent loan from an international bank, sometimes part of the same banking group.

However, clean (unsecured) lines of credit are difficult to obtain for commodity importers located in emerging markets. If the creditworthiness of the importer is deemed insufficient, the local bank would only lend on a secured basis backed up by a traditional security package (such as a pledge on fixed assets). These security requirements are onerous in more than one respect, including possible restrictions on the use of the pledged asset and stamp duty costs.

Pre-shipment financing for exporters

In addition to enabling post-shipment financing, letters of credit can be used by the exporter to raise pre-shipment financing. The amount of the financing would be a percentage of the expected export sales proceeds. This percentage would vary with the security package provided by the exporter and the creditworthiness of the importer. Some types of letters of credit (red-clause and green-clause L/Cs) are specifically designed to provide pre-shipment financing to exporters. They are discussed in Chapter 2.

Even without the support of letters of credit, exporters are more likely than importers to obtain pre-shipment lines of credit from local or international banks at competitive terms to finance their marketing cycle, especially with hard-currency loans.

Evaluation of basic trade financing instruments

Exporters and importers located in emerging countries can rely on a variety of instruments to pay for their trade-related needs, some of which can be further used to obtain post- and pre-shipment financing.

Trade paper that is provided by highly creditworthy counterparties, or that has been guaranteed by reputable banks, is actively traded in the forfaiting markets, discussed in Chapter 2.

Exporters and importers should discuss their business patterns with their bankers to obtain recommendations with regard to the range of financing methods available and most suitable for their particular situation. In certain cases where raising financing is difficult (for example, for small trading companies), borrowers may have to provide banks with a satisfactory security package, including not only the typical pledge of assets but also a certain level of control over the commodities being financed and the financial flows. Ultimately, when the control obtained by banks is very significant, the commodity trade financing transactions can be referred to as structured commodity finance.

---

1 A draft is an unconditional order issued by the importer to pay on demand a specified sum at a fixed or determinable future date. Drafts are usually drawn 'on demand', either 'at sight' or as a 'term' draft (also called 'time' or 'deferred payment' or 'usance' drafts).

2 Society for World Interbank Financial Telecommunications (Swift), a membership-based organisation located in Belgium, which provides telecommunications infrastructure for a very large volume of transactions, including payments, L/Cs and collections. Swift messages are structured and formatted messages that facilitate clearer communication, and have assisted in the automation of transaction processing within banks.

3 See the UNCTAD publication *Documentary Risk in Commodity Trade*, 1998, which provides an extensive overview of the main documentary risks, errors and frauds, and provides some means to reduce these risks.

4 Canadian Imperial Bank of Commerce (CIBC), quoted in 'Trade finance outsourcing', *Trade Finance*, July/August 2001. (Actually, CIBC has solved its own profitability problem by entering into an agreement with Bank of New York for the latter to issue L/Cs on its behalf to beneficiaries throughout the world.)

5 The UCP consists of quasi-regulatory articles governing all aspects of the use of L/Cs, from the definition of the obligations of all key parties to the detailed terms and conditions that may be included in an L/C. The UCP is published and updated periodically by the ICC. While adherence is voluntary, the vast majority of L/Cs are issued explicitly subject to the UCP and many legal traditions (including the UK's common law) have given increasing weight to the UCP in adjudicating disputes involving international commerce conducted on the basis of an L/C.

Chapter 2

More advanced instruments and techniques

In this chapter the discussion centres on additional instruments and markets that can be used to support a wider range of trade finance situations. The techniques and applications of more complex letters of credit are presented and analysed, together with forfaiting and, due to its increasing use to finance cross-border trade, factoring.

Tailored letters of credit

This section introduces letters of credit (L/Cs) that are tailored to meet specific contractual arrangements. Notwithstanding their particularities, these more complex L/Cs can also be used to obtain financing in the same manner as simple letters of credit. (Note that standby letters of credit are not discussed in this section, but in Part III, along with other forms of third-party guarantees.)

Revolving letters of credit

Revolving letters of credit represent a commitment on the part of the issuing bank to restore the L/C to the original amount once it has been used (that is, drawn down). Revolving L/Cs can be either cumulative, meaning that amounts not drawn during the time stated (a revolving period) can be added to the next revolving period; or non-cumulative, meaning that partial amounts expire if not used in the stated revolving period.

For importers, the issuance of revolving L/Cs is cheaper than the issuance of a documentary L/C for the same cumulative amount for the overall period of shipment, both in terms of administrative costs and, more importantly, in terms of issuing fees. Similarly, for an exporter the confirmation of a revolving L/C is cheaper than for a documentary L/C. This is due to the fact that L/C issuing and confirmation fees are generally calculated quarterly in advance on the L/C amount committed for that revolving period.

This instrument, however, is not applicable to every type of trade pattern. Revolving L/Cs can be used to cover the continuous shipment of relatively similar goods over a designated period. They are not designed to handle erratic shipments of diverse goods with complex documentation.

In short, revolving L/Cs are geared to specific commercial transactions. They do not provide access to additional financing for importers or exporters compared with straightforward L/Cs. Moreover, in practice the exporter (beneficiary) remains exposed to the risk that the issuing bank may find an excuse, at the end of a revolving period, for not rolling over the revolving L/C. For instance, the issuing bank may decide not to re-establish its commitment for the next revolving period if the importer (applicant) has been late or has defaulted altogether on its previous reimbursements to the issuing bank. The situation is even more risky for the exporter if the rollover structure requires the rollover L/C to be increased at the time of a subsequent revolving period.

Back-to-back letters of credit

Back-to-back letters of credit are typically used by trading companies or by processing companies. They enable these intermediaries to use a first L/C, issued in their favour by the importer or end-buyer of commodities, as collateral for their issuance of a second L/C in favour of the exporter.

Transaction flows of back-to-back L/Cs (see Exhibit 2.1) can be summarised as follows.

1. The importer or end-buyer applies for issuance of L/C no.1 in favour of the intermediary.
2. L/C no.1 is issued by issuing bank no.1 and sent to advising/confirming bank no.1.
3. L/C no.1 is advised or confirmed by advising/confirming bank no.1.
4. The intermediary requests issuance of back-to-back L/C no.2 in favour of the exporter.
5. L/C no.2 is issued by issuing bank no.2 (which is advising/confirming bank no.1) and sent to advising/confirming bank no. 2.
6. L/C no.2 is advised or confirmed by advising bank no.2.
7. The commodities are exported.
8. Documents are presented by the exporter to advising/confirming bank no.2 for negotiation.
9. Advising/confirming bank no.2 effects payment to the exporter and claims reimbursement on issuing bank no.2 (which is advising/confirming bank no.1).
10. Documents are presented by the intermediary for negotiation to advising/confirming bank no.1.

Exhibit 2.1

Back-to-back letters of credit

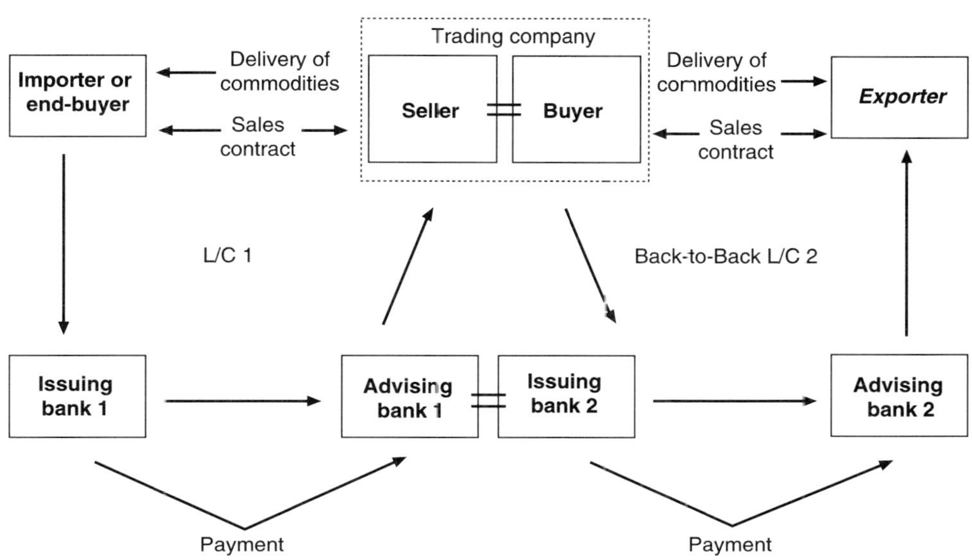

11. Advising/confirming bank no.1 effects payment to the intermediary and claims reimbursement on issuing bank no.1
12. The importer or end-buyer pays issuing bank no.1.

The order of the financial flows (8–12) depends on the financial terms negotiated between the parties. Because the issuing bank of the second L/C will be reimbursed under the first L/C, it is essential that the terms and conditions of both L/Cs match, except that (i) the amount of the first L/C (also called the master or prime L/C) is generally greater than that of the second L/C (the back-to-back L/C or counter-credit), to allow the intermediary to take its profit; and (ii) the shipment dates and validity of the first L/C should be later than those of the second L/C, to allow time for the substitution of invoices and examination of documents. For commercial reasons, the intermediary may require that documents be issued without disclosing the names of the exporter and importer or end-buyer.

This back-to-back mechanism is favoured by trading companies whose credit risk may be deemed insufficient by banks to issue L/Cs on their behalf in favour of exporters. Differing payment terms in back-to-back L/Cs can also enable the intermediary to pay the exporter before payment is received from the importer or end-buyer.

On the minus side, performance of the back-to-back L/C is highly dependent upon timely execution of the first or master L/C. For instance, a discrepancy in the documents under the first L/C can result in the issuing bank of the first L/C refusing to effect payment, in which case the issuing bank of the second L/C becomes extremely reluctant to effect payment as well. As a result, many banks would rather issue an L/C for a creditworthy trading company than rely on a back-to-back L/C opened in favour of a second-rate trading company. Alternatively, some banks advise trading companies to conduct their trade transactions under a transferable letter of credit (described in the next section). Also, there are no special provisions in the UCP for back-to-back L/Cs, and thus banks are uncertain about their rights and responsibilities. Transferable L/Cs, on the other hand, are covered by the Uniform Customs and Practice (UCP).

Can trading companies use back-to-back L/Cs to obtain financing? As with straightforward L/Cs, trading companies can request deferred payment terms on the back-to-back L/C and by seeking pre- or post-shipment financing on the back of the prime L/C, for instance by discounting or negotiating any term draft in their favour.

As a payment and financing alternative to back-to-back L/Cs, a trading company can borrow from a bank and effect an advance payment to the exporter. The benefit of using a prepayment structure over the back-to-back L/C mechanism would be that it enables the trading company to effect payment to the exporter before it has finalised the sale to the importer or end-buyer, which may not even be identified yet. This is because the bank lending in a prepayment is often willing to take the market risk. Moreover, in a prepayment the bank lends with limited recourse to the trading company (that is, the bank must bear the performance risk of the exporter). Inversely, in a back-to-back L/C the issuing bank of the first L/C only pays the trading company if the goods have been shipped as specified. (See Part II for a detailed discussion of prepayments.)

Transferable letters of credit

Transferable letters of credit are an alternative to back-to-back L/Cs as a method of facilitating transactions arranged by a trading company, for instance to cover the sale of oil products between two countries. In the area of project finance, transferable L/Cs can be used to pay subcontractors.

With transferable L/Cs, the first beneficiary (for example, the trading company) instructs the advising bank to transfer all or part of the L/C to the second beneficiary (for example, the exporter or supplier). The first beneficiary's rights and obligations under the master L/C are transferred to the second beneficiary (transferee), which must comply with the terms and conditions of the transferred L/C in order to receive payment. As in a back-to-back L/C, only certain terms of the original L/C can be changed.

Summarised transaction flows of transferable L/Cs (see Exhibit 2.2) are as follows.

1. The importer issues an L/C in favour of the intermediary (first beneficiary).
2. The L/C is issued by the issuing bank and sent to the advising/confirming bank.
3. The L/C is advised or confirmed by the advising/confirming bank.
4. The intermediary instructs the advising/confirming bank to transfer all or part of the L/C to the exporter or supplier (second beneficiary).
5. The commodities are exported.
6. The documents are presented by the exporter or supplier to the advising/confirming bank for negotiation.
7. The advising/confirming bank informs the intermediary that it is holding the documents.
8. The intermediary may substitute its own invoice and documents.
9. The advising/confirming bank effects payment to the exporter or supplier and claims reimbursement on the issuing bank.
10. The importer pays the issuing bank.

Again, the order of financial flows (6–10) depends on the financial terms negotiated between the parties. The terms and conditions of the transferred L/C must be identical to those of the principal L/C, except that (i) the amount of the transferred L/C may be lower so that the intermediary (first beneficiary) may substitute its own invoices and make a profit, and (ii) the

Exhibit 2.2

Transferable letters of credit

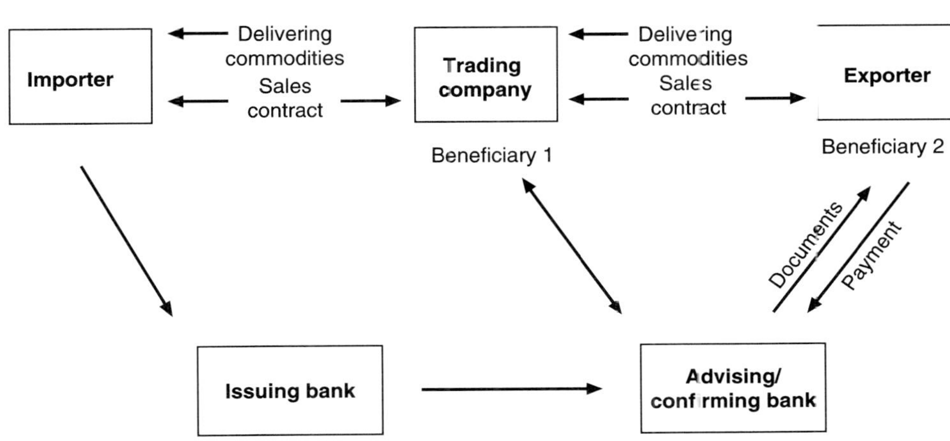

expiry date of the transferred L/C may be earlier. The advising or confirming bank can transfer an L/C provided that the word 'transferable' is explicitly stipulated on the L/C at the time of issuance. The transfer requires a written request by the first beneficiary to the advising or confirming bank. The transferring bank, however, is under no obligation to execute the transfer until it is paid for its services.

Transferable L/Cs can be used in circumstances similar to those supporting back-to-back L/Cs, that is, when the beneficiary is not the ultimate supplier of the goods but an intermediary between an exporter and an importer. Transferable L/Cs are more transparent and more secure, from a credit standpoint, than back-to-back L/Cs. As already mentioned, another relative advantage of transferable L/Cs is that they are governed by the UCP.

One drawback of transferable L/Cs is that the identity of the original exporter or supplier is typically disclosed to the importer, and this may weaken the commercial position of a trading company using this payment method. Also, the intermediary is unable to control the performance of the exporter or supplier compared with the terms of its original contractual obligations vis-à-vis the importer, for instance as regards the period of shipment.

Red-clause letters of credit

Red-clause letters of credit are structured specifically to enable an exporter (beneficiary) to obtain pre-shipment finance from the advising or confirming bank, expressed as a percentage of the L/C amount.

Upon instruction from the buyer, the issuing bank would authorise the advising or confirming bank to make an advance payment to the exporter, typically to assist in the production, acquisition or shipment of the commodities. This advance payment can be made against either a simple written statement of purpose (clean red-clause) or against an undertaking to provide certain specified documents (for instance, warehouse receipts).

After presentation of documents by the exporter, the issuing bank would transfer the payment to the advising or confirming bank, which would in turn pay to the exporter the amount specified on the documents, less the amount of the prior advance payment (and less interest and fees). If the exporter does not comply with the terms of the L/C (for example, if it fails to ship the commodities as specified), the advising or confirming bank can seek reimbursement of the advance payment (plus interest and fees) from the issuing bank. In turn, the issuing bank would ask for payment from the importer. Thus, under a red-clause letter of credit, the importer is actually granting an unsecured loan to the exporter. (See Exhibit 2.3 illustrating red-clause L/Cs.)

Secured (or documentary) red-clause L/Cs can be compared to some loosely structured forms of commodity financing. The main difference is that with secured red-clause L/Cs banks rely on an undertaking to provide the required security (such as warehouse receipts or the export sales contract), whereas with structured commodity financing such documents are actually a condition precedent to the granting of the loan. Lastly, red-clause L/Cs can also support prepayments if the exporter (beneficiary), instead of obtaining a loan from the advising bank, obtains a direct prepayment from the buyer (applicant) backed by a bank loan. Under a prepayment, the lending bank has recourse to the importer only to the extent that the exporter has performed its obligations, which makes both instruments similar for importers in terms of risk.

From the perspective of the exporter, red-clause L/Cs combine access to pre-shipment financing with coverage of the importer's payment risk. But these advantages can also be

Exhibit 2.3

Red-clause letters of credit

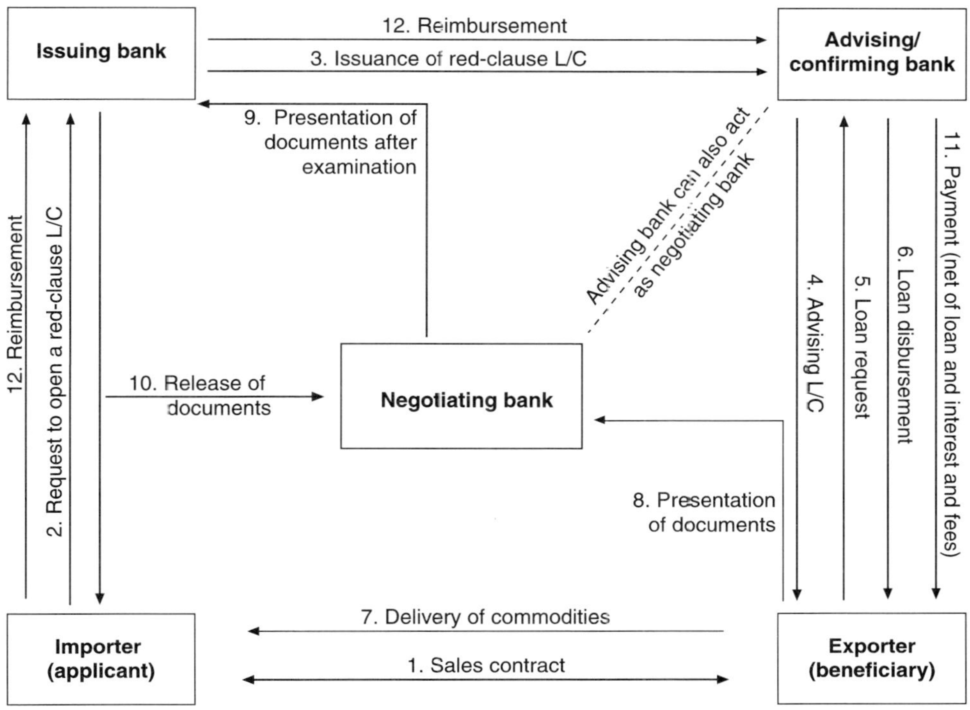

achieved without the support – and the cost – of a letter of credit, using structured pre-export financing. Moreover, structured pre-export financing transactions have the advantage of functioning with more than one buyer and for more than one transaction. In addition, the advance provided by red-clause L/Cs is usually only a small percentage of the L/C amount, typically around 20 per cent. From the perspective of banks, red-clause L/Cs have the advantage of providing full recourse to both the issuing bank and the buyer. In short, red-clause L/Cs would be used where the exporter is in a position of strength or where the importer seeks to attract potential exporters and secure their commercial relationships.

Red-clause L/Cs were originally developed to allow wool buyers in Australia to obtain financing to buy wool from growers. They are still used in the wool and cotton trades, where local buyers have to incur substantial pre-shipment costs.

Green-clause letters of credit

Green-clause letters of credit serve the same purpose as red-clause L/Cs but differ in that the exporter can only obtain an advance payment from the advising or confirming bank against the actual production of – ie, not just the undertaking to produce – certain documents.

These documents evidence that the commodities are held to the order of the bank. In this respect, green-clause L/Cs are a form of structured commodity financing. From the perspective of banks, green-clause L/Cs are more secure than red-clause L/Cs because the documents are presented to the banks and thus the loan is also with full recourse to the commodities. From the perspective of exporters, green-clause L/Cs are more attractive than red-clause L/Cs because the amount of the advance can be much higher, typically up to 80 per cent of the L/C amount. Advance payments may also be drawn down on a rollover basis, say as and when warehouse receipts are presented. However, banks may require that each advance be supported by an existing sales contract for the corresponding commodities. Additional financing can sometimes even be obtained once the commodities are shipped. As with red-clause L/Cs, green-clause L/Cs can be used to support prepayment structures.

Evaluation of more complex letters of credit

Some of these more complex, tailored letters of credit are used primarily to meet certain payment and security needs, although they can also provide post-shipment financing to the parties involved. Red- and green-clause letters of credit are specifically used to obtain pre-shipment financing, and green-clause L/Cs in particular can be regarded as a form of structured commodity financing. But letters of credit do not come cheap and a financing arranged on the back of them will often be more expensive than a structured alternative arranged without letters of credit. In short, structured commodity finance can be arranged without letters of credit, but there can still be perfectly valid motives for requesting them.

Forfaiting and factoring: the fraternal twins

Both reliant on sales receivables, forfaiting and factoring are often confused with one another. Forfaiting is specifically a method of financing international trade, while factoring was first developed as a domestic finance tool. Yet both instruments and markets have enjoyed exponential growth over the past decade in the area of international trade finance, although forfaiting has suffered from the worldwide economic slowdown of the early 2000s. Their growth is comparable to that of structured commodity finance, but these instruments serve different financing needs. Participants in the forfaiting markets are still completely different from providers of factoring services.[1]

Forfaiting

As mentioned in Chapter 1, trade receivables from highly creditworthy counterparties, or guaranteed by reputable banks, are actively traded in the forfaiting markets.

Principles and characteristics

This market is called 'forfaiting' simply because the purchaser of the debt has forfeited (ie, surrendered) its right of recourse to the exporter or to the previous holders of the debt. In other words, forfaiting is a non-recourse form of financing. The institution that first buys the debt can hold it for a time, or until maturity, or, alternatively, sell it in the secondary forfaiting markets.

The forfaiting markets typically trade paper of medium-term maturities (three to five years), but this trade finance instrument can also provide very short-term (90 days) and long-term (up to 10 years) financing. Transactions average a few million US dollars, and amounts range between US$1 million and US$50 million, denominated in US dollars, euros or Swiss francs.

The interest rate charged on forfaiting paper can be a fixed discount rate of a floating rate (generally based on Libor). Its level is based on the credit risk of the importer's country, the currency of the transaction and, since most forfaiting paper is avalised (guaranteed) by a bank, the credit risk of the avalising bank. In all cases, the default risk of the importer is also taken into account. Pricing varies greatly, ranging in the case of floating rates from a few basis points above Libor to very large spreads, such as the Libor plus 9 per cent charged in 1998 for 180-day paper from a Russian bank.

Raising financing with forfaiting

Used mainly in the trading of capital goods and (less so) commodities, forfaiting appeals because of its simplicity. Documentary requirements are straightforward and forfaiting agreements generally do not exceed a few pages. When the exporter is known to the forfaiter, the financing transaction can even close in a day. Moreover, the exporter can obtain a commitment with indicative financing terms before finalising the terms of its commercial contract with the importer, and thus adjust the related contract price accordingly. Compared with other sources of medium-term to long-term financing, such as export credit agencies, forfaiting has the advantage of providing financing for 100 per cent of the export contract (less interest and fees) and does not exclude high-risk countries. Note that syndication of primary level forfaiting deals is becoming increasingly common, thus enabling exporters to finance even large commercial contracts.

On the minus side, some countries do disappear almost overnight from the forfaiting markets. This happened for instance with Zimbabwe in 1998. Also, interest rates can rapidly exceed short-term bank loans, especially for good credits.

In the forfaiting markets bank guarantees are more the rule than the exception. Nevertheless, receivables due from companies with relatively good credit ratings can sometimes be traded in the forfaiting markets without the aval of a bank. In sub-Saharan Africa, for example, Ashanti Goldfields does not require an aval to be traded in the forfaiting markets.

Evolution of markets and participants

The forfaiting markets suffered from the financial crises of Asia in 1997 and Russia in 1998. At the end of the 1990s the markets had still not fully recovered the volumes transacted before the emerging market financial crises. Then came a glimpse of hope at the beginning of 2000, when liquidity began returning. At the same time, there was a recognition that the quality of assets booked was improving. Spreads for short-term quality counterparties were finally moving down, from around 300–400 basis points (bp) in mid-1999 to around 130bp in March 2000.

In an effort to standardise market practices, the International Forfaiting Association (IFA) was formed in 1999. The aims of the IFA include harmonisation of documentation, facilitation of e-commerce/trading and the introduction of education programmes designed to raise standards. The IFA also aims to develop a comprehensive set of rules similar to those of the Uniform Customs and Practice of Documentary Credits, but this may take some time.

Another recent development has been the emergence of many investment funds specialising in forfaiting paper. Commenting on the Tricon WestLB Forfaiting Fund launched in December 2000, one of the sponsors explained: 'The fund provides a means whereby individuals and institutions can place money in forfaiting receivables without having to concern themselves with the technicalities of the documentation for each deal . . . we believe that our fund should be attractive to many since trade-related debt characteristically yields somewhat better returns than purely financial instruments'.[2] Not all market participants, however, shared this optimistic view, mentioning possible liquidity problems due to the irregularity of shipment dates and different forms of documentation.

Despite these efforts at widening investor interest for forfaiting paper, the volume of secondary forfaiting markets has steadily decreased, mostly as a consequence of recurrent emerging markets financial crises. When the first signs of economic recovery in the emerging markets became apparent at the beginning of 2000, one market specialist observed that: 'With banks having a more positive perception of country risk they are more inclined to hold onto their deals'.[3] Paradoxically, the more widespread worldwide economic slowdown that began in 2001, combined with particular economic problems faced by some countries (for instance, Argentina), seemed to have a similar negative impact on the secondary forfaiting markets, eventually causing a fall in the number of primary transactions worldwide. As observed by one market practitioner: 'Margins have grown very thin because of the large number of funds looking for deals in which to invest and the small number of primary operations being generated by exporters. Accordingly, it is very difficult to structure a deal that will give a reasonable return and that can be sold into the secondary markets. Therefore, most deals concluded at the moment are kept on the book of the original forfaiter'.[4]

Finally, after some difficult years, in 2002 the forfaiting markets slowly picked up again, thanks to a new surge of primary transactions. However, it is unclear to what extent the forfaiting markets can fully recover from successive emerging market financial crises with banks in developing countries being increasingly reluctant to issue guarantees. One consequence of this series of crises, as noted by Martin Greenwood, head of forfaiting at BBVA in London, has been 'a move back towards pure trade forfaiting and away from balance sheet transactions because of concerns over asset quality'.[5] Interestingly, a different perspective is taken by BNP Paribas, which considers forfaiting 'as a service to the bank's exporting customers in the wider context of the bank's international corporate financing activities, rather than as an essential trading activity'.[6] BNP Paribas claims to keep most of its forfaiting deals on its books because its customers appreciate the fact that the bank does not have to build an extra margin to be able to sell the forfaiting paper in the secondary market.

Despite this sometimes gloomy environment, many banks have started a forfaiting business, often by poaching an entire forfaiting team from a competitor. This was the approach of the subsidiaries of two South African banks – Standard Bank London (SBL) in 1994 and ABSA in 2000. The strategy worked well for SBL, which came second in a poll conducted in 2000 by *Trade Finance* magazine. In the same poll, the best primary forfaiting institution in 2000, 2001, 2002 and 2003 was WestLB Forfaiting. Other recognised providers of forfaiting included Finanz AG Zurich, Nedbank, AWT, and Euro Trade & Forfaiting.

Like many other trade finance instruments, the forfaiting markets are becoming more structured, developing away from plain vanilla transactions towards hybrid and more complex trade operations. However, in spite of its recent advance within the portfolio of banks' offerings of trade finance instruments, forfaiting is still little known and little used. It should be noted that one important advantage of the forfaiting markets is that they actually do take emerging market payment risks. Therefore, forfaiting can enable an exporter to access pre-export financing of cross-border sales to emerging countries, which is not possible in the basic structured commodity finance transactions presented in Part II of this book.

Factoring

Factoring is the sale at a discount of accounts receivable on a daily, weekly or monthly basis in exchange for one or more payments as per an agreed schedule.

Principles and characteristics

In a basic factoring arrangement, also known as maturity factoring, a factor and a company agree on credit limits for each customer (buyer) and on the average collection period. The company then notifies each customer (buyer) that the factor has purchased the debt. Thereafter, for any sale, the company sends a copy of the invoice to the factor and the customer (buyer) makes payment directly to the factor. The factor pays the company on the basis of the agreed average collection period regardless of whether the customer (buyer) has paid. This form of factoring is non-recourse to the company, and thus provides both assistance with collection and insurance against bad debts. Under an arrangement known as with-recourse factoring, the company is liable for any delinquent accounts. In this case the factor provides collection, but not insurance.

Factoring is used mostly for consumer goods, in particular in the clothing industry. Yet nothing in principle should prevent factoring from expanding in the field of commodity finance. Indeed, over the past few years factoring has risen exponentially as a means to finance cross-border trade.

Raising financing with factoring

In addition to these services, the factor is generally also willing to advance a percentage (generally between 50 per cent and 85 per cent) of the value of the receivables. The interest rate charged on such advance is usually high compared with clean bank financing. In addition, fees typically range between 0.75 per cent and 2.5 per cent of factored receivables.

Factoring that provides combined collection, insurance and finance is generally called old-line factoring. In the area of international trade, old-line factoring would require the assignment by an exporter of receivables against an advance payment. The process usually involves the reassignment of such receivables to a correspondent factor in the buyer's country, which collects payment from the buyer and remits it to the export factor. Factors usually require access to a large percentage of an exporter's business and work mainly with short-term receivables (up to 180 days).

Factoring is similar to forfaiting in that receivables are sold to a third party, but, unlike in forfaiting, payment is usually not cash but as per an agreed schedule. Also, factoring does not require a bank guarantee and can cover very small amounts. Factoring can be an attractive short-term financing alternative for small companies, which may not be able to afford to employ a specialised credit manager whose job it is to manage receivables in the best possible way. Finally, factoring is obviously not limited to trade financing, but can provide general purpose short-term financing.

Evolution of markets and participants

Many factors are subsidiaries of commercial banks. In the mid-1990s the international factoring industry was dominated by a small number of factoring networks and houses, principally Factors Chain International (FCI), the world's largest network of factoring companies, which accounts for about half of worldwide factoring. Other market participants include International Factors Group, Heller International and Lombard Natwest Commercial Services. In the *Trade*

Finance magazine poll mentioned earlier, HSBC Invoice Finance was voted best factor in 2000, 2001 and 2003, overtaken by Fortis Commercial Services only in 2002.

In the 1990s the factoring market quadrupled its annual volume of business activity to a figure in the region of US$550 million in 2000, more than twice that achieved just four years earlier. The largest market continues to be Europe, which represents 64 per cent of world volume. Within Europe, the largest market is the United Kingdom, which is the world's second largest factoring market (behind the United States) with an annual volume of US$103 million (1999 figures). At last factoring is being used to finance international trade: the growth of the factoring market is evidence that more companies are switching to international factoring as a way of moving away from letter of credit terms to open account trading.

Like the forfaiting markets, factoring suffered from the 1997 and 1998 emerging market crises, especially in South-East Asia. In Indonesia, in particular, the volume of business fell from US$2.78 billion in 1996, when it was the largest factoring market in the region, to just US$33 million in 1999; over the same period the number of factoring companies fell from 55 to just two. In The Philippines, international factoring all but stopped as a result of the crisis. Some markets bounced back strongly, however; for example, China grew by nearly 700 per cent in 2000.

The volume of factoring increased steadily in central Europe in the late 1990s, the biggest market in terms of size being Turkey, with US$2.27 billion-worth of transactions in 1999. Part of the reason for this growth in Turkey was that 'for a period of time there were considerable tax advantages to exporters in using it instead of the more traditional banking methods'.[7] Among ex-communist bloc countries, the Czech Republic showed the largest increase in factoring volume, in part due to shortcomings of the local banking market as a result of the privatisation process and the fact that factoring enables exporters to obtain financing while bypassing banks. Similarly, factoring has generally experienced steady growth recently in western Europe, especially in countries to the south. Italy, in particular, experienced double-digit growth and became the third largest factoring market in the world.

Looking further west to Latin America, factoring is still relatively new. This enabled the volume of factoring business to grow exponentially in the second half of the 1990s, rising for instance in Argentina from none in 1994 to US$1.49 billion in 1999 and in Chile from US$289 million to US$2.61 billion over the same period. 'The region holds excellent potential for international factoring, although in some countries a lack of experience and a generally cautious attitude may hold back its development.'[8]

In Europe, the factoring market has experienced several important changes, starting with a consolidation of factors leading to Europe-wide businesses in northern Europe, as a result of bank mergers and acquisitions. Another development has been that 'factors are starting to work more closely with insurers in order to assist with their international and domestic credit risk'.[9] In Denmark, for instance, the credit insurer NCM bought Forenede Factors. This trend is also apparent in the UK international factoring market, where participants have moved away from the two-factor system and are increasingly using credit insurers to provide them with credit protection. This innovative practice has also been adopted in Italy: 'Whilst it still uses correspondent factors to handle the collection of export invoices on behalf of its clients, [Medio Factoring] now uses one of the credit insurers to take care of the credit protection side of their export business'.[10] Market specialists also expect the Basle II Accord (discussed in Part IV of this book) to result in more companies seeking financing through factoring. In summary, despite the worldwide economic slowdown that began in 2001, factoring has achieved consistent growth and one can expect its continued expansion into cross-border trade financing.

Trade finance in the new economy

At the beginning of 2000, although some banks already had web sites where they advertised their trade finance capabilities, none had yet launched a fully fledged forfaiting electronic market-place. On the other hand, the trading of commodities was rapidly moving online.

Electronic market-places for commodities

At the end of 2000, just before the bursting of the internet bubble took its toll, electronic market-places and exchanges had been established for most kinds of commodities and semi-finished products, ranging from soft commodities such as coffee, fish, flowers and grain, to hard commodities including steel, base metals, oil products and chemicals.

One landmark deal was a coffee export transaction conducted through the bolero.net electronic trading platform by the Federación Nacional de Cafeteros de Colombia (FNC)[11] in October 2000.[12] NatWest (now part of Royal Bank of Scotland) was the importer's bank. Because Royal Bank of Scotland was a member of bolero.net, the shipping documents and banking instruments, including a negotiable bill of lading, were not required in paper form. In 2001, bolero.net continued its development by expanding into the metals and mining sectors.

Emergence of electronic trade finance platforms

One of the first banks to invest in systems to meet the specific demand for online financing of commodity transactions was the Dutch bank Fortis (which includes the former Mees Pierson). As explained by Fortis's Walter Vollebregt: 'There is a lengthy logistics process in a commodity trade ... The right "total fulfilment solution" for commodity transactions is vital to drive liquidity. Besides logistics, issues such as credit and marine insurance and quality inspection have to be addressed'. Citibank was also at the forefront of developing online market-places for trade finance.

In the specific area of forfaiting, as at the early 2000s several e-platforms had been launched, including LTPtrade.net and TradeSurface in London, and LoanQuorum, IPFEX and FXTrade in the United States. LTPtrade.net, for example, a few months after its establishment was already posting offerings from more than 200 registered banks and successfully conducting deals on an auction basis, with market participants being able to view electronic copies of documentation and market information (such as news and banks' financial statements). More recently a new platform named Global Trade Finance Network (GTFNet) was launched specifically to enable banks to finance and distribute trade debt receivables. As observed by Tara Kimbrell Cole, founder of GTFNet:[13]

> There are a variety of private initiatives seeking to develop internet platforms to redress the current trade finance climate. While each has its merits, none of them seems a complete solution. Over time the various initiatives on this front will need to come together

> to provide a truly global organisation with a comprehensive approach. Only a truly integrated international approach can break down the old barriers and create a viable, trade finance platform that will be open to all markets – both developed and emerging.

Another development closer to the area of factoring has been the use of 'tracked asset finance', which enables companies to raise finance by selling invoice receivables, thus 'taking advantage of the technology developed for automated sales ledger input and strict reporting routines to provide a real-time basis for corporate health evaluation'.[14]

Impact of the internet on trade finance

Most market specialists view the electronic enabling of trade finance as a necessary development: 'We believe that the time has now come to apply techniques to the trade finance market that are already used in other sectors to create more liquidity, efficiency and transparency . . . Forfaiting is already less important as a means of raising trade financing than it was 10 years ago . . . the forfaiting markets will die unless there is more liquidity'.[15] Other market participants adopt a more positive perspective regarding the impact of electronic trading on the secondary forfaiting markets: 'By enhancing transparency, price discovery and liquidity, the new online ATSs [alternative trading systems] for trade finance assets will lay the ground work for participation by institutional investors . . . by the end of 2003 online trading will account for nearly 19 per cent of the secondary market in trade finance assets'.[16] Yet others predict even more profound changes, expecting electronic trade of commodities to hasten the decline of many existing trade financing instruments:

> We can now begin to see a feasible alternative for L/C-type transactions. L/Cs could be replaced by what amounts to electronic deferred payment certificates. Interestingly, because of the potential difficulty in agreeing standard formats for other instruments, items such as bills of exchange might suffer the same fate on the web. What we may also expect to see are that deferred payment certificates might be lodged with a trusted third party, such as Bolero or TradeCard, for example, and even discounted.[17]

Reality has not yet been that bleak for letters of credit, which now enjoy their own electronic market-place with LCconnect. The company that launched LCconnect claims that more than US$100 million-worth of transactions were executed in 2001 (the platform went live in May 2001). They believe that 'corporate subscribers can benefit by saving a significant amount of time originating letters of credit, more easily developing new relationships with banks and accessing aggregated L/C reports online'.[18]

In any case, the electronic enabling of trade finance can be expected to have at least an indirect impact on the more structured transactions – like a two-speed development of trade finance. As anticipated by SG: 'Big deals are big money, but we are client-driven and small deals are the bread and butter, so we need to keep doing them. The challenge is to standardise the process for smaller deals so that we can concentrate on the bigger, structured deals'.[19]

---

[1] An exception is a joint venture recently formed by WestLB and the Export-Import Bank of India – Global Trade Finance – to provide forfaiting and factoring products for Indian exporters. Their reasoning is that 'factoring provides credit assessment and protection, financing, and collection services to exporters for regular sales on open

account terms. As the demand for open account trading expands globally, the need has arisen for Indian exporters to offer similar terms to importers in order to remain competitive. Alternatively, forfaiting enables exporters to offer longer-term financing to importers of capital goods from India. Both products, being complementary and available at a one-stop-shop, will therefore provide greater client servicing and support through tailor-made financing packages'. (Quoted in 'Trade finance outsourcing', Trade Finance, July/August 2001.)

[2] Margrith Lutschg Emmenegger, quoted in 'Blinking in the bright lights', *Trade Finance*, March 2001.

[3] Janine Barber, quoted in 'Confidence returns' by Philip Carter, *Trade Finance*, March 2000.

[4] Daniel Vignial, head of forfaiting at Crédit Agricole Indosuez, quoted in 'Simmering quietly' by Michael Rowe, *Trade Finance*, July/August 2001.

[5] 'Simmering quietly' by Michael Rowe, *Trade Finance*, July/August 2001.

[6] Ibid.

[7] 'All the right ingredients', *Trade Finance*, December 2000.

[8] 'True frontier territory', *Trade Finance*, January/February 2001.

[9] 'Consolidating home base', *Trade Finance*, May 2001.

[10] 'Italian design earns rewards', *Trade Finance*, June 2001.

[11] National Federation of Coffee Growers of Colombia.

[12] 'E-trade cash: The race is on', *Trade Finance*, November 2000.

[13] 'GTFNet brings in top management', *Trade Finance*, March 2002.

[14] 'Taking the direct route' by Tim Nicolle, CEO of Demica, *Trade Finance*, February 2002.

[15] Richard Tull, director and marketing chief of LTPtrade.net, quoted in 'Blinking in the bright lights', *Trade Finance*, March 2001.

[16] Neil Katkov, analyst with online financial research firm Celent Communications, quoted in 'Simmering quietly' by Michael Rowe, *Trade Finance*, July/August 2001.

[17] Citibank's Peter Sargent, Vice President ebusiness, quoted in 'E-trade cash: The race is on', *Trade Finance*, November 2000.

[18] 'LC connect boosts deal volumes', *Trade Finance*, February 2002.

[19] 'Keeping the deals flowing', *Trade Finance*, November 2001.

Chapter 3

Evolution of traditional trade finance

The developments of the past few years have enabled trade finance to finally shake off its rather dull mantle and live up to its true, exciting nature. One important change in the way cross-border trade is conducted is that recurring trade transactions are increasingly carried out on an open account basis, even if occasional economic problems in a particular country once again push letters of credit to the forefront. In Chapter 1 the mechanics by which traditional letters of credit and basic trade finance instruments continue to support the provision of post-shipment financing to both importers and exporters were explained. This availability of post-shipment financing compares with the dearth of traditional trade finance instruments capable of meeting market demand for attractive pre-shipment financing. In this respect, we saw that the philosophy behind the development of certain tools, such as green-clause letters of credit, is the same as that supporting the recent development of structured commodity finance.

The more direct relationship between exporters and importers provided by open account trading has in turn spurred the development of cross-border factoring and trade credit insurance. Moving on to longer-term financing, the forfaiting markets have experienced profound changes, ranging from the consolidation of market participants to the harmonisation of standards through the International Forfaiting Association. While forfaiting has suffered from the economic slowdown worldwide in general, and from emerging market misfortunes in particular, as far as medium-term financing is concerned it still represents an attractive alternative to export credit agencies.

Finally, the common feature of all these traditional trade finance markets and instruments is the rapid move to standardise and facilitate electronically all aspects of the trade finance process. We are seeing only the beginning of this process and cannot yet predict its long-term impact on trade finance. Nevertheless, in the future only deals that bring real added value will be able to remain outside these fast-developing, highly liquid, low-cost electronic market-places. This is the ambition of structured commodity finance transactions, presented in Part II.

Part II

Techniques

Introduction to Part II

In the 'Introduction' to this book the following general definition of structured commodity finance was proposed: 'financing transactions whereby an inventory and/or flow of commodities can be isolated from its owner and used as collateral for security and repayment'. The purpose of the structure is to give lenders greater control over the commodities being used as security and to put in place a repayment mechanism based on the sale of the commodities, so that the financing becomes self-liquidating.

The lending bank has control if the commodities are stored in a safe place and remain so more or less until the financing is extinguished. This is the principle underlying inventory financing and is covered in Chapter 4. Banks can also lend against a commitment by the owner to deliver the commodities at a later time to one or more acceptable offshore buyers. The various techniques based on this principle are covered in Chapter 5 under the heading of pre-export financing. Chapter 6 discusses countertrade, a particular form of structured commodity finance that also serves certain commercial objectives. Chapter 7 presents more complex structures and explains how the principles of structured commodity finance can also achieve accounting or tax benefits, or attract new classes of investors through securitisation. The next chapter, Chapter 8, examines the due diligence process and the increasing role of collateral managers. Part II closes with an overview of the legal aspects to be considered when organising a structured commodity finance transaction (Chapter 9) and an evaluation of structured commodity finance (Chapter 10).

Before discussing specific techniques, it is important to stress that there are no standardised types of structured commodity finance transactions because one essential principle of this financial product is the ability to tailor the structure to the particular needs and circumstances of the parties involved. Likewise, many structured commodity finance transactions actually rely on a combination of techniques. Nevertheless, to help put some order into the web of structured commodity finance transactions executed over the past decade or so, this book will present these techniques under the broad classification detailed in the previous paragraph. Also, it should be noted that in this Part II references to a particular form of financing are concerned with its structured finance expression. For instance, 'prepayments' described in Chapter 5 relate to a structured form of the advance payment mechanism covered in Part I.

Commodity finance is needed at various stages of the production and marketing cycle. However, for simplicity, the techniques presented in this book will start from the assumption that the financing is raised from an international bank for a commodity exporter located in an emerging country that sells to one or more buyers located in an OECD country. Extrapolations to other types of operations will be made when relevant.

Chapter 4

Structured inventory financing

Principles and background

With inventory financing, the owner of the commodities raises finance against the assignment to the lending bank of the commodities stored in a warehouse and repayment comes from sales proceeds payable by future buyers directly to the bank. Because storage of the commodities is generally evidenced by warehouse receipts, this technique can also be referred to as warehouse receipt financing.

While this technique is actually very old (warehouse receipt for grains were first recorded in 2400 BC in Mesopotamia[1]), it has not spread evenly to every region of the world. In particular, as observed by the Food and Agriculture Organisation (FAO) and the Natural Resource Institute (NRI) in a joint paper,[2] inventory credit for agricultural produce is widely used in Latin American countries and in some Asian countries.

In the early 1990s inventory financing experienced a new impetus thanks to widespread liberalisation and privatisation in emerging markets. In this respect, the FAO/NRI paper noted that 'government marketing boards and parastatals usually had ready access to finance to enable them to purchase and to store food and industrial crops. Following liberalisation, such finance has not been easily available to private traders who are expected to take over the marketing functions previously carried out by the state . . . Inventory credit is one way of overcoming financing constraints'.[3]

In its most sophisticated versions, inventory financing can also form the basis of asset-backed securities issued through the capital markets (see Chapter 7 for a discussion of securitisation).

Basic transaction flows

Financing is obtained against commodities already produced but not yet sold. Basic transaction flows are as follows.

- The owner stores commodities in a warehouse.
- The bank takes a security interest in the commodities (for instance, a warehouse receipt).
- The commodities are inspected and found to be acceptable.
- The bank makes a loan to the commodities' owner (the borrower).
- The commodities are sold by the owner to one or more first-class buyers.
- The bank obtains acceptable new security and gives a release order to the warehouse.
- The commodities are released and delivered to the buyer(s).
- Sales receivables are paid by the buyer(s) into an escrow account controlled by the bank.
- The loan is repaid to the bank from the escrow account.
- The bank releases excess funds to the borrower.

Term sheet

Using the outline of a standard term sheet, the following are some of the key features and terms and conditions of structured inventory financing. (Legal aspects are also discussed in Chapter 9.)

Amount

Inventory financing can be used for small to large loans. Note that in the case of agricultural commodities the cumulative amount of the loans would tend to be limited by the value of the commodities that the borrower could store from the current crop. Exceptionally, loans can be available for longer periods when arranged on a rollover basis.[4]

Borrower

Typically, the borrower under an inventory financing is a local trader seeking financing for the purchase of locally produced commodities pending their export to offshore buyers. End-buyers must be first-class credits and agree to effect payments, preferably in hard currency, into an escrow account. This technique can also be used by commodity importers to pay for the cost of imported commodities. In this case, the lending bank would either make a loan (sometimes called a produce loan) to the importer or effect a direct payment to the supplier on behalf of the importer. Transaction flows are essentially the same as listed above, with the added complexity that the importer (for example, a state-owned refinery) can sell the commodities either as they are, or after processing or manufacturing.

Commodities

Inventory financing can be used to finance commodities at all stages of the production and marketing cycle: 'The collateral system can be effectively applied to any commodity required to be stored or remain idle for a period of time [and] is commonly used today in numerous forms and at various stages of the commodity, that is, during the natural flow of goods from producer to consumer, for example (i) pre-export financing; (ii) processing of raw commodities; (iii) trade, frequently financed through a bill of lading (B/L); and (iv) financing of local distribution channels'.[5]

Disbursement

The loan would be disbursed upon satisfaction of conditions precedent giving the bank a certain level of comfort with regard to the value and availability of the commodities being financed. The owner would typically assign to the bank warehouse receipts evidencing ownership of the commodities. In a less secured form of inventory financing, a loan could be extended before the commodities are actually stored in a warehouse, although, in the case of agricultural commodities, banks would normally disburse funds only after the commodities are produced or at least once weather conditions affecting the crop are known. When inventory financing is used before the commodities are actually stored in a warehouse, the bank would require as a condition precedent to disbursement either shipping documents or other documents evidencing ownership of the commodities and upcoming delivery to a warehouse. Banks may require that the commodity be sold before the loan is disbursed, although this requirement somehow defies the very purpose of inventory financing. Inventory financing can also be structured to allow multiple drawings, each time against new warehouse receipts or other documents evidencing ownership. With this procedure, it was observed in the FAO/NRI paper mentioned earlier: 'The bank loan can be used to purchase further produce, which can itself be pledged as security for a further loan. In this way the borrower's stocks can be increased well beyond his or her initial means'.[6]

Financing ratio

The amount that the bank would disburse would be based on the expected value of the commodities held or to be held in a warehouse, less anticipated liquidation costs. This expected value would take into consideration the level of liquidity in the particular commodities market. A discount would be applied for highly perishable commodities, for commodities with high price volatility – unless price risk is properly hedged (see Part III) – or for loans with longer maturities. Obviously, the financing ratio would be higher if buyers have already been identified or if there is a liquid market for the commodities pledged as security. The loan should be less than the market value of the commodities so that the borrower continues to have some equity tied up in the transaction.

Tenor

Tenors (that is maturities) of inventory financing transactions typically range between three and 18 months. As will be discussed later, tenors can be longer for certain commodities (such as aluminium) if the borrower has a good track record under its commercial and financial obligations, or if the structure is geared towards institutional investors (for example, asset-backed securitisations). Tenors are also linked to provisioning requirements, discussed in Part IV. For agricultural commodities, it would be very difficult to obtain financing for a tenor extending beyond the end of the marketing cycle of the current crop.

Cost

Financing cost is typically expressed as a spread over a floating rate, such as the three-month or six-month London interbank offered rate (Libor).

Repayment

Repayment should come from commodities sales receivables payable by the buyer(s) into an escrow account controlled by the bank. In this regard, to the extent possible the commodity owner should sell the commodities during good market conditions. Although inventory financing is generally self-liquidating, the bank retains full recourse to the borrower in case the sale proceeds are not sufficient to meet the loan obligation. Alternatively, the bank could accept direct repayment from the borrower with an adequate security structure (see below).

Security

The backbone of inventory financing is the control that the bank has over the commodities held as collateral. The security package would require, among other things, the following.

- A satisfactory security interest in the commodities being financed, including a pledge agreement, assignment of warehouse receipts, shipping documents and/or any other documents evidencing ownership of the commodities. If the financing extends prior to or after the time when the commodities are stored in the warehouse, the bank should retain a full set of negotiable shipping documents issued 'to order' and blank endorsed, to be forwarded directly to the bank. If non-negotiable transport documents are involved, the commodities should be consigned to the banks. In any case, the bank should ensure that, as soon as the commodities leave the warehouse, its security interest in the commodities (or the sales proceeds thereof) is maintained until all obligations of the borrower have been extinguished.
- Satisfactory reports from a reputable inspection service company and/or collateral manager having inspected the commodities stored in the warehouse or tank. The bank should be in a position to have some recourse to the warehouse operator to compensate for any loss in the value of the commodities for which the warehouse operator is responsible.
- Agreement that the commodities will not leave the warehouse without a proper delivery order from the bank. This delivery order should include instructions to collect all charges before releasing the commodities in order to avoid the establishment of any legal interest in the commodities by the warehouse operator. Release of commodities should be conditional upon receipt by the bank of either (i) repayment of all principal, interest and fees due under the loan; or (ii) assignment of sales contracts and receivables with the buyers' agreement to pay the proceeds into an escrow account; or (iii) assignment of irrevocable letters of credit issued in favour of the borrower covering the sale proceeds; or (iv) any other payment security agreed by the bank. The new security structure will progressively replace that provided by the warehouse receipts and related documents. Sometimes the bank may accept trust receipts, which are undertakings from the commodity owner to sell (as the bank's trustee) the commodities within a specified time limit, possibly to identified buyers, and to hold them to the bank's order in the meantime. However, the inventory financing transaction is fully structured only if the bank retains control over the sale proceeds.
- Noting of the interest of the financing bank in payments under the commercial insurance, for instance with the lending bank named as loss payee under the policy.
- Assignment to the bank of the proceeds of firm sales contracts between the borrower and one or more acceptable first-class buyer (acknowledged by the buyers). To guarantee a minimum receivables value for the contracts, the bank would typically require either fixed or hedged sales prices, or a commitment on the part of the borrower to assign more sales contracts to the bank if the expected value of sales receivables falls below an agreed level. The owner of the commodities may even be obliged to purchase the commodities directly from the market to make up for any loss in the value of expected receivables.
- Sales receivables should be payable into an offshore escrow account, controlled by the bank and supported by irrevocable payment instructions given by the owner of the commodities to the commodity buyer(s) and confirmed by such buyer(s). The bank should have a satisfactory security interest in sums standing to the credit of the escrow account and to any additional reserve account supporting the borrower's loan obligations.
- If the payment risk of certain buyers is deemed unacceptable, the bank may require that sales to those buyers be supported by a letter of credit.
- The bank should take any additional guarantee deemed necessary, such as a local bank guarantee or surety bond, or political risk insurance cover. In many cases the bank does

not rely exclusively on inventories as collateral, but tends to use them in combination with more conventional guarantees.

The next sections discuss the benefits and limitations of structured inventory financing techniques. A more general evaluation of structured commodity finance is provided at the end of Part II.

Benefits of structured inventory financing

Exporters can raise attractive financing earlier in the marketing cycle

Inventory financing is probably used by a greater number of borrowers than other forms of structured commodity finance, primarily because this technique works for small loan amounts, and because its principles and basic structures are simple and readily understandable. The underlying concept is so straightforward that small, unsophisticated farmers and traders with little or no financial track record increasingly turn to it.

A valuable side benefit of inventory financing is that it enables commodity owners to store the commodities and wait for better market conditions in order to sell them at a higher price. Borrowers can also obtain financing before the commodities have been sold and even before potential buyers have been identified. Provided that sufficient security is obtained (for example, assignment of shipping documents), banks can sometimes disburse funds even before commodities have actually reached the warehouse.

Inventory financing enables soft commodity exporters in emerging markets to raise financing at attractive terms, in particular at a lower cost than under traditional loans. For a start, amounts lent under inventory financing can exceed the borrowing capacity offered by the balance sheet. As summarised by one market specialist, inventory financing is: ‘a highly cost-effective way to borrow money and raise working capital since (a) interest rates on the borrowing are less onerous than securing credit by conventional means, and (b) it is a vehicle by which a bank can lend money to companies even though they may have exhausted all other means of raising a loan by way of mortgage, balance sheet borrowing, etc’.[7] This market specialist presented the example of a three-month financing against ownership of US$7 million-worth of coffee in Kenya to argue that using warehouse receipt financing techniques with collateral management would result in extra credit availability of US$2.1 million at interest charges of Libor plus 2.5 per cent instead of Libor plus 15 per cent, against the cost of extra collateral management fees of US$59,000.

Lenders have more control over the commodities

In general, the commodities already exist in a saleable form when the loan is disbursed and thus their value can be easily assessed. In case of performance default on the part of the buyers, the bank can seize and sell the commodities to extinguish the loan. Since the bank has full recourse to the borrower, the bank can expect its cooperation to solve any commercial or political problem linked to the liquidation of the commodities. To the extent that, in general, to extinguish financial obligations of the borrower, inventory financing ultimately relies either on the sale of the commodities or on the assignment of export receivables from OECD buyers (or local first-class credits able to pay in hard currency), it can also be regarded as more secure than export receivables financing, thanks to the initial security provided by the thorough inspection of the commodities. There is also a stronger incentive for borrowers to reimburse financing than under clean loans, as failure to do so should result in a loss of the commodities or their proceeds to the benefit of the bank.

Limitations of structured inventory financing

Required logistics are time-consuming and costly

Funds are only disbursed upon delivery of satisfactory warehouse receipts or shipping documents, which may take time to reach the bank. Fortunately, copies of relevant documents and transfer instructions can now be provided by fax, by telex and even in electronic form (via e-mail or on B2B market-places). Still, there are additional costs related to the warehouse component (higher insurance costs, collateral manager's and inspection service fees, possible stamp duty, and so on).

Additional exposure to volatile commodity markets

Moreover, there are risks that the borrower may not be in a position to repay the loan if the commodities cannot be sold. This would be the case, for instance, if the commodities were physically damaged or if the government repealed a necessary export licence. The borrower may also be compelled to hold onto the commodities for longer than expected, either because no reputable buyers can be found, or because prices have collapsed and are now too low for the sale proceeds to be sufficient to repay the loan and enable the borrower to make a profit or even to stay in business.

Banks remain exposed to third-party fraud and performance risk

When financing is granted against commodities stored in a warehouse, the risk of fraud by the borrower or the warehouse operator (for example, the risk of multiple pledge) cannot be completely eliminated and can leave the bank with recourse only to the balance sheet of the borrower. The same risk applies when the financing covers the period during which the commodities are transported. An alternative to warehouse financing could be the use of International Federation of Freight Forwarders Association (FIATA) forwarders' certificates of receipt (FCRs), which may also include the financing through the transport period.[8] FIATA FCRs are commonly used in eastern Europe. However, due to increased fraudulent activities in this sector, FIATA eventually prohibited the issuance of all FCRs for steel shipments. In fact, some freight forwarders were issuing forged FCRs without disposing of the commodities.

Banks are also exposed not only to fraud but also to simple non-performance by third parties, such as warehouse operators, inspection companies and collateral managers, as well as any other key third party involved in the inventory financing chain (such as freight forwarders, processing companies and loading terminals). In this regard, as stated in the FAO/NRI paper quoted earlier: 'A key to getting banks to make a serious commitment to this sort of lending is the presence of warehouse operators of outstanding reputation'.[9] Bank risks also markedly increase with less than perfect legal documentation and poorly managed back offices: 'To manage collateral properly requires significant back and middle office effort on the part of the lender, since the collateral needs to be not only controlled but also monitored for value on a daily basis'.[10]

Even if banks eventually come to control the commodities, liquidation costs can be unexpectedly high: 'Some banks and traders estimate that on average about 30–40 per cent of the market value of the goods may be lost because of discounts that have to be taken on the price, and because storage until the time of sale, transportation, etc. have to be paid. These liquidation costs will be less if the goods can easily be sold on at auction or delivered to an exchange'.[11]

---

1 Christian Joerg, Head of Collateral Management Services at Société Générale de Surveillance (SGS), an international inspection services company based in Geneva, quoted in 'Securing the frontier supplies', *Trade Finance,* April 2002.

2 *Inventory Credit: An Approach to Developing Agricultural Markets* by Jonathan Coulter (NRI) and Andrew W. Shepherd (FAO), FAO Agricultural Services Bulletin No.120, 1995.

3 Ibid.

4 For instance, early in 2003 the European Bank for Reconstruction and Development (EBRD) arranged a US$15 million revolving credit facility for the Russian and Ukrainian subsidiaries of Nidera Handelscompagnie, a Rotterdam-based commodity trader, based on warehouse depositary receipts.

5 Christian Joerg of SGS, quoted in 'Securing the frontier supplies', *Trade Finance,* April 2002.

6 FAO Agricultural Services Bulletin No.120, ibid.

7 'The collateral advantage', *Trade Finance,* November 2001.

8 SGS's Christian Joerg, quoted in 'Securing the frontier supplies', *Trade Finance,* April 2002.

9 FAO Agricultural Services Bulletin No.120, ibid.

10 *Structured Trade and Commodity Finance in Emerging Markets* by John McNamara, Woodhead Publishing Limited, 2001.

11 Lamon Rutten, Chief, Finance and Energy, UNCTAD, quoted in *Collateralised Commodity Financing: With Special Reference to the Use of Warehouse Receipts,* report by the UNCTAD Secretariat, 1995.

Chapter 5

Structured pre-export financing

Principles and background

This chapter covers financing structures whereby the owner of the commodities raises finance against the assignment to the lending bank of existing export sales contracts and receivables (called export receivables financing) or directly through prepaid export sales contracts for future delivery (called prepayment financing), and repayment comes from export proceeds payable by dedicated buyers directly to the bank. In structured pre-export financing, lenders rely on the ability of the commodity owner to perform under an underlying commercial transaction.

In effect, the commodity exporter raises a loan against future exports. However, in the case of export receivables financing the exporter borrows from the bank and assigns export proceeds as security, whereas in the case of prepayment financing the exporter receives payment from one buyer against an undertaking to deliver commodities in the future to this buyer for the value of the prepayment. In turn, the buyer raises a bank loan to effect the prepayment. Pre-export financing may be regarded as the original form of modern structured commodity finance. In a way, inventory financing is a variation on the same theme, with the added control over the commodities that has proved necessary in some transactions.

In its most sophisticated versions, pre-export financing can also form the basis of securitisations (see Chapter 7).

Export receivables financing

The phrase 'export receivables' is used for simplicity and refers to sales receivables from exports. Thus export receivables financing simply refers to self-liquidating loans secured by export proceeds. Export receivables financing is also commonly referred to as pre-export financing or pre-shipment financing.

Export receivables financing transactions were pioneered in the late 1980s by Bankers Trust Company and Union Bank of Switzerland (UBS) for clients in sub-Saharan Africa. In Angola, for instance, Bankers Trust arranged the first syndicated pre-shipment financing facilities for Banco Nacional de Angola against the assignment of crude oil receivables by Sonangol. Similarly, for several years in a row, the bank arranged a coffee pre-export financing facility for Tanzania's National Bank of Commerce, with the loans being used to finance the country's oil imports. At the same time, in Zimbabwe, Bankers Trust arranged or co-arranged several syndicated facilities for the Agricultural Marketing Authority of Zimbabwe, drawn against bankers' acceptances related to various agricultural exports. Finally, in 1991 Bankers Trust arranged and syndicated the first pre-export financing transaction against cocoa receivables due to the Ghana Cocoa Board (Cocobod); at that time, the funds were used to pay for Ghana's oil imports. The Cocobod pre-export financing facility remains one of the most popular of its kind. Thanks to these breakthrough financing structures, for the first time in the aftermath of the 1982 world debt crisis high-risk African countries were able to raise commercial loans from international banks. In all cases, country risk was mitigated via the assignment of export receivables, leaving lenders exposed to performance risk. At that time, loans were made either to state-owned or central banks, or to commodity boards, and were further supported by government guarantees.

Prepayment financing

In most prepayment financing transactions (or simply 'prepayments') the buyer raises a loan from a bank and uses the proceeds to effect prepayment to the commodity exporter. In this case, the lending bank would normally require a further security interest in the commodities from the time of production to their future delivery to the buyer. Prepayments therefore propose a different relationship between the ultimate lender and the ultimate beneficiary of the funds. Prepayment is the name given to this type of transaction from the perspective of the buyer. It can also be called production payment or advance payment. From the perspective of the exporter, this technique can also be referred to as 'forward sale of future production' or 'prepaid forward sale'.

Prepayments used to be a very common form of commodity financing for large transactions. Banks were lending to commodity buyers, primarily large trading companies, which would in turn finance exporters. However, with the demise of several trading houses in the late 1980s and related bank losses this form of financing all but disappeared under its original unsecured form. Over the past few years, prepayments have made a marked comeback, but under a new structured form. This recent development came not only as a way to perfect the security interest of banks in the commodities being financed but also as a consequence of new emerging markets being opened up by trading companies long before international banks dared to enter them.

Basic transaction flows

Financing is obtained against commodities already produced and sold. Basic transaction flows for export receivables and prepayment financing are set out in the following subsections.

Export receivables financing

1. The commodities are sold by the owner to one or more dedicated buyer(s).
2. The owner assigns the export sales contracts and receivables to the bank.
3. The bank makes a loan to the owner of the commodities (the borrower).
4. The commodities are exported to the buyer(s).
5. Export sales receivables are paid by the buyer(s) into an escrow account controlled by the bank.
6. The loan is repaid to the bank from this escrow account.
7. The bank releases excess funds to the borrower.

Prepayment financing

1. The commodities are sold by the owner to the buyer (with a prepayment agreement).
2. The buyer assigns the prepaid export sales contracts to the bank.

3. The bank takes a security interest in the commodities.
4. The commodities are inspected and found to be acceptable.
5. The bank makes a limited recourse loan to the buyer (the borrower).
6. The buyer prepays for commodities to the owner.
7. The bank gives a release order to the warehouse.
8. The commodities are released and exported to the buyer.
9. The buyer repays the loan to the bank.

Note that steps 3, 4 and 7 reinforce the structure, but are not present in all forms of prepayments.

Term sheet

Using the outline of a standard term sheet, the following are the key features, terms and conditions of both structured export receivables financing and structured prepayment financing. (Legal aspects are also discussed in Chapter 9.)

Export receivables financing

Amount
Export receivables financing can be used for medium to large loans. In the case of agricultural commodities, the cumulative amount of the financing would again tend to be limited by the amount of export receivables that could be generated from the current crop.

Borrower
Typically, the borrower under an export receivables financing is a local producer seeking financing for the commodity marketing cycle pending receipt of export proceeds from offshore buyers. However, export receivables financing techniques can also be used by any company exporting commodities or even by commodity importers. When used by importers, this technique would require the onward sale of the commodities to local or regional first-class buyers, such as subsidiaries of multinational companies willing to pay hard currency into an offshore escrow account.

Commodities
Export receivables financing can be used to finance any type of commodities.

Disbursement
The loan would be disbursed in one or more tranches upon satisfaction of certain initial or continuing conditions precedent, giving the bank a certain level of comfort with regard to the value and availability of the export sales contracts and receivables being financed. In a less secured form of export receivables financing, a loan could be arranged before export sales contracts are signed, but subsequent assignment of sufficient export sales contracts would be a condition precedent to loan disbursement. In the case of agricultural commodities, banks would usually disburse funds only after the commodities have been produced or at least once weather conditions affecting the crop are known.

Financing ratio

The amount that the bank disburses would be based on the expected value of the export sales contracts and receivables. A discount would be applied for highly perishable commodities and for commodities with high price volatility, unless price risk is properly hedged (see Part III for a discussion of commodity price risk hedging), or for loans with longer maturities. Obviously, the financing ratio would be higher where commodities have already been sold or if there is a liquid market for them.

Tenor

Tenors of export receivables financing transactions typically range between six and 24 months. Up to the late 1990s, tenors would generally not exceed 18 months, but the limits are being continuously extended thanks to innovative structures, including embedded rollover mechanisms up to four or even five years. Tenors can be longer for certain commodities (such as gas) or if the structure is geared towards institutional investors through securitisation. Tenors can be limited by provisioning requirements, discussed in Part IV. For agricultural commodities, it would be very difficult to obtain financing for a tenor extending beyond the end of the marketing cycle of the current crop (except on a rollover basis, with some strict conditions attached).

Cost

Financing cost is typically expressed as a spread over Libor.

Repayment

Repayment should come from export sales receivables paid by one or more identified buyers into an offshore escrow account controlled by the bank. Although export receivables financing is self-liquidating, the bank retains full recourse to the borrower in case sales proceeds are not sufficient to meet the loan obligations.

Security

The security package would require *inter alia* the following.

- Assignment to the bank of the proceeds of firm export sales contracts between the borrower and one or more dedicated first-class buyers (acknowledged by the buyers). To guarantee a minimum receivables value for the export contracts, the bank would typically require either fixed or hedged sales prices, or a commitment on the part of the borrower to assign more export sales contracts to the bank if the expected value of sales receivables falls below an agreed level. The owner of the commodities may even be obliged to purchase the commodities directly from the market to make up for any loss in the value of expected receivables.
- Payment of export sales receivables into an escrow account, preferably located offshore, controlled by the bank and supported by irrevocable payment instructions given by the owner of the commodities to the buyer or buyers. Buyers should confirm such payment instructions. The bank should have a satisfactory security interest in sums standing to the credit of the escrow account. There are typically two escrow accounts: a collection account, in which export sales receivables are paid; and a reserve account, in which a minimum balance is kept once the loan has been serviced, for instance to cover the next

interest payment, and excess funds returned to the borrower. The reserve account can also be used to fund shortfalls in loan servicing, margin and settlement payments under hedging programmes, and so on. The reserve account should be replenished as and when required by the loan agreement.

A much less secured form of export receivables financing is through the use of evidence accounts, in which export receivables flow through briefly only to demonstrate the reality and value of the underlying exports. They are not used to support loan servicing and banks do not have a security interest in sums standing to their credit. Evidence accounts are therefore not consistent with the premises of structured commodity finance because the security and repayment mechanism do not rely on the underlying transaction, but on the balance sheet of the borrower. Yet they may ultimately replace escrow accounts in cases where the exporter is in a better negotiating position (for example, a long and positive track record in export performance and debt servicing, a stronger balance sheet, or fierce competition between lending banks). From the point of view of exporters, evidence accounts have the advantage of not blocking funds into the escrow account. In fact, exporters often complain about the absurdity of paying borrowing rates on a loan when, for a period of time, export receivables sit idle in an escrow account and are remunerated at a much lower interest rate. This opportunity cost can be minimised with a schedule of loan servicing (fees, interest payment and capital repayment) consistent with export receivables payment dates. Nevertheless, unless the loan is structured as an overdraft, there will be a necessary time lag between the date on which payment receivables are received in the escrow account and the date on which the loan is serviced and the balance of funds released to the exporter. Borrowers should however try to negotiate that only agreed minimum amounts remain in the collection and reserve accounts at all times.

Exceptionally, the export receivables financing structure could be used to raise hard currency financing against assignment of domestic sales contracts and receivables expressed in local currency, for instance by involving the local subsidiary of the lending bank as local collection bank. According to one market practitioner, referring to a successful transaction arranged along these lines: 'The foreign exchange risk was mitigated by [the local bank's] ability to provide forward cover against the local currency'.[1] As this form of foreign exchange hedging expands and foreign exchange controls are further lifted in emerging countries, some of the advantages of hard currency payments will start to erode. On the other hand, the massive default of local Russian banks on forward currency covers in August and September 1998 also showed the limits of relying on local banks to provide hard currencies. Paradoxically, it was Russia again that saw one of the first syndicated structured loans in hard currency secured by local currency receivables. Finalised at the end of 2001, the structured transaction enabled Russia's Transneft, the world's largest crude oil pipeline operator, to raise US$150 million on the back of rouble receivables paid by Russian oil producers' transit fees.[2]

Other requirements for the security package would include the following.

- In cases of loans with long tenors and high financing ratios, the bank may require that the commodity exporter hedges not only the commodity price risk but also the foreign exchange risk if the loan is not in the same currency as the export sales receivables.
- Noting if the interest of the financing bank in payments under the commercial insurance, for instance with the lending bank being named as loss payee under the policy.

- If the payment risk of certain buyers is deemed unacceptable, the bank may require that sales to these buyers be supported by a letter of credit.
- The bank may require any additional guarantee deemed necessary, such as a local bank guarantee or surety bond, or political risk insurance cover.

Prepayment financing

Amount

Prepayment financing can be used for medium to large loans. Again, in the case of agricultural commodities, the cumulative amount of the financing would be limited by the amount of export receivables that could be generated from the current crop.

Borrower

The borrower under a prepayment financing would typically be the commodity buyer (for example, a trading company or a commodity importer). Proceeds from the bank loan would in turn be used by the buyer to prepay the exporter for commodities to be exported at some point in the future. As an alternative to a bank loan, the bank could also enter into a back-to-back contract with the buyer and in effect prepay the commodities to the buyer. Of course, prepayment financing can also take place without the involvement of banks, but in practice commodity buyers are generally unable or unwilling to prepay commodity purchases with their own internal funds. Inversely, the bank could bypass the buyer and prepay the commodities directly from the exporter, although, in practice, the bank would necessarily involve a commodity buyer in the structure to take physical delivery of the commodities.

Prepayment financing techniques can also be used to raise funds for importers, provided as always that the commodities can be onsold to first-class buyers. For example, a prepayment financing transaction could be arranged whereby a bank would make a hard currency loan to the local subsidiary of an international oil company for prepayment of petroleum products to the local refinery (the importer).

Commodities

Prepayment financing can be used to finance any type of commodities. There is even a prepayment market for certain French wines sold *en primeur*, whereby investors receive ownership certificates that give them the right to take delivery of the wine three or four years later, once it has properly aged.

Disbursement

The loan would normally be disbursed in one tranche upon satisfaction of conditions precedent, giving the bank a certain level of comfort with regard to the value and availability of the commodity exports being financed. Disbursement would obviously take place only after the export sales contract has been signed. In case of agricultural commodities, banks would generally disburse funds only after the commodities have been produced or at least once weather conditions affecting the crop are known.

Financing ratio

There is no financing ratio *per se*, since the amount of the loan should correspond to the value of the commodities sold by the exporter. However, this approach is only valid for fixed-price contracts, which are less frequent given the highly volatile commodities markets. Increasingly, the prepayment structure would enable the exporter to sell the commodities at spot prices and would include a hedging programme to guarantee a minimum value of such export sales to service the loan obligations. In any case, the amount of the prepayment should be less than the export capacity of the exporter, especially for perishable commodities, in case of illiquid commodities markets or for loans with longer maturities.

Tenor

Tenors of prepayment financing transactions typically range between six and 36 months. As in the case of export receivables financing, maturities are being continuously pushed forwards thanks to innovative structures. Tenors can be longer for certain commodities thanks to innovative structures or through securitisation. For agricultural commodities it would be very difficult to obtain financing for a tenor extending beyond the end of the marketing cycle of the current crop.

Cost

Financing cost is typically expressed as a spread over Libor.

Repayment

Repayment should come either from the borrower or, if the borrower is not the end-user of the commodities, from sales receivables paid directly by the end-buyers into an escrow account controlled by the lending bank. The bank loan is generally made with limited recourse and the borrower is responsible for servicing the loan only to the extent that the commodities have been delivered by the exporter as per the terms of the export sales contract. However, repayment can also be split, say 20 per cent with full recourse and 80 per cent with limited recourse. The decision as to which risks should be shared by the borrower is a complex and negotiable issue. Nicholas Budd of law firm Denton Wilde Sapte has identified four categories of essential limited recourse provisions: (i) risks that are always shared are cancellation of an export licence, confiscation of commodities and contract repudiation by the supplier; (ii) risks that are sometimes shared are commercial non-performance (commodities that do not meet contract specifications), occurrence of *force majeure* or lack of transport, insured political risk losses, increases in duties and excess costs, and the inability to obtain an export licence; (iii) risks that are (almost) never shared include losses covered by casualty insurance, delay in exporting commodities if no shared risk occurred, exercise of set-off rights by the supplier and decline in commodity prices; and (iv) risks that are never shared include commercial non-performance by the borrower and nuclear war or contamination.[3]

Security

The security package would require, among other things, the following.

- Assignment to the bank of the proceeds of prepaid export sales contracts. To guarantee a minimum receivables value for the contracts, the bank would typically require either fixed or hedged sales prices.
- Either direct loan repayment to the bank by the borrower (the buyer) or, if the borrower is not the end-user of the commodities, payment of re-marketed export sales receivables into an escrow account, exactly as for export receivables financing. A more secured structure

Exhibit 5.1

UBS/BPOI US$310 million prepaid forward sale financing (1995)

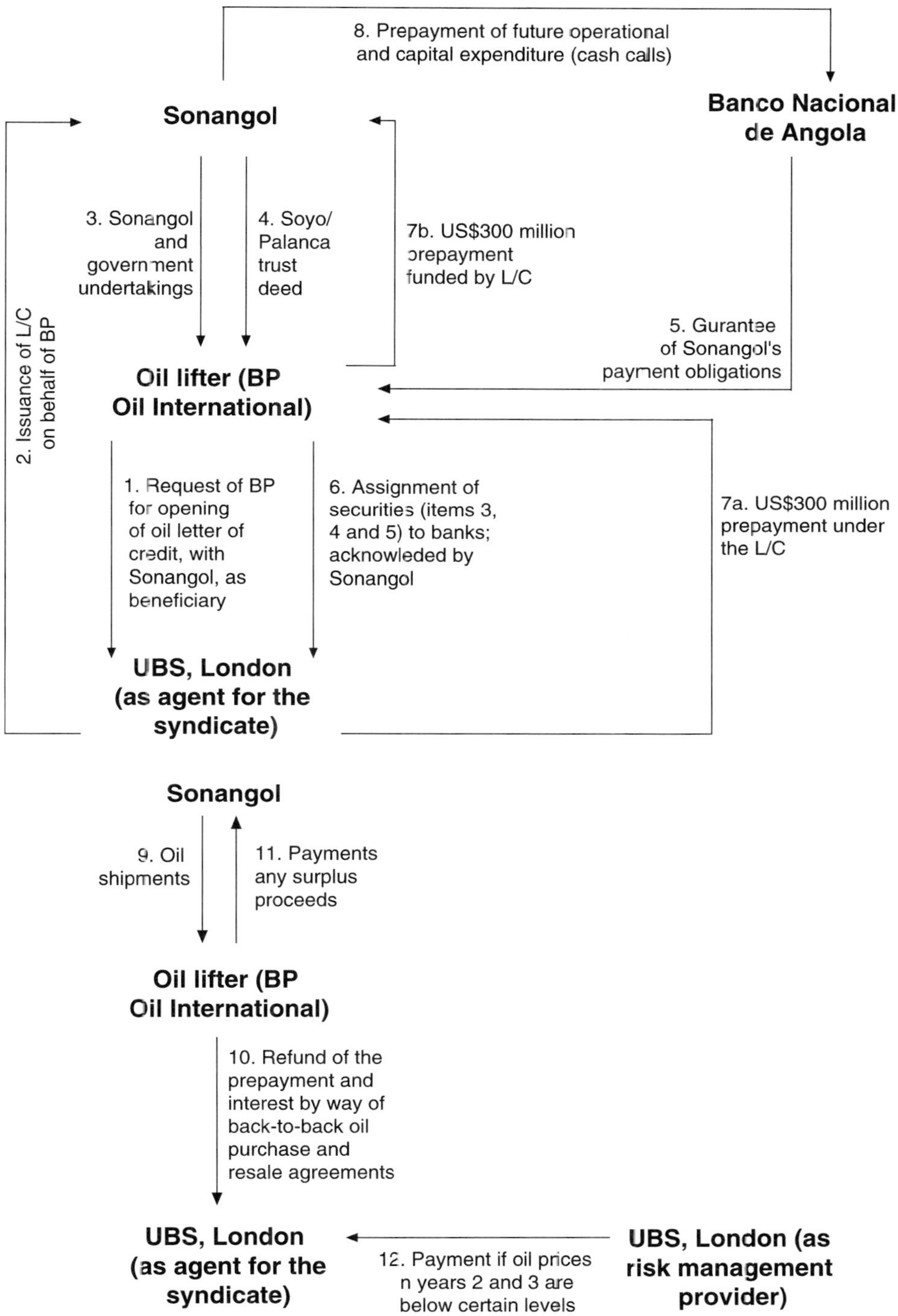

would be for the lending bank to issue on behalf of the borrower (the buyer) a confirmed letter of credit in favour of the exporter (L/C beneficiary). The L/C would be with recourse to the buyer only if exports are made as per the terms of the L/C. In fact, prepayments are sometimes structured on the back of red- or green-clause L/Cs. Exhibit 5.1 illustrates the benchmark US$310 million medium-term prepaid forward sale transaction arranged in 1995 by UBS and BP Oil International. When the prepayment is ultimately in favour of an importer, the borrower (for example, a local oil company) can issue an L/C for the benefit of the importer (for example, a refinery), such L/C to be with recourse to the applicant only if petroleum products have been delivered as per the terms of the L/C.
- To obtain more control over the commodities being financed, the bank may require a satisfactory security interest in the commodities being financed, exactly as for inventory financing. In this case, the bank would also require a satisfactory report from a reputable inspection company and/or collateral manager who has inspected the commodities stored, and a secure procedure for the release of the prepaid commodities from the warehouse or tank storage.
- Noting of interest of the financing bank in payments under the commercial insurance, with the bank being named as loss payee under the policy.
- The bank may require any additional guarantee deemed necessary, such as a local bank guarantee or surety bond, or political risk insurance cover.

Benefits of structured pre-export financing

Exporters can leverage their buyer relationships

Commodity buyers generally have stronger relationships with commodity exporters than do international banks. Structured pre-export financing transactions build on these relationships and on the willingness of buyers to support the financing. Financing terms can be further improved by the involvement of buyers with strong credits or that are strategically important to the lending bank.

Pre-export financing is used mainly by medium and large commodity exporters that can demonstrate a positive track record in performing under their commercial obligations. More than access to cheaper pricing, the main benefit of structured pre-export financing is its ability to give borrowers access to longer-term financing. As in the case of inventory finance, disbursement under structured pre-export financing can be flexible and linked to each new contract, shipment or warehousing.

Furthermore, being essentially trade financing, these transactions can be structured to enable banks to comply with provisioning requirements usually applicable for loans in excess of one year to non-OECD borrowers. Banks would do so on competitive terms that allow them to share the resulting cost benefits with the borrower.

Banks take payment risks of OECD buyers

Structured pre-export financing transactions enable banks to transfer the payment risk from commodity exporters to OECD buyers, remaining exposed mainly to an exporter's ability to perform in the normal course of business. Most structures also eliminate virtually all transfer risks and exchange control risks for the bank. This is not the case, however, in Russia, where a regulation commonly known as 'passporting' results in lenders to Russian borrowers remaining exposed to transfer risk, even if only for 24 hours. As pointed out by John

McNamara: 'this last leg does give you an element of transfer risk – but banks have been accepting this for some time'. In fact:

> There is still payment risk, but in this scenario it is the payment risk of the OECD offtaker, who is typically also an important client of the financing bank, and who in many cases has brought the deal to the bank in the first place. In any case, this OECD payment risk should not be the most challenging risk of the structure and can be considered a credit enhancement. Such a combination of OECD payment risk and emerging market performance risk can also be achieved by the bank lending to the offtaker on a limited recourse basis, for the offtaker then to prepay the export of goods from the emerging market producer, and such a structure may provide lenders with additional comforts in certain countries.[4]

Besides the ability to lend directly to more familiar OECD borrowers, prepayment financing can bring specific additional benefits due to its particular structure, including:

- the possibility of avoiding withholding tax due on bank credits;
- stronger security rights in the commodities being financed due to the fact that the bank is not merely a creditor but actually owns the commodities (for example, in case of bankruptcy or contract repudiation);
- cheaper political risk insurance and simple assignment to the bank of the proceeds of commercial insurance;
- easier liquidation of commodities (to obtain export licences and comply with other regulations);
- the possibility of avoiding the implications of negative pledge covenants; and
- less risk that the financing will become part of a rescheduling agreement or general moratorium, especially with an L/C structure.

These benefits mean that in some markets, such as Angola, structured prepayment has by and large replaced structured export receivables-backed financing. In Angola more than US$6 billion has been raised since 1995 for Sonangol on the back of prepayment – forward oil sale – structures.[5]

Limitations of structured pre-export financing

Exporters are tied to existing buyers

The corollary to the benefits drawn from leveraging the special exporter–buyer relationship is that this relationship can become a burden. Banks require a positive track record with the very buyers that will be asked to support the new transaction, leaving exporters with a limited power of commercial negotiation with its buyers. Sometimes banks will not accept existing buyers deemed insufficiently creditworthy. The most basic prepayment structures also makes the financing conditional upon a steady commercial relationship with only one buyer.

All-in cost can be high

Putting in place a structured commodity deal, in particular a structured pre-export deal involving international buyers and offshore escrow accounts, does not come cheap. The overall cost is a factor of not only the all-in interest rate, which is often reasonable, but also bank fees and expenses, legal costs, fees paid to third parties such as inspection companies, and the opportunity cost of the resources spent on the due diligence. If the structure is supported by a letter of credit, the overall financing cost goes even higher. Arranging such transactions requires management time and effort from the borrower. While the concept may be easy to understand, the details of a structured pre-export finance transaction can become extremely complex. Moreover, there is often a long list of conditions precedent to the disbursement of the funds, including receipt of all governmental authorisations, copies of commercial contracts, opening of escrow accounts and so on. Therefore, unless the borrower can negotiate very low arrangement and related fees, and commit the necessary time and resources, this type of financing only makes sense either for large amounts or when the transaction can be repeated in some form in the future.

Even the interest rate spread of structured commodity finance transactions can be higher than that of conventional financing, to the extent that borrowers who can afford it may switch back later to straight loans. Borrowers may still have to pledge additional assets as security. For instance, in October 2001 Pan American Silver Corporation (PASC) retired a US$12 million structured financing granted in August 2000 by Standard Bank London. The outstanding balance of US$6.3 million was repaid from a new loan that enabled PASC to have lower monthly interest and repayment instalments. In addition, under the new financing, the assets of Huaron (one of PASC's three silver mines) were the only collateral pledged. However, the earlier financing by SBL had served its purpose and allowed Pan American to complete the reconstruction of Huaron in April 2001.[6]

While structured commodities financing can be expensive for borrowers, it may be even more so for banks. Transactions are time-consuming to design, arrange and execute (a large qualified team, frequent trips and so on), while their success rate (from proposal to execution) is not very high because borrowers can take months or years to provide the information requested and give a mandate to proceed with the transaction. Often borrowers shop around with many banks just to put pressure on a bank they have already elected in order to improve its terms. For some deals (such as the annual Cocobod financing) there can be so much competition between banks wishing to act as arranger that the resulting fees and spreads are not sufficient to adequately cover the costs and risks involved.

Banks remain exposed to performance risk

Structured commodity finance rests on the premise that exporters will perform as expected. However, even with 'watertight' structures, production or delivery delays can occur and slow down the payment of export receivables, thus affecting loan servicing despite top-up clauses. The quality of the commodities produced may not attract the expected price. Fraud is also an issue. Some of the causes of non-performance are under the control of the exporter. For instance, the strong relationship existing between commodity exporters and buyers can also work to the detriment of the bank in that the commodity buyers may choose to accommodate exporters (for example, by accepting new payment instructions) to safeguard their long-term commercial relationship.

Lenders are also vulnerable to the impact on performance of completely independent occurrences, such as electricity shortages, strikes at the port of loading and so forth. To minimise the impact of these risks, lenders should contemplate taking insurance cover. (For further discussion of insurance cover see Chapter 8 on due diligence and Part III.)

---

[1] Presentation entitled 'Oil Trade Finance: Traditional and Non-Traditional Techniques' made by Simon Mansfield (then Director and Head of Structured Trade Finance, Standard Chartered Investment Banking) at a conference on the African Oil Trade organised by UNCTAD in Harare (Zimbabwe), April 1996.

[2] 'Russia', *Trade Finance,* December 2001.

[3] Presentation made by Nicholas Budd (then with Denton Hall Wilde Sapte) at a conference on Structured Commodity and Trade Finance organised by the IBC in Geneva, December 1996.

[4] 'Performance risk deals' by John McNamara, *Trade Finance,* April 2002.

[5] Presentation on Angola made by Cynthia Witcombe, a partner with the law firm Norton Rose, at a conference entitled 'Financing Oil and Gas Projects in Africa', organised by CWC, June 2002.

[6] 'Russia', *Trade Finance,* December 2001.

Chapter 6

Countertrade

The term 'countertrade' involves obligations on the seller either to accept goods or trade instruments in partial or full payment for its products, or to generate foreign exchange for the buyer. Countertrade is one of the oldest methods of payment in international trade. The term covers a wide range of business arrangements where payment is received in forms other than cash. Countertrade arrangements are not easy to make. They usually involve two or more separate contracts (or 'protocols') that often necessitate the participation of third parties, and by their nature they call for additional payments or financing as part of the transaction.

The use of countertrade by importers is more common in countries experiencing a decreasing demand for their commodity (or industrial) exports, lack of foreign exchange and/or local currency inconvertibility. Countertrade takes different forms, but the most popular in the area of structured commodity finance is tolling. Other frequent types of countertrade involve counter-purchase, switch trades and buy-back agreements. Although barter is the most widely known form of countertrade, today it is also one of the less common. A decade ago, most countertrade business was located in Asia and eastern Europe. Now, over 100 countries have formal or informal countertrade policies.[1]

Existing forms of countertrade

Tolling

Tolling is the exchange of raw materials for a finished product produced with these raw materials. A typical tolling transaction would take place with the intervention of a trading company that would borrow from a bank to purchase raw materials to be delivered to a processing company, which would in turn deliver the finished product back to the trading company. The trading company would then sell the finished product into the market and repay the bank loan. The loan would be with limited recourse to the trading company: the bank would take the performance risk of the processing company and the payment risk of the trading company.

Tolling is typically used when the finished product is also a commodity, for example, raw sugar into white sugar or alumina into aluminium. In Russia, processing of raw materials under tolling is practised mainly in the non-ferrous metal sector. In 1996, the share of production of non-ferrous metals arranged on a tolling basis was 69.5 per cent for aluminium, 51.4 per cent for zinc, 29.0 per cent for lead and 5.0 per cent for refined copper.[2] In past years, tolling deals have been much criticised in Russia for political reasons, but old habits do not die easily. In 2001 a landmark 12-month US$125 million revolving tolling facility was arranged in favour of Rual Trade, the trading company of the Russian Aluminium (RusAl) group. The arrangers put in place a very complex disbursement and security structure to take advantage of Rual's offshore location, which made it immune to Russian foreign exchange requirements. The facility was disbursed on a cost-incurred basis to finance the actual costs of tolling alumina into aluminium. 'Because Rual Trade signs sales contracts with aluminium buyers on a calendar year basis and tolling contracts with smelters throughout the year, it was essential to have a structure flexible enough to be able to seamlessly replace maturity tolling and sales contracts.'[3] A dynamic security package was set up 'to mitigate the risks embedded in Rual Trade's commercial practices, including the aluminium price risk'.

Tolling can also be structured around letters of credit. For example, in 1995 an international bank arranged a medium-sized tolling transaction to finance the import by a Romanian company of billets (steel semi-manufactured products) to manufacture into tubes for export to Russia. Payment for tube exports was made through a letter of credit.

Barter

Barter is the exchange of one product for another of equivalent value, with little or no money exchanged. It involves one transaction and occurs on a short-term basis (see Exhibit 6.1[4]).

Straightforward barter transactions are uncommon, especially since the liberalisation and privatisation of commodities markets. Nevertheless, they can still be found where foreign exchange or raw materials are difficult to source, and specifically under government-to-government arrangements to further economic cooperation. For example, in 1999 Hungary signed an agreement with Russia to export US$60 million-worth of goods (mainly foodstuffs and medicines) in return for Russian gas.[5] Owing to the insolvency of Russia, Hungarian exports to Russia had fallen drastically after 1998, while the Russians were receiving less foreign currency for their gas because of falling international gas prices. The barter agreement therefore provided opportunities for Hungarian exporters to increase their sales in Russia and for Russia to import goods without the need for foreign currency.

The use of barter involves considerable risk to the exporter and the importer, as goods are shipped and documents exchanged directly, with usually one party initially carrying out an obligation (usually the exporter) before the other party does its part of the transaction. However, in most barter deals an escrow account is required so that the exporter can be sure of receiving the bartered goods. This means that, in general, a bank intervenes to take a cash deposit from the importer (once the exporter has duly shipped the goods) that will be maintained in an escrow account until the importer has, in turn, delivered the goods in accordance with the barter contract. However, since most barter deals are cash-free, the bank can simply create an 'evidence account' that will show a balance in favour of one of the parties (that is,

Exhibit 6.1

Barter

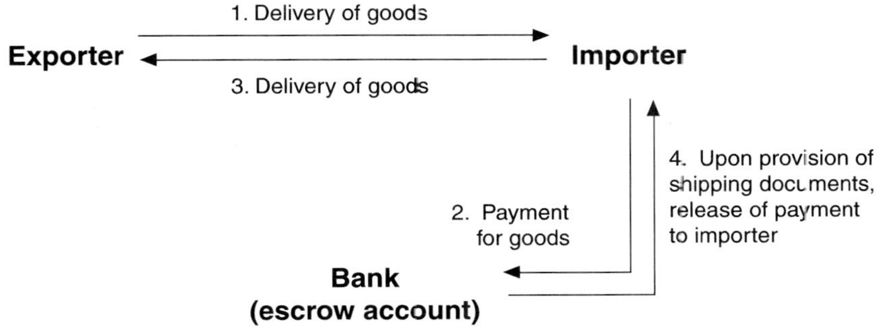

whichever has shipped). This balance can move in either direction. Whether the bank underwrites the balance depends on the relationship with the parties and any security given. Risks can also be reduced through the issuance of standby bank letters of credit or performance bonds on behalf of the parties to guarantee performance. Another control mechanism is simultaneous shipments, with the bank holding the shipping documents until both vessels have arrived. Alternatively, the exporter can require the assistance of a trading company to take delivery of the goods received through the barter deal, sell them to a third party and remit payment (less the trading company's fees) to the exporter.

Barter between two commodity producers can also be supported by commodity price swaps in which the floating price of each commodity is transferred to a hedge provider. Assuming no default on performance, this guarantees one or both sides of the barter with fixed volume and prices for each commodity. (See Part III for a discussion of commodity price risk management.) The arrangers of the barter deal may also swap deliveries of equivalent commodities to reduce certain transaction costs such as transportation costs. For example, if Mexico has agreed to ship oil to Germany and Ukraine has agreed to ship oil to Cuba, a swap deal may be arranged under which Mexican oil will be sent to Cuba and Ukrainian oil to Germany.

Counter-purchase

Counter-purchase involves an agreement between an exporter and an importer to make reciprocal purchases of goods for cash within a given period of time. Counter-purchase therefore involves the use of two separate contracts: the commodity sales contract between the exporter and the importer; and a separate, although technically related, contract between the importer and the exporter that obliges the commodities exporter to buy a defined value of goods (or services) from the importer or from a company nominated by it (usually in the same country) over a fixed time period. If the exporter fails to perform, a penalty is normally payable. The Coca-Cola Company has used counter-purchases worldwide to invest in certain emerging markets, for example trading syrup for cheese from a factory it had built in the former Soviet Union; syrup for oranges it had planted in orchards in Egypt; and syrup for tomato paste made from plants it had installed in Turkey.

The counter-purchase obligation may involve a third party to handle the commodities. The fact that transactions do not form part of one single contract makes it easier for the companies involved to obtain traditional bank credit. The contracts are normally implemented through clearing or evidence accounts maintained with selected banks in each of the exporter's and importer's countries. These accounts provide an umbrella for continuous trade flows and permit monitoring of purchases by the exporter.

Compensation trade

Compensation trade is a protocol arrangement between industries in two countries linking exports and imports. In a typical compensation transaction, a supplier from an industrialised country sells manufactured goods to a buyer from an emerging market country and a monetary claim is registered against that buyer. This claim is cancelled by a compensating delivery of commodities by the buyer. Both transactions are part of the same contract. Where the manufactured goods are supplied first, the transaction would be supported by a cash deposit made by the buyer of manufactured goods into an escrow account. This cash deposit would be released to the buyer/commodity exporter once the commodity has been delivered, possibly under a letter of credit arrangement. If the commodity is exported first, as is often the case, the initial cash deposit would be made by the supplier/commodity importer.

Romania has traditionally sourced much of its iron ore requirements through compensation deals. In 1996, a barter deal was entered into with Brazil whereby the supply of six million tonnes of iron ore was to be paid for with manufactured Romanian products. Another arrangement with Venezuela involved export from Venezuela of one million tonnes of iron ore per year, over a five-year period, in exchange for delivery by Romania to Venezuela of cars, buses, tractors and some rail rolling stock. Both deals were arranged by the Romanian government at the request of the Romanian metallurgical industry. Compensation can be total (that is, the financial value of the goods exported is equal to that of the goods imported), or partial (the party making the first delivery receives part of the payment in cash).

In a triangular compensation, a supplier may agree to sell manufactured goods to a buyer and at the same time agree to take commodities as compensation, but not necessarily from the same party. Alternatively, as in straight barter deals, if the supplier of the manufactured goods does not want the commodities, and yet entering into a compensation contract may be a regulatory or competitive requirement, this supplier can require the assistance of a trading company to take delivery of the commodities, sell them to a third party and remit payment (less the trading company's fees) to the supplier. An example of such a triangular compensation

Exhibit 6.2

Alternative compensation structures

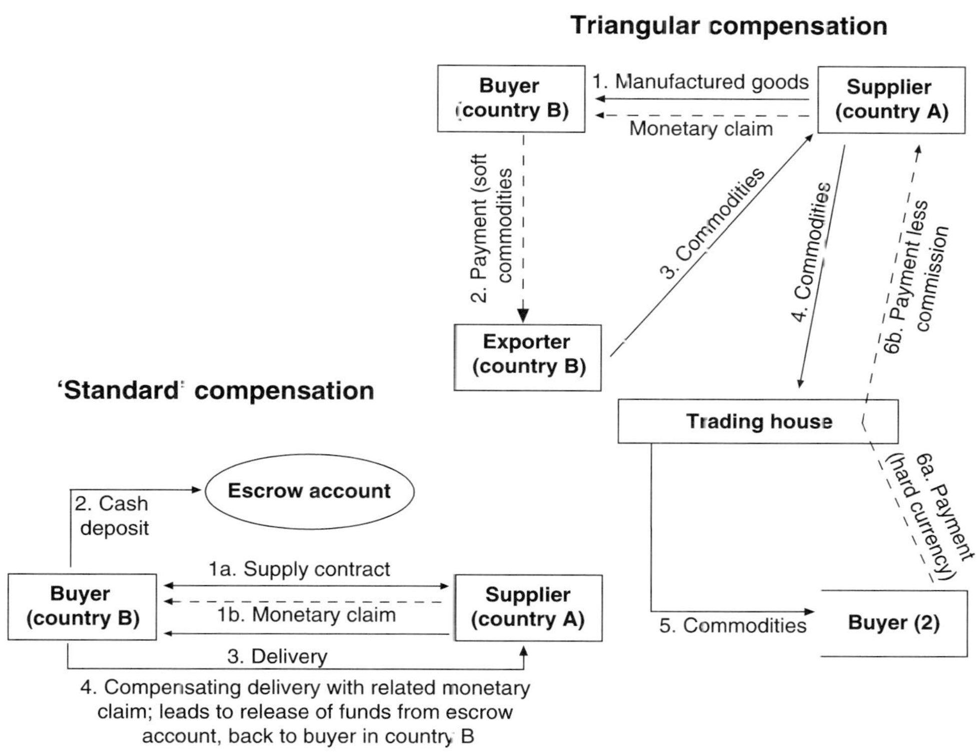

was an agreement signed in 2001 whereby the Philippine Associated Smelting and Refining Corporation (Pasar) was to export copper cathode to China's Minmetals group worth US$12 million, with the cost of the exports to be offset by delivery by Minmetals of coal to The Philippines' National Power Corporation (NPC) for Pasar's energy requirements (Pasar's copper smelting facility has an average monthly electricity bill of US$1 million).[6] Alternative compensation structures are illustrated in Exhibit 6.2.

Buy-back

Buy-back (which can be considered a form of compensation trade) is the exchange of capital goods for a finished product produced with these capital goods. A typical buy-back transaction would support a new project with the obligation for the supplier of capital goods to repurchase (buy back) the output of the new project. At the end of 1996, for example, a US$104 million expansion project for the Latakia cotton yarn spinning plant (Syria) was arranged whereby 10 per cent of the contract value was to be paid through a buy-back structure with the contracting company Peco Trading (Germany). The remaining 90 per cent was to be financed by the opening of a standard line of credit. A larger €300 million buy-back was arranged at the beginning of 2000 for the Mobarakeh steel complex, an affiliate of National Iranian Steel Company, and provided for the import of production equipment from Germany and Italy, supported by a steel offtake contract from the Balli group.

Buy-back arrangements are often concluded at government level for new projects supported by export credit agencies. Some see buy-back as a way to develop industrial capacity in Africa, noting that: 'Even the IMF have given tacit approval to some countertrade, in particular buy-back deals, where export production supports the import of additional production machinery'.[7]

Offset

Offset transactions (which can be considered a form of counter-purchase) occur when a supply contract is conditional upon the incorporation into the contract of certain goods or services from the buyer's country that should be offset from the final price. There are two forms of offset: direct and indirect. Direct offset involves co-production arrangements based on transfer of production technology to the importing country. Indirect offset occurs when the selling country agrees to purchase unrelated products from the importing country.

Offset is often used in large export transactions, in particular in transactions where suppliers of aerospace or military equipment agree to procure goods or services from the buyer. Offset has now become a major industry and few intergovernment deals are entered into nowadays without some form of offset. A number of countries such as South Africa, Malaysia, the UAE and India have major offset policies.

Switch trade

Switch trade is the multilateral use of bilateral trade imbalances. In certain cases, governments can enter into bilateral or multilateral trade agreements under which agreed volumes of goods are imported and exported over a specific time period. Mutual trade flows would be monitored through evidence or clearing accounts maintained in state-owned banks (to the

Exhibit 6.3

Switch trading

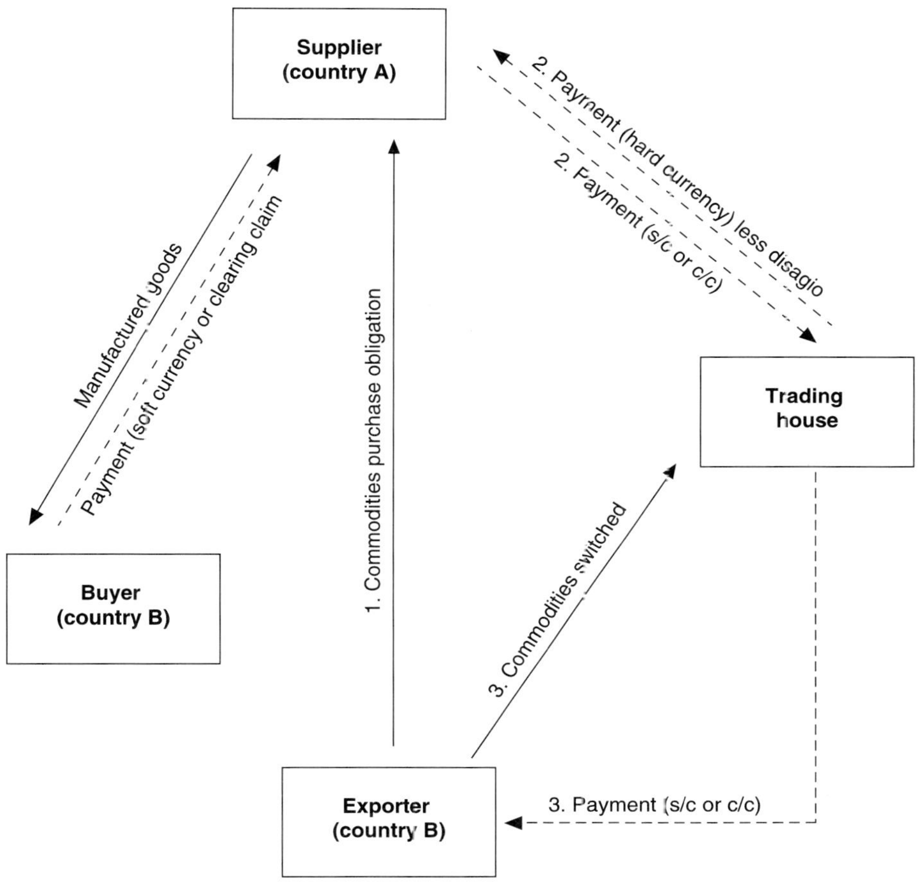

Country B has a net purchase obligation *vis à vis* Country A

extent that they still exist). At the end of the agreed time period, the balance, if any, would be settled in the currency of the accounts (usually US dollars) or carried forward into a new agreement. In 1994, for example, China and Saudi Arabia negotiated a bilateral agreement with a US$1 billion trade imbalance target.

In a typical switch trade transaction a supplier would accept payment in the form of a clearing claim or a non-convertible currency which could then be exchanged with a switch dealer (a trade company) for hard currency, less the switch dealer's fee (called 'disagio'). Switch dealers will only exchange clearing claims if they can either use them to offset against purchase of goods or sell them to another party. A switch trade can also be part of a triangular compensation transaction (see Exhibit 6.3).

Evaluation of countertrade

Countertrade is not confined to any particular situation or environment. Large and small companies in developed and developing countries may benefit from different forms of countertrade arrangements. Typically, exporters would use countertrade to gain access to new prosperous markets and/or expand their sales potential in existing markets. Countertrade is not a thing of the past, as shown by the recent establishment in the United Kingdom of the first countertrade unit within the Department of Trade and Industry to help British companies compete in markets more effectively 'where they may be either faced with a countertrade demand, or where a company is using countertrade proactively as part of its own marketing strategy to capture an export order'.[8] As noted by one market specialist: 'Interesting countertrade business still exists in a sizeable number of former Soviet Union countries, for example, Moldova, Kyrgyzstan and Turkmenistan. These transactions still prevail in the CIS or other former communist countries, for instance Vietnam and Cuba, due to a lack of international funds made available to those countries'.[9] Note that some export credit agencies have started to offer specific barter cover based on future exports of commodities. Private insurers are also involved in providing insurance on countertrade deals.

Importers would seek to use countertrade to buy manufacturing imports when they do not have enough foreign exchange and/or cannot find a liquid market in which to sell their commodities. However, this could mean that the supplier may have difficulties liquidating these commodities and may increase the price of its exports as a result. This is why countertrade is often criticised for being inflationary. If the supplier dumps the commodities received on the world market, this will also undermine the normal commodity export business of the buyer. When barter is involved, countertrade often becomes a means to get rid of goods that are otherwise unlikely to find a market and that governments want to keep producing in order to maintain jobs. In one of the Romanian barter deals referred to earlier, the Brazilian company had to accept as payment the shipment of 1,200 Dacia cars.

Although the structure of countertrade may be complex, the main characteristic it shares with structured finance is that of making financing available in difficult situations (poor credit risk, reduced access to foreign exchange, and so on). More than providing finance, countertrade replaces financing with the delivery of the goods themselves. Additionally, countertrade often results in the transfer of technology and know-how from the exporter to the importing country. Moreover, as with structured commodity finance, payment risk is essentially replaced by performance risk – thus countertrade requires marketable commodities and needs to be supported by export contracts with reliable counterparts. Countertrade can also be useful to circumvent certain regulations (such as foreign exchange controls and quotas), although due to the worldwide tendency to deregulate commercial and financial flows this benefit is becoming less attractive. Finally, at the country level countertrade can be a temporary means of financing in case of a foreign exchange shortage and also as a means of improving the balance of trade.

Compared with structured finance, however, countertrade carries the inconvenience of blurring the various cost and risk components of a commercial transaction. This is in direct opposition to structured commodity finance, which, as will be shown, helps to identify these elements.

---

1 Refer to the UNCTAD publications entitled *Countertrade Regulations in Selected Developing Countries* (UNCTAD/ECDC/200), 1989, and *Countertrade Policies and Practices by Selected African and Latin American Countries* (UNCTAD/ST/ECDC/32), 1991.

2 Presentation made by Alexander A. Tikhonow (then General Director, Enterprise 'Interrural') entitled 'Financing Russian Metal Exports Through Foreign Investment' at a conference on Structured and Commodity Trade Finance in Russia, organised by IBC in Moscow, September 1997.

[3] Eric Saux, head of the metals group at SG Commodities, quoted in 'Hedge laying provides strong base', *Trade Finance,* March 2002.

[4] Diagrams in this chapter are all provided by UNCTAD.

[5] Economic, technical and scientific protocol signed during the third meeting in Bucharest of the Romanian–Russian intergovernmental committee.

[6] 'Philippines strikes copper deals with China', *Trade Finance,* November 2001.

[7] 'Jumping the stop light', *Trade Finance,* December 2000.

[8] 'UK gears up countertrade unit', *Trade Finance,* April 2002.

[9] Armin Eckermann, head of global structured commodity finance at WestLB, quoted in 'Award for Excellence 2001: Part One', *Trade Finance,* June 2001.

Chapter 7

More complex structures

This chapter begins with a discussion of reinforced structures giving lenders more comfort that they will be repaid. Next is an overview of securitisation of structured commodity finance transactions. The chapter continues with a presentation of structures that cannot be construed as simple extensions or variations of the three models presented earlier and yet can be relevant to the needs of the commodity sector. These include structures relying on flows other than commodity flows, as well as structures that have accounting or tax benefits (in particular, leases).

Reinforced structures

The advantage of the security package provided under structured commodity finance transactions, compared with that supporting more traditional commodity financing, is that it can be a win-win situation. The security provided to the lenders is not necessarily costly to the borrower. That being said, in difficult situations the lending bank may still require additional guarantees. Particular commercial and political situations may also prompt even more complex structures, notably with the use of special purpose vehicles.

Combining structured commodity finance techniques

Pre-export financing relies on first-class buyers for the repayment of the loan. Inventory financing deals are generally liquidated with the sale of the commodities stored, typically while the commodities are still in the country of the producer. Some finance deals, however, have successfully combined various structured commodity finance techniques to cover the entire marketing cycle, even when the commodities are sold to second-rate buyers and/or after temporary offshore storage.

For example, at the end of 2001 WestLB arranged a pre-export financing for a cotton exporter in Uzbekistan, to cover the entire flow from the gin in Uzbekistan until the arrival at the spinners (final buyers), through transportation to and storage in third-party warehouses in Latvia and Iran. The security for this transaction evolved over time, from a guarantee from the National Bank of Uzbekistan, to warehouse receipts and finally credit insurance to cover the payment risk of the spinners. The major challenges were (i) to establish an enforceable and legally valid pledge over the goods during storage in the Baltics and in Iran, and (ii) to set up a monitoring system to control the flow of each bale from the gin (in Uzbekistan) until arrival at the spinners. To quote one of the key figures behind the deal: 'It is not sufficient to provide only the classic pre-export financing facilities. This is especially the case in soft commodities, where we do not see many big-ticket, syndicated facilities . . . tailor-made financing structures are necessary'.[1]

Another example of a reinforced structure is provided by the aluminium tolling transaction examined in Chapter 6, with a security structure that included the following elements.[2]

- Recurrent short-term contracts with first-class pre-approved eligible aluminium buyers to be assigned to the lenders from time to time throughout the term of the facility.
- Recurrent short-term tolling agreements with attached tolling licences approved by Russian customs between the borrower and the RusAl group smelters, to be assigned to the lenders from time to time throughout the term of the facility.
- A four-month standby sales contract signed between SG (as LME broker) and Rual Trade to give the borrower sufficient future cash flows during the first months of 2002 to permit utilisations under the facility. This standby contract was to be exercised only in the event that the borrower would be unable to provide sufficient sales contracts with its traditional clients.
- As an additional security, the delivery obligations of the borrower were guaranteed by the RusAl smelters and their holding company Russkiy Aluminy, and a pledge on the alumina and aluminium in circulation, storage and processing throughout the tolling process.
- Hedging on the aluminium price was another crucial element.

What these examples share is the willingness of the arrangers to find a financing solution that takes advantage of the strengths of the various parties involved and closely mirrors the underlying commercial transaction. Another illustration of this 'can do' philosophy is provided in Exhibit 7.1 with the example of a hypothetical fishing plant that, thanks to structured commodity finance, succeeds in increasing its production despite an apparently blocked situation.

Requiring additional guarantees

Structured commodity finance transactions can involve additional credit enhancement features, such as surety bonds issued by a local bank, political risk insurance or outright third-party guarantees. These types of credit enhancement are discussed in Part III. Transactions can also be strengthened by ensuring that lenders control at all times the shipping, transport and warehouse documents.

Traditional guarantees (like mortgages) can be added to the security package. In other cases, lenders may require control over a higher percentage of the commodities produced and exported by the borrower or related parties. For example, in a recent pre-export financing of cotton arranged by Société Générale for the Compagnie Malienne pour le Développement des Fibres Textiles (CMDF) in Mali, lenders required 'a tripartite pledge of sale contracts, a pledge of 100 per cent of the cotton produced in Mali, a third-party pledge of an inventory cotton in Abidjan, and a payment of 100 per cent of export proceeds of CMDF directly through SG's escrow account in Paris'.[3] These types of additional guarantees are generally required by lenders when the borrower or the country of the borrower is considered very high risk or when it is relatively new to the international loan market. This is, for instance, the case with second-tier Russian oil producers, where, 'on top of export contracts, it is advisable to take a fixed or floating charge over the company's assets'.[4]

Other structures have also shown their reliability and efficiency. For example, in Angola the Offshore Cabinda Trust became the flagship of the oil-field development financing of Sonangol, the state-owned oil company. Under this structure, the offshore trustee (an inde-

Exhibit 7.1

Deal structure as a risk mitigation tool

Innovative ways of structuring a transaction can make even very difficult-looking financings possible. Imagine that, as a bank, you get a financing request from a fish-processing plant in a small West African country. The plant processes fish bought from local fishermen, and sells them to well-established buyers in Spain and Sweden. These buyers have indicated that they are interested in buying more, but the processing plant is now constrained by the limited supply from fishermen. It considers buying its own fishing boats, but finally rejects this as too risky. Instead, it requests the bank for pre-financing, which will be used to pre-finance the fishermen so that they will be able to increase their production.

As such, this transaction looks very risky. Among other things, there is no guarantee that the fishermen will use their funds to catch more fish. Nevertheless, you decide to take a closer look at the sector, and you find that the major constraint for fishermen is that they need diesel for their engines, and this diesel needs to be paid for in cash. The cash flow of most fishermen is such that they can only buy enough to go out for short, one-night fishing trips, thus foregoing the further-away richer fishing grounds.

All the fishermen take their diesel from two central terminals (this is the only way for them to be able to get subsidised diesel). You find that it is possible to lease these terminals and that you can recruit a trustworthy local bank to control the stocks.

You now have the basis of the financing. You finance diesel imports; the diesel is provided on credit to the fishermen; the fishermen deliver to the processing plant, which deducts the costs of the diesel from their payment; the processing plant exports the processed fish; and the foreign buyers pay to an escrow account established for the reimbursement of the initial loan used for the diesel imports. There are still many details to be worked out, but you have a structure with strong incentives for all parties not to default, simply because each single one of them has a strong incentive to continue being part of the structure.

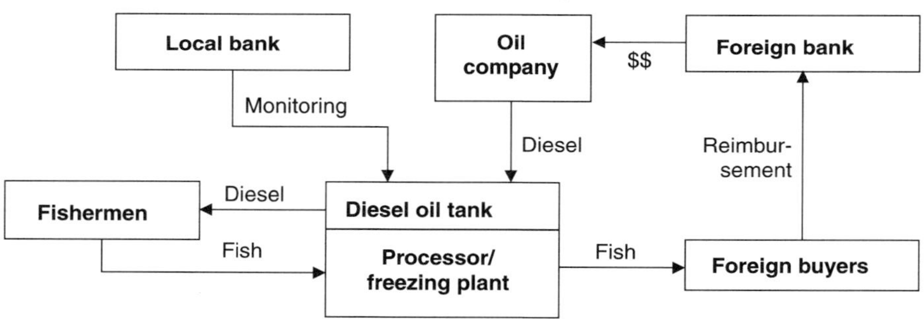

Source: UNCTAD.

pendent bank or trustee company) collects the oil revenues on a continuing basis until they are sufficient to meet the debt service notice requirements (including reserve funds) submitted by the lenders. The trustee then makes loan repayments on a regular basis from these oil revenues, and all lenders (except for specific contracts) are *pari passu*.[5]

Using a special purpose vehicle (SPV)

Although not frequent, SPVs can be part of structured commodity finance transactions arranged by banks. An SPV essentially puts in place an intermediary between the lenders and the borrower.

There can be various reasons for using an SPV. For example, having no assets, the SPV structure can ring-fence certain flows of funds from third-party creditors, and thus both mitigate attachment risks and limit compliance covenants otherwise applicable to corporate borrowers. The SPV structure also easily supports a larger number of lenders.

The interesting thing is that SPVs are increasingly being used for commercial reasons, in what could be called 'second-generation' structured commodity finance transactions, to enable a borrower to retain a certain commercial autonomy with regard to the selection of the underlying commodity buyers. As noted by Carla Jakoby, regional head in the structured commodity team at WestLB:

> An important issue is to provide more flexibility to our customers, who in Russia nowadays are more likely to be producers than traders . . . . This means, in particular, flexibility with regard to the commercial partner – ie, the offtaker. The longer the tenor of a loan, the more uncomfortable the producer feels with the traditional one-way offtaker route. This problem limits the scope of commercial negotiations. To answer it we have modified our contracts with several new elements, including framework contracts and SPV structures.

Cynthia Witcombe, a partner with Norton Rose, the law firm advising Angola's Sonangol, made a similar analysis when the firm decided to amend the traditional prepayment/forward sale structure of recent Sonangol deals to incorporate an SPV. An important consideration was indeed to give Sonangol the 'flexibility to sell the crude oil not to a single dedicated lifter but "spot" to many lifters'.[6] The SPV structure was also instrumental to reduce other risks faced by lenders. As explained by Cynthia Witcombe: 'No purchaser [wanted] to commit on a medium- or long-term basis to the structure or to take the environment risk. [There was also a] political reluctance on the part of some export credit agencies to have a direct contractual relationship with certain countries' – for which read a war-torn country like Angola! She also added that rescheduling risks are arguably mitigated and that the SPV 'may assist ability to raise political risk insurance (including "rating" of the transaction, if applicable)'.

In the next section the discussion centres on structured commodity finance transactions for which the lenders are capital markets participants. The concept remains essentially the same, but the structure is generally more complex when marketable securities are involved. For example, the intervention of an SPV is more likely and the due diligence is more detailed.

Securitisation

Companies that want to issue more marketable types of debt, yet without losing the benefits of asset-backed structures (which in this context includes receivables-backed structures), should consider issuing asset-backed securities (ABS). This process is called securitisation and relies on the substitution of marketable securities for privately negotiated instruments. Commodity-based asset-backed securitisations rely, just like structured commodity finance, on the assignment or the outright forward sale of commodity inventory or future production and associated receivables. There is a continuing trend towards securitisation of receivables in structured trade finance deals, because: 'this enables companies to raise finance in the markets as an alternative to bank borrowing. The technique is often suitable for sectors like energy and commodities, in cases where there is a reasonable degree of creditworthiness on the buyer's side'.[7]

Principles and background

Securitisations allow the owner of the commodities to raise finance by packaging the receivables and selling them into the market-place as asset-backed securities. The originator creates a special purpose vehicle (SPV) to which all the receivables are transferred and then issues capital market debt instruments (bonds or notes) backed by security on the trade receivables in the SPV. In summary:

- there is a bond issue (in the capital markets);
- repayment is made from the cash flow of defined assets;
- borrowing is usually channelled through a bankruptcy-remote special purpose vehicle;
- the originator is not responsible for repayment (off-balance sheet financing); and
- the likely future performance of the assets will (generally) be credit-rated.

Typically, the securitisation is either fully underwritten by the arrangers or provides for a standby bank facility in case the deal is not entirely placed in the markets.

Asset-backed securitisations became popular in the United States at the beginning of the 1980s, when privately negotiated instruments, such as home mortgages or car loans, were bundled up together and used as collateral for the issuance of securities. By 'securitising' future cash flows, companies were able to access financing over the medium term, generally through the issuance of floating-rate notes (FRNs) in the Eurobond markets. Today, the US market for ABS and MBS (mortgage-backed securities) is enormous, which contrasts with the situation in Europe where asset-back securitisation has remained marginal.

At the beginning of the 1990s there was a realisation in the US markets that asset-backed securitisations could be extrapolated to all sorts of predictable future cash flows, provided that the right conditions were in place. Thus securitisation moved to finance emerging markets borrowers by relying on cross-border flows in what is commonly referred to as 'international future flow securitisation'. Compared with traditional asset-backed securitisation, international future flow securitisation relies on payments due from an international (offshore) obligor. One of the first transactions of this type was arranged in 1987 on the back of telephone receivables due to the Mexican telephone company Telmex. By the end of 1995, already an estimated US$7.5 billion-worth of securities had been issued, mostly in Latin America but also in Asia and central and eastern Europe (particularly in Turkey). At the beginning of the 2000s, commodity-backed securitisations emerged in Russia and other CIS countries. Unfortunately, international future flow securitisations are still virtually non-existent outside mainstream emerging markets; in particular very few have been arranged in sub-Saharan Africa.

The principle of international future flows can be applied to any type of foreign exchange receivables, such as receivables due to a local telephone company by foreign networks involved in international calls, international credit card receivables, electricity receivables and so on. Financial future flow securitisations have also been structured on the back of individual remittances or travellers' cheques. In other words, any type of foreign exchange receivables can be accepted as collateral for a securitised deal provided that the right conditions are in place.[8]

Commodity-linked securitisations

In the commodity sector the first significant export receivables-backed securitisation was probably a deal closed in 1993 by Pemex, Mexico's state-owned oil company. The transaction was structured around a newly created Pemex Receivables US Masters Trust that issued certificates privately placed among large investors. Payments from this trust were secured by the assignment to the trust of the proceeds of the sale of Mexican oil to a number of American oil companies.[9] The market for commodity-based international future flow securitisations took off very rapidly and in 1995 already accounted for one-third of all international future flow securitisations, actually more than telephone receivables and credit card receivables put together. The continued expansion of this market ever since is very much comparable to the growth of bank-based structured commodity finance. Securitised bond issues on behalf of commodity exporters are often called securitised export notes (SENs).

Exhibit 7.2

US$330 million securitisation for Mobil Nigeria (1996)

In a context where securitisations were still virtually non-existent in Africa (with the exception of South Africa), the export receivables securitisation closed in 1996 by CS First Boston for Mobil Producing Nigeria Unlimited (MPB) received, paradoxically, the 'deal of the year' award from the magazine *Project and Trade Finance*. Using a traditional securitisation structure on the back of existing and future hydrocarbon production, MPN, a wholly owned Nigerian subsidiary of Mobil Corporation (USA) and the 40 per cent shareholder and operator of a joint-venture (JV) with the Nigerian National Petroleum Corporation (NNPC), was able to raise a portion of the cost of the JV's Oso natural gas liquids (NGL) project. Given that the climate was particularly difficult at that time, the success of this deal proved that well-structured securitisations can open new financing roads for strong African companies.

The securitisation was structured around the issuance by MPN of US$330 million secured export notes to a New York grantor trust which, in turn, issued certificates evidencing beneficial ownership in the notes. The certificates were offered through a traditional US private placement to a group of 14 institutional investors (11 US, two European, one Japanese). The issue was split into two tranches: (i) US$280 million of fixed-rate bonds with a maturity of 10 years and an average life of seven years and (ii) US$50 million floating-rate bonds with a maturity of 12 years and an average life of eight years. The first tranche was priced at 265 basis points over US Treasuries and the second tranche at 275 basis points over Libor. Amortisation was to take place with 12 equal semi-annual instalments beginning 54 months after the issue date.

The features listed below helped further reduce production, commercial and sovereign risks, thus enabling the transaction to secure a Baa3 rating from Moody's (and to be more than three times oversubscribed):

- Crude oil production was offshore and MPN had over 25 years history of uninterrupted crude oil production and export. The JV was Nigeria's second largest producer of hydrocarbons, which represent the country's main foreign exchange earner.
- MPN was an important strategic asset for Mobil, accounting for almost one-third of its proven liquid reserves.
- The offtaker (obligor) was another wholly owned Mobil subsidiary. Its performance under the sales contracts, extending to the life of the notes, was guaranteed by Mobil.
- MPN assigned agreed volumes of exports of crude oil and NGL (from the Oso project) as security for the notes. A set volume of crude oil production was to be maintained free and clear of liens.
- MPN gave irrevocable instructions to pay export proceeds directly into a New York account from which debt service was to be effected.
- MPN agreed to pre-fund a 12-month debt service reserve supported, if need be, by incremental crude sales.
- The sales contract proceeds were anticipated to generate healthy debt service coverage (2.5 times in the base case, and 2.1 times in the downside case), thus providing over-collateralisation.
- CS First Boston gave investors the option to redeem their certificate in case of an embargo within six months from the issue date

Source: CSFB.

Exhibit 7.3

Some examples of commodity receivables-backed securities

Issuer	*Country*	*Country's rating*	*Issue rating*	*Type*	*Market*
Pemex	Mexico	BB	A	Oil exports	Private placement
AHMSA	Mexico	BB	BBB-	Steel exports	Banks / private placement
Corpoven	Venezuela	B+	BBB	Oil exports	Banks / private placement
Bitor	Venezuela	B+	BBB-	Orimulsion	Banks
Alcoa do Brasil	Brazil	B	BBB-	Aluminium exports	Private placement
Shell Minerals	Brazil	B	A	Mineral exports	Banks / private placement
Aracruz Celulose	Brazil	B	BBB	Pulp exports	Private placement
Samarco	Brazil	B	BBB-	Iron ore exports	Private placement
Yacimentos Petroliferos Fiscales	Argentina	BB-	BBB	Oil exports	144a placement

Note: Country ratings from UNCTAD Secretariat, 1996.
Source: Structured Finance Group, Paribas Capital Markets presentation entitled *Securitisation of Commodity Flows* at a December 1995 IBC conference.

A landmark African commodity-linked securitisation was the Mobil Nigeria transaction arranged by CS First Boston at the beginning of 1996 (see Exhibit 7.2). Not only was the Mobil Nigeria securitisation oversubscribed at the time, but also it fared exceptionally well throughout the political changes that took place soon after. Another important commodity securitisation was arranged in 1997 for Empresa Colombiana de Petroleos (Ecopetrol). The securitisation relied on an SPV set up in the Cayman Islands that privately placed Eurobonds worth US$290 million with an average life of 2.66 years. The SPV was to receive a predetermined stream of oil from Ecopetrol's share of joint venture fields in Cuisiana and Capiagua (Colombia) and to sell the crude oil to a AA-rated oil company at the market price (hedged separately). Arranged by Salomon Brothers, the deal was more than three times oversubscribed.

From the crude oil sector, commodity-based securitisations have expanded to serve other commodities sector, in particular iron ore, steel, copper, aluminium, pulp and cement (see Exhibit 7.3). The ongoing success of commodity-linked securitisations shows that, despite highly volatile commodity prices, investors still have a good appetite for well-structured securitised deals in the commodity sector.

Basic transaction flows

The following transaction flows are those of the securitisation deal arranged in the mid-1990s by JP Morgan for Triton Colombia (owner and exporter of the commodities).

1. A bankruptcy-remote SPV is established.
2. The commodities are sold by the owner to an SPV (with a prepayment agreement).
3. The SPV issues certificates or notes that are then offered to investors.
4. Investors make payment to the SPV, which is then passed on to the owner.
5. The SPV signs a re-marketing contract with the commodity buyer(s).
6. The commodities are exported to the buyer(s).
7. Export sales receivables are paid by the buyer(s) into an escrow account controlled by the SPV.
8. Debt service is effected via debit from this escrow account.
9. The SPV releases excess funds to the owner.

Variations

Just like structured commodity banking transactions, commodities-linked securitisations must minimise payment and political risks while being tailored to accommodate the needs of all parties.

For instance, commodity buyers dedicated to the financing can be either end-users of the commodities or trading companies. There can actually be more than one buyer, and buyers may be located in more than one country. Dedicated buyers are typically based in industrialised countries, but there can be exceptions. For example, a securitisation of export receivables was arranged in 1995 on the basis of an export contract between a Chilean company and an Argentinean company (see Exhibit 7.4). In another securitisation deal, a portion only of the receivables was denominated in local currency.

Exhibit 7.4

ENAP and YPF secruitisation of export receivables, 1995

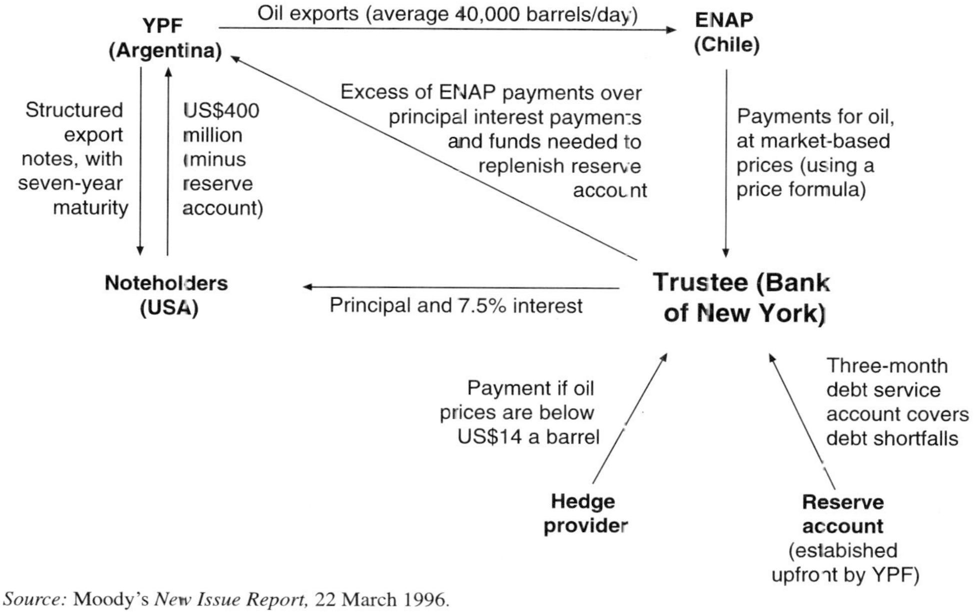

Source: Moody's *New Issue Report,* 22 March 1996.

If the securitisation is supporting a prepayment structure, the exporter can sell the future receivables either to the SPV or to the commodity buyer(s). In the latter case, both the export sales contract and the export receivables are then assigned to the SPV, and this assignment is acknowledged by the commodity buyer(s). Alternatively, the exporter can borrow from the SPV and assign export sales contracts and future receivables to the SPV as security. Securitisations can also be backed by commodities held in inventory, in which case the commodity owner can sell its inventory to an SPV and obtain the right to borrow. Proposals have been made in this regard to various EU member countries to securitise part of their crude oil permanent reserve requirement. One such proposal gave a large southern European oil company the right, for a period of five years, to issue short-term floating-rate asset-backed notes (up to 90 days) by selling the stored crude oil to an SPV with an option to repurchase the crude oil for strategic reasons or *force majeure*.

Finally, commodity-linked securitisations can rely on a mix of assets involved in the marketing cycle of the commodities. For example, a proposal was made a few years ago to a large international trading company to raise several hundred million US dollars for three years on the back of a combination of (i) pools of eligible sales receivables from a large steel company, (ii) eligible steel inventory (both exchange and OTC-traded) and (iii) London Metal Exchange (LME) warrants.

Once a securitisation structure is in place, it can also be used by the originator to borrow short term, each time against the sale of eligible assets. Structured securitised commodity deals can also be further reinforced, for instance with third-party surety bonds (see Part III). For security, tax or regulatory reasons, certificates or notes can be issued by a second SPV such as an offshore trust.

Originators of commodity-linked securitised transactions can include commodity producers, exporters, trading companies or even processing companies and local banks.

Evaluation of commodity-linked securitisations

Most of the advantages of structured commodity finance are present – and sometimes amplified – in securitisations.

More flexibility and better terms for the commodity owner

Like structured commodity finance, securitisations backed by commodities enable access to financing in difficult situations. Securitisations using prepayment structures can also share certain benefits with their bank equivalent, such as the ability to circumvent negative pledge restrictions and their off-balance sheet status for the originator. However, commodity-linked securitisations do not come cheap. This is because of the relatively onerous due diligence, legal and marketing costs of arranging securitisations. On the other hand, funding in the international capital markets can enable the originator to avoid certain taxes payable on bank loans. For example, in a securitisation for the Mendoza province (Argentina), the originator was able to avoid a value-added tax of about 20 per cent that would otherwise have been payable on this prepayment structure. This particular securitisation was collateralised by oil royalties and priced to yield a spread of 400 basis points.

Borrowers wishing to keep their new financing confidential appreciate the fact that securitisations can provide anonymous funding. Inversely, securitisations can also be high-profile transactions that expose originators to a new environment and broaden the investor base, thus paving the way for corporate clean bond issues. Whereas the tenor of bank loans is limited by provisioning requirements, securitisations make use of inventory and/or receivables to facilitate medium- to long-term financings at fixed or floating interest rates.

Finally, asset-backed securitisations are generally more attractively priced than comparable plain vanilla bonds. For example, in the mid-1990s a securitisation was arranged for Triton Colombia to raise US$125 million for five years at a cost of US Treasuries plus 220 basis points. This compared with an estimated stand-alone margin of 490 basis points. The transaction was rated BBB, a credit rating improvement above the rating of both Triton (BB-) and Colombia (BBB-).

More security attracts a wider range of lenders

Compared with bank financing, securitisations widen the range of lenders through public offering or private placement in the capital markets, which is an advantage where large sums are sought or where an equivalent bank loan would attract high provisioning requirements. Properly structured export receivables securitisations where the originator is based in emerging markets can even support an investment grade security issue. Moreover, arranging financing on securitisations can enable banks to reduce their use of country lines and access new funding sources. Well-structured securitisations often attract a rating higher than that of the originator's country. See for example the Exhibit 7.3 comparison made a few years ago of asset-backed securitisations arranged in the mid-1990s by the old Banque Paribas versus the country rating of the originator.

Securitisations address a more sophisticated and diverse pool of investors, and thus have evolved to provide flexibility as and when needed. Because capital market investors are generally not liable to provisioning requirements, securitisations have the potential to develop further in high-risk countries, especially with the advent of Basle II.

Dependence on multinational sponsors or 'established' emerging markets

International future flow securitisations have evolved and proliferated primarily in response to the capital needs of operationally strong companies located in developing countries, but securitisations have so far failed to take off in developing countries that are still outside the focus of emerging market investors. For example, in sub-Saharan Africa, where commodity exports account for the bulk of foreign exchange earnings, export receivables securitisations are almost non-existent. As mentioned, a rare exception was the Mobil Nigeria crude oil securitisation closed at the beginning of 1996 by CSFB, in which Mobil Corporation was involved both as local joint-venture partner and as international crude oil buyer.

Another reason for the absence of securitisation in regions such as Africa is that local capital markets are still underdeveloped. Because international institutional investors are not knowledgeable about the country as an investment target, they are unlikely to be in a position to appreciate the risk of local issuers or of securitisations originated on the back of local exports.

In transition and industrialised countries, the reliance on international investors is less important given the ability to structure securitisations backed by domestic sales. This is a possible alternative for the few commodities that are not always exported, for example wine. Indeed, a few years ago a successful US$11 million bond and warrants issue was arranged by Italian investment bank Mediobanca on the back of the entire 1997 wine production of the Marchese Piero Antinori due for delivery in 2001.

Other available flows for structured finance

As illustrated throughout this Part II, the commodity sector can gain access to financing at attractive terms on the back of structured transactions. Although the bulk of structured financing still relies on the assignment of the commodities to the lenders, we are seeing more and more deals now structured as true sales of commodities. As already discussed, prepayments are especially worth considering when there is a strong relationship between a buyer and an exporter or in an otherwise uncertain or restricted environment (involving, for example, risk of fraud, over-commitment of export receivables, negative pledge covenants and so forth). In both cases, the financing is granted on the back of reserves or flows of commodities. There are, however, other flows that borrowers in the commodity sector can use to obtain financing, principally transport fees and tax receivables.

Transport and transit fees

Companies operating in the commodity sector include not only producers, exporters, importers, trading companies and processing companies, but also transport companies. Depending on their characteristics, commodities are mainly transported by rail (train), road (truck) or sea (tanker, ship). Oil and gas for their part are increasingly transported through pipelines. The price paid by the commodity owner to transport the commodities can in turn be employed by the transport companies to obtain financing.

Loans raised by transport companies can be used for general working capital purposes or to obtain longer-term financing for capital expenditures. ING Bank, for instance, once arranged financing for rail cars against transport fees.[10] As already mentioned in Chapter 5, in 2001 Russian pipeline operator Transneft borrowed US$150 million on the back of rouble receivables paid by Russian oil producers' transit fees.[11]

Tax receivables

Structured financing supported by commodity-related tax receivables is becoming increasingly frequent and, since governments are always very creative in raising new taxes, we can expect this type of structured commodity financing to develop further.

Companies operating in the commodity sector are exposed to various types of taxation, for example value-added tax (VAT), income tax, royalties, withholding tax and customs duties. Exhibit 7.5 illustrates a complex structured financing arranged in 1997 by WestLB to raise hard-currency financing for government-owned companies to pay for imports of wheat whereby the loan was supported by tax claims from the government on the country's crude oil exporters. The transaction took place in one of the republics of the Commonwealth of Independent States and can also be regarded as a particular form of countertrade.

A simpler transaction was arranged in 2000 by Standard Bank London to provide financing for a strategic fuel terminal in Zanzibar owned by a joint venture between Eco-Tec International (Gibraltar), a company servicing the oil and power industries, and the government of Zanzibar. Repayment of the financing would come primarily from fuel taxes collected by Eco-Tec. Other scheduled sources of repayment were payments to be made by oil marketers to the borrower for rented storage space. Security for the finance included guarantees from the joint-venture partners (Eco-Tec and the government of Zanzibar), a pledge over fuel stocks and a mortgage over the fuel terminal. As explained

Exhibit 7.5

Tax receivables-based structured financing

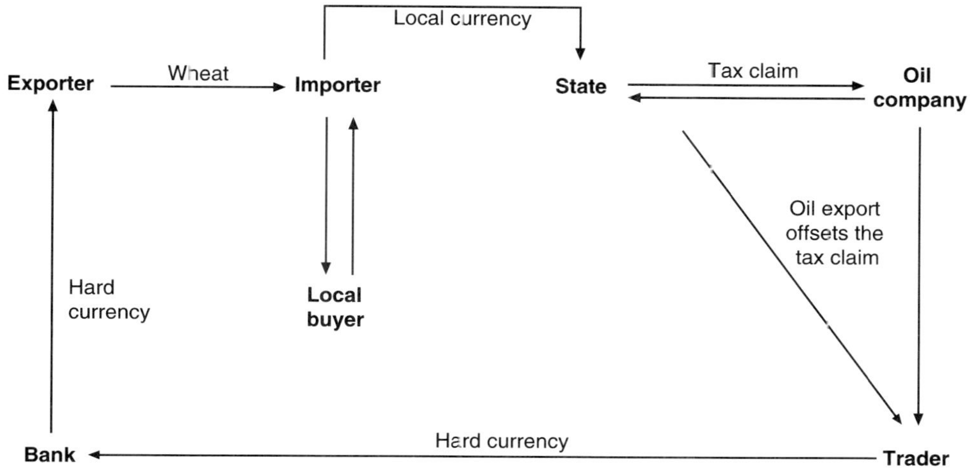

Source: West LB, *Project Finance*, December 1997.

by one of Eco-Tec's managers: 'By taking over the sole responsibility for supplying Zanzibar with all its petroleum product needs and also for the collection of the government's petroleum taxes within their supply price, Eco-Tec has removed Zanzibar's problems of fuel supply shortages, black market pricing and lack of tax accountability'.[12] The tax receivables-backed structured financing was successfully put in place despite a highly risky political and economic environment.

Other potentially useful tax receivables to obtain financing include oil royalties due by crude oil producers to governments.

Balance sheet-enhancing structures

Structured commodity finance can be used not only by high-risk borrowers in emerging markets to raise financing in difficult situations, but also by creditworthy borrowers to benefit from certain accounting and/or tax advantages. For instance, certain structures enable the financing not to show as a liability on the balance sheet, while others provide tax benefits to the borrower. Structured financing can also bring about certain industrial or commercial benefits.

Off-balance sheet transactions

A financing is off-balance sheet when it does not have to be reported as debt on the liability side of the balance sheet. The only reference to off-balance sheet transactions would be in the notes to the financial statements. Companies may seek off-balance sheet treatment primarily to improve their debt ratios.

Off-balance sheet treatment can be obtained by the commodity owner and financing beneficiary when commodities are sold to the lending bank or to a commercial buyer with a simple 'commercial' obligation to deliver the commodities in the future – as opposed to being pledged against a loan. This is the case with prepayment structures (forward sales). Limited recourse loans to commodity buyers or trading companies for the purpose of making a prepayment to the commodity owner may also sometimes be off-balance sheet for the offshore borrower as well. Likewise, securitisations are generally off-balance sheet for the originator. Off-balance sheet treatment can also be obtained for certain types of leases (see below). Some banks are encouraging off-balance sheet financing even for soft commodities, acting directly themselves as the buyer of the commodities and entering into re-marketing contracts with commercial buyers. The benefits of off-balance sheet structures are particularly salient for large corporate clients: as explained by Jasper van Schaik of Fortis, they provide 'a smaller balance sheet for our client, more control over the commodity' while 'Fortis can take the country risk for our clients and reinsure it'.[13]

These remarks were made, however, before the Enron and WorldCom scandals. Off-balance sheet financing arranged mainly for tax or accounting purposes may now become less fashionable for quite some time. This new situation can be illustrated by a remark made by Sandy Weill, chairman and chief executive of Citigroup, as a response to criticism of Citigroup's role in financing Enron, in which he pledged to 'turn down deals that disguise debts'.[14] In any case, regulators are not fooled easily and, in most countries, it is not possible for a transaction to be classified as 'off balance sheet' if it is deemed to be in reality a financing transaction.

Tax-advantageous structures

In our imperfect world, taxes are affected by the sources and structure of financing. For example, dividends are not tax-deductible while interest payments are. The tax implications of certain forms of structured commodity finance must certainly be addressed.

Prepayment, for example, can be construed as a strictly commercial transaction and thus the exporter can be liable to pay VAT immediately. In such a case, the structure could be adjusted to look more like a loan or, if that is not possible, the arranger could seek an exemption from the tax authorities.

On the other hand, structured finance can also save or defer taxes, and in fact some more sophisticated forms of structured finance are specifically designed to achieve this objective. If a transaction is structured in such a way that one of the parties involved derives a tax benefit, a portion of this tax benefit can be passed on to the borrower, thus reducing its borrowing cost.

One area of structured finance that dramatically affects the timing and amount of taxation is leases.

Leases

A lease is just an extended rental agreement. The owner of the equipment (the lessor) allows the user (the lessee) to operate the equipment in exchange for regular lease payments.

International leases are particularly used for exports of industrial equipment and other capital goods. In general, the leased assets would not come directly from the manufacturer but rather from a third-party leasing company (the lessor). Frequently this lessor would acquire assets directly from the manufacturer and leases them to the user (lessee). This is a direct lease. Alternatively, the lessor can acquire assets from their user and then lease them back to the same user. This is a sale and lease-back.

Leases come in a variety of forms. Short-term cancellable leases, also known as operating leases, put the risk of obsolescence on the lessor. Inversely, with long-term, non-cancellable leases, also known as full pay-out, financial or capital leases, the lessee bears the risk of obsolescence. Leases that include insurance and maintenance are full-service leases (as opposed to net leases).

Why are leases an alternative form of financing? Because instead of raising debt or equity finance to buy equipment or other capital goods, their user is going to lease the required assets. Comparing lease payments to interest payments helps to explain why leases can in effect replace financing. If the asset is very costly, it may be convenient to arrange a leveraged lease, in which case the cost of the leased asset is financed by issuing long-term debt or equity. A financial lease is like a secured bond.[15]

From a tax viewpoint, a lease also makes sense when the lessee cannot use its depreciation tax shield, in which case the lessee can sell the asset to someone who can. The leasing company (the lessor) would hold title to the equipment, claim depreciation for tax purposes, and lease it to the user (the lessee), who in turn would be able to claim lease payments as an expense. The lessor may also pass some of its tax benefits onto the lessee in the form of lower rentals.

Structured financial leases now form part of the portfolio of asset-backed financing instruments offered by major banks. Recent transactions have been structured with (or with a combination of) US leveraged leases (USLL), German leveraged leases (GLL), French leveraged leases (FLL), Irish tax leases and Swedish leases, many of which are cross-border deals. The relative attraction of a particular type of lease, reflected in its average net present value benefits, is a complex matter that varies, for instance, with the size and characteristics of the deal, and the accounting rules and tax capacity, rate and regulations pertaining to the various parties. Japanese leveraged leases (JLL), for example, once very popular, are now all but dead, one of the reasons being the dramatic fall in the tax capacity of Japanese financial institutions. Financial leases can also be combined with export credit agency (ECA) cover.

Leases also have benefits that extend beyond their tax or financial advantages. For example, a lessor may be better able to bear the risk of obsolescence, or be in a better position to resell second-hand assets, or be able to offer a very good deal on maintenance. From an accounting standpoint, operational leases increase book income in the early years of an asset's life, but should have no effect on the value of the company. This is because only lease payments are deducted from revenues whereas, with the buy-and-borrow alternative, both depreciation and interest payments are deducted. In addition, for standard items of equipment, it may be much cheaper and less time-consuming to arrange a simple lease contract than to arrange a normal loan and buy the equipment. Moreover, lessors and secured creditors may be treated differently in bankruptcy. For example, the lessor may not be able to get back its equipment if the latter is deemed essential. Finally, under certain conditions leases may also be off-balance sheet financing.

Companies in the commodity sector could investigate the possibility of leasing some of their assets. To start with, computers are often leased and they are certainly needed by everyone today, yet they represent a marginal investment. Trucks, railway cars, aircraft and ships can also be leased. These means of transportation are vital to the commodity trade: for example, railway wagons to deliver oil products to landlocked countries. Outside the commodities sector, a successful securitised financial lease of railway cars worth US$167 million was, for instance, arranged in 1997 for the US company GATX Corporation, secured by underlying cash flows from the subleasing of the railcars. Leasing can also be used in the case of warehouses. For example, in 1997, the Chicago Transit Authority closed sales and lease-backs totalling US$133 million for three bus garages and a warehouse.

Without involvement in similar amounts or levels of complexity, the commodity sector should investigate the opportunities offered by structured financial leases for its transport and storage needs. For example, at the beginning of the 1990s the Ghana National Petroleum Company (GNPC) might have considered leasing a vessel instead of entering into a costly financing to buy its vessel *North Sea Pioneer*. Besides weighing less on the balance sheet of GNPC, a lease might have enabled GNPC to share with the lessor some of the costs and consequences of the very long seizure of the vessel by the Angolan government following a commercial dispute. In short, storage (especially offshore) and transport (especially moveable) assets provide structured financial lease opportunities for the commodity sector.

While the commodity sector has not yet fully utilised these opportunities, some companies have already used this type of structure for their processing or manufacturing plants. For example, in January 1996 the South African company Sappi signed a three-year US$100 million loan structured around the sale and lease-back of one of its paper mills in South Africa. In the former CIS countries, leases are also expanding as a means of financing agricultural machines. For example, the recent sale of 100 grain harvesters by Rostselmash of Russia to Agrocentre-Astana of Kazakhstan for a total cost of US$3.6 million was proposed to Rostselmash by Regiton Leasing of Russia. The lease payments were guaranteed by Turan Alem Bank, which issued a letter of credit in favour of Rostselmash (confirmed by Commerzbank and the EBRD).[16]

Another area where leasing could become a significant means of financing is gas-fuelled power stations. In the United States, for example, energy companies identified a few years ago up to US$100 billion of power facilities that could be sold off, with the plants being put on a form of operating lease. Finally, lease structures can also provide financing on the back of existing assets.

---

1 Markus Fuchs, head of the soft commodity desk of the Structured Commodity Finance unit of West LB, quoted in 'Sowing the seeds in new ground', *Trade Finance*, November 2001.

2 'Hedge laying provides strong base', *Trade Finance,* November 2001.

3 'Reinforcing the structure', *Trade Finance,* March 2002.

4 Natasha Isakova, senior manager of Standard Bank London, quoted in 'Onwards and upwards', *Trade Finance,* March 2002.

5 For further details see the presentation on Angola made by Cynthia Witcombe, a partner with law firm Norton Rose, at a conference entitled 'Financing Oil and Gas Projects in Africa', organised by CWC, June 2002.

6 Ibid.

7 Michael Kenny, partner with law firm Watson, Farley & Williams (London), quoted in 'Lawyers win again', *Trade Finance,* February 2002.

8 For example, in 1997 a 10-year US$90 million securitised bond was launched on the back of securitised earthquake insurance premiums payable by Japanese companies, with the added feature that principal repayment would vary as a function of the size, depth and location of the earthquake.

9 Report by UNCTAD Secretariat, 1996.

10 'Finding a football', *Trade Finance,* May 2001.

11 'Russia', *Trade Finance,* December 2001.

[12] Steve Herbert, East African trading manager at Eco-Tec, quoted in 'Jumping the stop light', *Trade Finance,* December 2000.

[13] Ibid.

[14] 'Citigroup focus could bring banking spin-off', *Financial Times,* 12 August 2002.

[15] If a company issues a bond, the cost of interest payments to investors is the after-tax interest rate. Therefore, to value a lease one needs to discount the incremental cash flow achieved by leasing, as opposed to borrowing to buy the asset, by the after-tax interest rate paid on long-term debt.

[16] 'Russian banks gain strength', *Trade Finance,* September 2001.

Chapter 8

Due diligence

Structured commodity finance transactions provide access to financing even in difficult situations, but they are certainly more onerous to put in place than traditional trade and commodity finance deals. In essence, structured commodity finance enables lenders to trade off payment risk for performance risk, and the latter depends on a wide variety of factors. As explained by one market professional: 'In order to make a transaction financeable one needs to identify all risks involved in the underlying commercial transaction and try to mitigate them. The more risks are mitigated and the better the way those risks are mitigated, the more the financing will become available'.[1]

Arranging a new structured commodity finance transaction is costly in terms of both time and money because of the due diligence that must be conducted on the key aspects of the proposed transaction. This requires a thorough investigation of the components of the marketing cycle and of the track records of the parties involved. The objective of the due diligence process is to provide the arranger with the means to achieve a near watertight structure in order to reduce risks to the minimum acceptable by the various parties. At one extreme, the cotton pre-export financing for Mali arranged by Société Générale and Banque de Développement du Mali in the early 2000s was 'the result of five years of intense marketing to allow the inclusion of specific securities of structured commodity finance, including risk mitigants, in order to make the deal operate smoothly and attractive to other institutions as participants'.[2] Thankfully, due diligence can generally be completed in less time.

The same principles apply to securitisation of structured commodity transactions. Both publicly and privately placed securitised transactions are generally rated to evaluate the likelihood of timely payment of principal and interest. This evaluation is based on a due diligence process similar to that supporting structured commodity finance transactions arranged by banks – only more complex and more thorough.

This chapter is divided into four parts. First, the components of the marketing cycle are examined, from the characteristics of the commodities being financed to the sales contract terms and inherent market risks. This is followed by an analysis of the parties involved in a structured commodity finance transaction, including in particular the commodity owner. Next there is a short discussion of how political risks can be minimised through proper structures and of the role of governments in promoting structured commodity finance deals. The last part of the chapter pinpoints some of the key structural aspects that enable structured commodity finance transactions to add value for the parties involved.

Components of the marketing cycle

Sometimes funds will be disbursed after the commodities have been transported to the port; at other times, funds will be disbursed at an earlier stage, once the commodities have been produced or extracted. Some lenders may even consider disbursing funds when the commodities are still in the ground or not yet produced. Obviously, the later the disbursement in the marketing cycle, the lower the risk for lenders.

To a different extent each time, lenders will need to assess the risks affecting the ability of the owner of the commodities to perform as contemplated. These risks relate to both intrinsic characteristics of the commodities and market risks. Are the commodities perishable? Are we sure that the owner will be able to sell the commodities to reputable buyers at a good price? Lenders should also identify circumstances under which the owner of the commodities may be unable or unwilling to perform.

Availability of the commodities

The lending bank should address factors that have an impact on the likelihood of future availability of the commodities being financed. This requires a detailed analysis of their physical integrity and movement.

The due diligence process should first ascertain the quantity of the commodities supporting the financing transaction (expressed in tonnes, ounces, barrels, and so on) and their quality (composition, grading, durability, etc). This will in turn reduce the risk that buyers may not accept the commodities. According to one market professional: 'Lenders will also seek to quantify the performance track record over time, and the relationship between reserves to production, production to exports, exports to the assigned contract value, in order to establish how plausible it is that the borrower will be able to sustain the levels required to achieve repayment under reasonable variations of commodity price and interest rates'.[3]

Before funds are disbursed, lenders would generally want these characteristics to be verified by a reputable inspection company. Particular attention should also be paid to the quality of storage and transport for the commodities, as these have often been a source of problems. All these aspects (discussed in more detail below) should be carefully monitored throughout the life of the financing, either directly by lenders or, more frequently, by specialised collateral managers.

If the commodities have not yet been produced, the due diligence should obviously extend to the production stage. Does the company have the facilities required to effectively produce the commodities? How reliable is the availability of necessary production factors, ranging from raw materials to electricity and labour? In the case of soft commodities, this requires an analysis of the weather conditions and other direct or indirect factors that may affect the future crop. For instance, the management of the most recent land reform in Zimbabwe had a disastrous impact on the production of food and tobacco crops. When processed commodities are involved, the due diligence should cover the operating cycle as well as processing techniques. Medium-term crude oil financing, for its part, should not rely on a volume of crude oil exceeding proven reserves whose proceeds have not yet been assigned to other parties. And so on.

Lenders should know at any time where the commodities supporting the financing are located. If the commodity exporter has a long and positive track record, lenders can assume that the existing inland transport system and shipment method are adequate. There should not be blind reliance, however. The due diligence should still identify transport companies and possible obstacles on the road, as well as loading and unloading facilities. If in doubt about a particular aspect of the transport system, lenders should not hesitate to suggest or impose alternative arrangements to the owner of the commodities.

As one should always hope for the best but prepare for the worst, the required insurance should always be in place. For a start, lenders should ascertain that the owner of the commodities has insured against commercial risks relating to the physical integrity of the commodities. These risks include:

- natural disasters, such as fire, flooding;
- vandalism or sabotage; and
- theft.

Commodities should always be insured for these risks once they are assigned as security for the financing, including during storage and transport. The due diligence conducted on the insurance component should also ascertain potential exclusion from insurance cover, the currency in which the insurance is denominated and paid (preferably hard currency), and the reliability and timing of insurance payments. In this respect, the creditworthiness of the insurance company and of the reinsurer, if any, should be checked. Finally, lenders should require – to the extent possible – to be named as loss payee or beneficiary under the insurance policy, or alternatively that insurance proceeds be assigned to them (or to the SPV in case of a securitisation).

Note that other insurance worth considering in order to strengthen the security structure of the financing includes quality risk insurance and insurance cover for political risk, credit risk or commodity price risks. These are discussed in Part III.

The next stage in the due diligence process is to assess the market risk involved in the sale of the commodities being financed.

Market risks

The value of commodities sales proceeds supporting the structured commodity financing depends on two factors: what commodities are being sold (discussed in the previous subsection); and under what terms and conditions.

Ideally, the commodities being financed should face a stable or increasing demand profile (adjusted for any seasonal pattern) and a low possibility of obsolescence. They should have an established and diversified market of OECD buyers, and a transparent and stable pricing mechanism. Market risks are potentially more significant for inventory financing, which enables the disbursement of funds before sales contracts are negotiated and sometimes even before acceptable buyers have been identified.

This due diligence process will provide lenders with the means to judge the quality of the commodities sales receivables earmarked to support the financing.

Commodity buyers

The result of the due diligence process on commodity buyers should shed light on their performance and payment risks, and establish the latitude of the commodity owner *vis-à-vis* the market. If the commodities are sold to a primary buyer with the purpose of being re-marketed, lenders should also conduct a similar analysis on the end-buyers.

First of all, lenders should look more favourably at commodities whose market is large and diversified (in terms of number of participants and their possible geographical concentration), as well as highly liquid. This is the case with crude oil. It is not the case with steel.

The next important matter is to decide whether the financing transaction is going to be supported by one or more commodity buyers. Obviously, diversifying contracts with more buyers enables the commodity owner to minimise the idiosyncratic risk that a particular buyer may become unwilling or unable to pay for the commodities sold, or may refuse to take delivery at all. On the other hand, certain structures such as prepayments are specifically founded on the strength of the existing relationship between the commodity owner and a single buyer, although, as discussed in Chapter 7, even prepayment structures can be adapted to enable the commodity owner to continue to sell to the entire market.

Once the commodity exporter has suggested one or more buyers to support the proposed financing, lenders should investigate the financial risk of these buyers. This requires an analysis of their financial statements and an investigation of their payment track record with the commodity exporter, which should be positive and consistent. If possible, the due diligence should also uncover the buyers' payment record with other exporters as well, based on the buyers' reputation in the market and on any additional source of information that lenders may have.[4] If the payment risk of a particular buyer is deemed too high, lenders may require that sales to this buyer be supported by a documentary letter of credit. On this argument, note that lenders have to be extremely careful before disrupting the commercial relationship that exists between a commodity exporter and its buyers. For example, when Bankers Trust Company arranged the first Cocobod deal in 1991, after more than 10 years of absence by Ghana from the international loan markets, the bank felt that the syndicated financing would have more chances of being accepted by participating banks if payments were supported by letters of credit. Therefore, the dozen or so traditional cocoa buyers of Cocobod were contacted by Bankers Trust with a request to establish letters of credit to pay for the cocoa contracts assigned to the financing. Until Bankers Trust came up with that request, cocoa export sales were mainly conducted on an open account basis. Needless to say, not only were the cocoa buyers extremely reluctant to incur the cost of issuing the letters of credit, but also some of them became extremely vexed by the implicit assumption that they could fail to pay for the cocoa purchases. The negotiations became very tense and at one point this issue almost jeopardised the success of the deal.

In a securitisation whereby sales to one or more dedicated buyers are assigned to the structured commodity financing transaction, each buyer should normally have a senior, unsecured credit rating at least equal to that of the transaction.

Next to the payment risk of the buyers is an assessment of their performance risk. Will the dedicated buyers actually take delivery of the commodities as agreed with the exporter? To answer this question, the due diligence should look at the strength of commercial relationships between the parties, and ensure that the terms and conditions of the sales contracts are conducive to good behaviour on the part of the buyers. One fundamental risk to evaluate – and minimise – is the probability that a particular buyer may unilaterally terminate its contract with the commodity exporter, say to take advantage of lower prices offered by a different exporter. Lenders should ensure that dedicated buyers have strong incentives to purchase stable quantities from the commodity exporter.

In some looser forms of structured commodity financing, there may not be an assignment of sales contracts from dedicated buyers. This situation could be acceptable if the commodities are sold on the spot market using a list of pre-approved acceptable buyers, and if the exporter shows a strong export track record, as well as a clear economic case for sustained export volumes and prices in the future.

Price risk management

Finding one or more reputable buyers is not sufficient to guarantee that the structured transaction will be sufficiently secure and self-liquidating. Lenders should satisfy themselves that the price realised on the future sale of dedicated commodities adequately supports the scheduled interest and capital repayment.

First, to enable a clear and accurate monitoring of the expected value of sales proceeds, lenders should encourage a transparent pricing mechanism, with a contract price preferably calculated with reference to an official spot market price. Obviously, the existence of a transparent pricing market does not in itself provide any guarantee that prices will not fall to unsustainable levels.

Price risk is usually addressed by dedicating excess export receivables to the transaction (over-collateralisation), by including top-up (escalation) clauses in the sales contract or by arranging an appropriate hedging programme. The level of over-collateralisation depends on the price volatility of the commodities and on the maturity of the transaction. A typical arrangement would be for the expected value of the export proceeds to equal 125 per cent of the value of the financing. With regard to top-up clauses, one should bear in mind that they guarantee that the overall value of the commodities exported will be sufficient to service the obligations of the borrower under the loan, not that these obligations will necessarily be serviced in a timely manner. As explained by one market practitioner: 'If your escalation clause is dependent upon additional quantities being delivered down a pipeline, but the pipeline schedule is fixed three months in advance, there is a strong possibility, assuming all other volumes are already committed, that "escalation" will result in a three-month delay, for which lenders had better be prepared'.[5] Also, top-up clauses may not work for a variety of other technical or political reasons – for example, with regard to second-tier Russian oil companies: 'A top-up clause doesn't work: the company would not produce that much oil. And for small companies, getting export allocations is much more difficult than it is for Lukoil'.[6] Actually, given the shortfalls of top-up clauses, lenders are increasingly encouraging borrowers to accept commodity price risk-hedging mechanisms as part of structured commodity trade finance transactions.

Once sales to certain buyers are dedicated to the repayment of a transaction, it is essential that the exporter continues to export to these dedicated buyers. If the sales price is fixed and commodity prices increase, the exporter might be tempted to default on its sales contracts. One way to avoid this situation is to insist that the price of the commercial sales contract be related to market prices at the time of shipment. The exporter's exposure to fluctuating commodity prices can then be hedged separately. Lenders should ensure that diversion of the delivery of the underlying commodities would be difficult, expensive and time-consuming.

Finally, the due diligence conducted on the price risk should also cover the currency in which the domestic or export sales or the commodities are denominated. To the extent that this currency (or currencies) might be different from the currency in which the financing was obtained, lenders could require that this foreign exchange risk be hedged. This would be the case, for instance, with the export contracts supporting the US dollar financing for the Ghana Cocobod deal because they are mainly denominated and paid in pounds sterling.

Contractual aspects

The due diligence should cover all aspects of sales contracts. Particular attention should be paid to the following features:

- the nature of sales contracts – preferably take-or-pay contracts;[7]
- maturity – preferably long-term contracts;
- revocability – preferably binding and non-cancellable contracts;
- currency – preferably hard currency contracts; and
- the scope to assign and transfer rights – if possible, this should be conditional upon the lenders' prior written consent.

Direct and indirect parties to the transaction

The success of a structured commodity finance transaction relies on the ability of the owner of the commodities and other parties to deal with any unforeseen problems. The due diligence process should attempt to measure this ability, taking into account principally the relevant experience and financial capacity of the parties involved.

Commodity owner

In most cases, the borrower is also the end-user of the new financing. However, this is not always the case, for instance in structures relying on an offshore borrower making a prepayment to its counterparty in an emerging country. This is why we generally use the term 'commodity owner'. However, for simplicity we will commonly refer to the 'borrower' to designate this commodity owner – that is, the true beneficiary of the financing raised on the back of the commodities.

Structured commodity finance transactions rely essentially on the good performance of the underlying commercial transaction. This means that, compared with other types of financing, lenders are less concerned with the payment risk of the borrower or with its balance sheet. This does not mean that lenders do not care to know who the borrower is – on the contrary. Lenders simply look foremost at other aspects of the borrower and, in particular, at the borrower's track record in the business concerned.

The due diligence on the performance risk should demonstrate that the owner of the commodities has good experience, and a positive reputation and track record, in (preferably) exactly the type of commercial transaction that will support the structured financing. More thorough due diligence would seek detailed and reliable information to confirm this, and the financing contract could even be supported by covenants obliging the borrower to maintain the business line or core operating assets generating the receivables, as well as the commercial relationship with the identified buyer(s). Ideally the borrower should be a major exporter with significant foreign exchange revenues. Clearly, lenders should not rely solely on the overall level of export revenues generated by the borrower, but should examine other export sales contracts entered into by the borrower, and find out the rights of other lenders under existing financing arrangements to receive these export contracts and related revenues. Likewise, lenders should be aware of the off-balance sheet commitments of the borrower and, in particular, of its outstanding derivative contracts. One just needs to remember the catastrophic impact that the recovery of gold prices at the end of 1999 had on the operations of Ashanti Goldfields. The magnitude of the problems faced by Ashanti at the time was actually due to the fact that its management had entered into gold price derivatives contracts not so much for the purpose of establishing a true hedge of the company's future gold exports but rather for speculation purposes, hoping to beef up the company's short-term revenues and its stock price.[8]

Moving on to corporate credit risk, the due diligence should uncover the factors that may influence the capacity and willingness of the exporter to perform. For a start, no money should ever be disbursed, even under a structured transaction, before lenders have ascertained certain key aspects of the borrower, such as its ownership and management – especially if there have been any recent changes – and have pinpointed any potential conflict of interest between these parties and the lenders: 'This includes checking that the managers have a clean history . . . banks should look out for eventual management squabbles, or for signals like high management turnover. One specific factor that banks should evaluate is whether key company officers are likely to withstand political and outside pressures'.[9] Also of management. This aspect is key to achieving the required performance of the commercial obligations supporting structured commodity finance deals.

Likewise, complex or opaque ownership structures act as deterrents to the granting of foreign loans in general, and in particular of loans based on the techniques of structured finance. Obviously, the offshore location of trading companies or special purpose vehicles is sometimes useful in order to circumvent onerous tax or regulatory requirements.

Lenders should also know the intended use of funds to be raised through the new financing, even if this information is not fully shared with participating banks. The long-term strategy of the borrower should also be evaluated. More generally, the due diligence should cover the know your customer (KYC) elements relating to money laundering.

Next, given that the structured financing arrangement relies on the cash generated by sales proceeds, a thorough due diligence should investigate the payment records of the exporter, including receivables ageing, dilution and write-offs, and should also review collection records as well (back 18 months to three years). Attention should also be given to any commingling of cash and related matters. The risk of intervention by other creditors should also be assessed. Finally, the due diligence should focus on the more classical analysis of the creditworthiness of the borrower, relying on its financial statements and key operational and solvability ratios. Obviously, corporate credit risk is more readily assessed if the borrower is already rated.

As mentioned earlier, securitisations relying on future export receivables will generally be rated. Transfer and convertibility risks being largely mitigated, the credit risk becomes closely related to the borrower's ability to service its local currency debt obligations. Local currency ratings depend in turn on factors affecting credit quality, such as management expertise, capital structure and cash flow generation, as well as the exposure of the originator to adverse economic or financial events (such as a devaluation). If the structure of the transaction properly mitigates these risks, and provided that the transaction is small in relation to the borrower's other debt, the rating of such an export receivables-backed securitisation can exceed that of the borrower's senior, unsecured local currency rating.

Warehouse operators

For structured commodity finance transactions relying at some point on the storage of the commodities, the due diligence should cover all aspects of the warehouse component to provide lenders with a reasonable guarantee of the integrity of the commodities stored.

- *Location.* Is the warehouse located inland or offshore? How far is it from the port and from other major transport links?

- *Type*. Is the warehouse bonded, semi-bonded or unbonded?[10] What is the quality of its infrastructure? Is it a terminal or a field warehouse? Field warehouses are established and controlled by a bona fide collateral management company on the premises of a borrower for the purpose of acquiring custodianship exclusively of the commodities owned by the borrower, with the advantage for the owner of having the commodities nearby. A terminal warehouse is separate from the physical plant of the owner of the commodities stored in the warehouse. It is usually based in a large storage area (such as a port) that serves many transactions and is owned by an independent warehouse company, with the disadvantages of added transport risks and costs.
- *Ownership*. Is the owner private or public? Is it a local or an international operator? Is the operator licensed or unlicensed? What are its experience, reputation and level of independence from political pressure? There should not be any conflict of interest between the lenders and the warehouse operator.
- *Operation*. Are the commodities stored commingled or differentiated? Banks should normally insist that the commodities used as collateral be physically separated from other commodities. What are the technical skills of the warehouse operator in storage management and pest control? What is its business ability? What is the security system? What are the release and other procedures? The commodities stored in the warehouse should be properly insured for commercial risks.
- *Warehouse receipts*.[11] Are they negotiable, transferable and/or discountable? Do they provide effective documents of title? Is there a possibility of registering the warehouse receipt in a central registry at low cost? Even if the answer to all these questions is 'Yes', lenders should still treat warehouse receipts with relative caution: 'A warehouse receipt is only as good as the company issuing it . . . the company issuing a warehouse receipt should be by all means financially viable to do so – ie, the risks taken should correlate to balance sheets'.[12]

As observed by market specialist Dan Day-Robinson, warehouse receipt financing relies on 'integrity, itself a function of local property rights, warehouse quality, security and inspection systems and proper administration. Without such integrity a banker cannot know if a receipt is genuine or really represents the goods claimed'.[13] Day-Robinson International Consulting (DRIC) is actually the project executing agency on a two-year pilot project (the Samara warehouse certificates pilot project) in Russia that fully combines farmers, grain elevators and local banks into a system that, in its view, can stand such scrutiny. The programme runs under the auspices of the International Grains Council, and is directly funded and supervised by the Common Fund for Commodities (discussed in Part IV).

To monitor the integrity of the commodities supporting the financing arrangement, the lending bank or its agent should regularly visit the warehouse, without prior notice. This task is increasingly delegated to inspection companies or more general collateral managers (discussed in the next subsection). However, banks more actively involved in structured commodity finance transactions may elect to establish their own warehousing subsidiaries to carry out a range of collateral management activities concerned with domestic or internationally traded goods.

Inspection companies and collateral managers

Inspection companies have traditionally been involved in cross-border trade to certify the quality and quantity of the commodities being exported. They are increasingly used in structured commodity finance transactions to provide inspection services at various points of time during the marketing cycle of the commodities being financed. Some of these inspection companies have expanded their role to act as comprehensive collateral managers. This is the case, for instance, of Geneva-based Société Générale de Surveillance (SGS). Collateral management can also be an extension of services provided by the warehouse operators discussed earlier. In other cases, collateral management companies, such as Audit Control and Expertise (ACE, also based in Geneva), have sprung up specifically to take advantage of the increased demand on the part of lenders for reliable and tailored collateral management services. The role of inspection companies and collateral managers will become even more important with the advent of Basle II, which sets strict operational requirements and eligibility criteria in order for a commodity loan to obtain the favourable treatment of specialised lending.

In addition, the combination of corruption, organised crime, and unreliable legal and regulatory local environments has created the need for first-class collateral management to efficiently support structured commodity finance transactions. In effect, privatisation and deregulation have created exporters and other local operators with insufficient track records. Because the ongoing and massive transformation of the modes of producing and trading commodities has raised the performance risk of doing business in emerging markets, the due diligence now required for arranging structured commodity finance transactions can become so overwhelming that an offshore bank on its own would be unable to conduct it in a timely manner or at a reasonable cost. This situation has also supported the development of collateral managers.

The core services provided by collateral management companies include (i) assuring the right quality and quantity of goods delivered into their custody, (ii) ensuring quality maintenance, (iii) guaranteeing proper storage, (iv) loading for export and (v) issuing certificates of delivery.[14] What lenders should look for in collateral managers is a good reputation, independence from local business or political interference, and the ability to provide in a timely manner the full range of collateral management services. Collateral managers should know the local market and have the ability to monitor the commodities throughout the life of the financing (warehouse, transport system and so on). The due diligence should also uncover any potential conflict of interest between the collateral manager and the lenders. Collateral management companies that have these qualities are often subsidiaries of multinational companies. There are, however, some limitations to the scope and benefits of collateral management companies, as noted by Jonathan Coulter in an article published at the beginning of 2003:

> The main users tend to be large operators, who own or can rent entire warehouses or silos, and can afford fees costing thousand of dollars (US) per month. Services are not available to farmer groups or traders who wish to deposit relatively small volumes of a commodity (for example, 50–100 tonnes). The system is predominantly used as a component in financing import and export transactions, but rarely used for non-tradables, except where the depositor is a large processor or major trading company. In most African countries, there have been very limited benefits to the domestic agricultural trade.[15]

While collateral management services started in the field of agricultural commodities, they have been successfully introduced in the energy and metal sectors. The range of services provided by collateral managers has steadily increased and they have sometimes become fully fledged partners of international arrangers of complex trade financing transactions:

> If an operation is situated in emerging markets with risks potential, or markets with political instability, collateral managers are included into the structure applying their designed risk control techniques . . . The underlying goods are often physically secured by a collateral manager which often facilitates access to trade finance in general . . . . The transfer of risks to the collateral manager can be the one effective tool to guarantee a pledge the financier has on the goods.[16]

The involvement of collateral managers can even extend beyond assisting offshore arrangers through inspection services, as they are increasingly becoming instrumental in widening the possibilities offered by structured finance transactions: 'The involvement of a local bank, and an independent agency able to carry out the necessary collateral controls, can enable a deeper penetration of the funds into the countryside. For example, through the local bank, the disbursement of funds can be controlled, with part being used to finance input suppliers'.[17]

Essential qualities for providers of collateral management services are professionalism, strength, integrity and impartiality. Besides SGS and ACE, other familiar names in the area of international inspection services and collateral management include Cornelder, Control Union, Steinweg (all three from The Netherlands), Warrant (Belgium) and Auxiga (France). Major collateral management providers are bringing their know-how into new regions:

> On a country level the international players compete with local entities like Sucofindo in Indonesia and USCO in Thailand . . . The Cornelder Group for example expanded into the Asian markets in the early 1980s . . . Cornelder Asia is now seen as one of Asia's leading service providers for the handling and storage of metals, soft commodities, plastics, edible oils and chemical products. As a collateral manager, Cornelder is involved in structured finance transaction in Thailand, China, Malaysia and Indonesia. It cooperates with the main trade and commodity finance banks, financial institutions such as Refco, and trading houses like Glencore, Gerald Metals, Cargill, Agrosin and ADM.[18]

The operations and procedures of the best inspection services and collateral management companies are ISO 9002 accredited by independent audit companies, which guarantees the integrity of their operations.

Finally, as in the more traditional fields of trade finance, supporting documents are increasingly established and sent electronically. For example: 'Zambia was able to leap-frog the existing paper-based systems by going directly to an electronic receipt system, which has recently emerged in the United States (so far only in the cotton industry) and the UK (London Metal Exchange). Electronic warehouse receipts offer greater security against forgery, are less costly and provide a ready-made audit trail'.[19]

Other commercial parties

Lenders should generally assess the strength of all local correspondents involved in the financing transaction in view of their proposed role. These correspondents include warehouse operators, inspection companies and collateral managers, as well as local banks and other parties selected to conduct part of the due diligence, advise lenders, arrange any local syndication, or act as administration or agent for the loan.

Finally, the due diligence should also investigate other third parties, such as transport companies or port authorities. As always, these parties should be checked for their reliability, integrity and creditworthiness, and lenders should be aware of any possible conflicts of interest.

Country/political risks

A major reason for the development of structured commodity finance has been the necessity of mitigating the political risk of the country in which the borrower is operating. Since the purpose of structured commodity finance is essentially to replace payment risk with performance risk, the underlying due diligence should look not only at the capacity of the borrower itself to perform but also at the risk that its government may impede such performance or manage somehow to restrict payments due to the lenders.

Impact on performance

The due diligence should investigate all country risks that potentially directly affect the ability of the exporter to perform under the commercial transaction, such as a confiscation of its assets or labour disruption. Next, lenders should have a good appreciation of general economic, financial and political risks, and of their potential impact on the transaction. This includes factors directly affecting the commodity producer or exporter, such as a sharp increase in inflation or export controls, as well as any event that has a potential impact on the capacity of the borrower to repay the loan, such as an international boycott on the country preventing the commodities being exported to the dedicated buyers.

Governments' actions or inaction can affect the very performance on which structured commodity finance deals rely. Sound macroeconomic fundamentals are helpful, especially in encouraging local banks to become more involved in the provision of financing to the local commodity sector. They are not essential, however, and structured commodity finance has proved its ability to flourish in adverse economic environments. War and high political instability are trickier, as they can directly undermine the ability of operators to perform on their underlying commercial contracts. In exceptional cases, production and exports can be successfully ring-fenced, as shown by Angola's uninterrupted access to the international bank markets on a structured basis in the 1990s, at a time when the country was being devastated by a civil war – but then more oil was discovered in Angola in the second part of the 1990s than probably anywhere else in the world.

As in the analysis of the owner of the commodities, the due diligence covering country risks should look at the incentives (political, financial or otherwise) for the country's government not to interfere in a particular transaction. A non-exclusive list of cues in that regard could include the borrower's economic weight in terms of foreign exchange generation and local employment, donors' support (direct or indirect) for the financing transaction, impact of any disruption by the government on the ability of other exporters or importers to secure commercial contracts and gain trade financing, and so on. As noted by one market specialist: 'Political risks also depend on the nature of the transaction. A transaction which is seen as good for the country is much less likely to be impacted by political changes than one which was negotiated under the table with the former governing group'.[20] Finally, even if a particular financing transaction is structured with the objective of being self-liquidating, lenders to that transaction should ascertain that the total of all export receivables-backed transactions issued out of the country of the borrower does not represent a significant portion of the country's foreign debt, otherwise the government may be under pressure when a financial crisis looms to redirect such receivables, in order to avoid any external debt default.

Transfer and other payment risks

Under structured pre-export financing transactions, transfer and convertibility risks are largely mitigated by the fact that the foreign exchange will not enter the borrower's country before the loan is duly serviced. That being said, it is virtually impossible to entirely remove the risk that governments may require foreign buyers to pay the foreign exchange proceeds to the central bank or a local bank before any other party (for instance, the 'passporting' requirement imposed by Russian authorities).

Governments that no longer have adequate incentives to support a particular structured commodity finance transaction, or that may urgently need to get their hands on foreign exchange, may also order the foreign commodity buyers to pay export proceeds into another bank than that originally contemplated by the financing. Although buyers may have confirmed original payment instructions to the lenders, they may prefer the risk of disrupting such agreement to that of being put on a blacklist by the emerging market government and losing out in an otherwise profitable market. This risk is higher when operating in countries with poor democratic checks, and where governments are still directly involved in the production and export of commodities.

Finally, every attempt should be made to explicitly exclude the particular transaction from any possible future debt rescheduling. Where applicable, sovereign immunity should also be waived explicitly. These aspects form part of the structural considerations surrounding the arrangement of structured commodity transactions (see the 'Structural aspects' section later in this chapter).

Note that most of the country risks discussed here can always be reduced with appropriate political risk insurance cover, discussed in Part III.

Legal and regulatory environment

The range of potential government impediments to the further development of structured commodity finance transactions spans many key elements of such transactions. In some countries, for example, stamp duties can prove prohibitively high, reducing the incentive for banks to perfect their security interest in the commodities being financed.

The due diligence should also investigate the rights of lenders in case of a default under, or with acceleration of, the financing transaction, especially regarding priority *vis-à-vis* third parties (government, other creditors, employees and so on). In particular, lenders should assess the clarity, adequacy, reliability and enforceability of commercial and bankruptcy laws and regulations affecting their ability to seize and sell the collateral, and/or be assigned export contracts and have first right on export receivables. For instance, lenders would find the value of their collateral discounted if export licences (if required) are not automatically transferred to them as the new owner of the commodities. Other forms of structured commodity finance, such as structured leases, can also be negatively affected by restrictive ownership laws limiting the rights of private owners – and in particular of foreigners – to own land. While the legal and regulatory environments have generally improved, banks are sometimes still confronted with major impediments, such as restrictions on the operation of offshore escrow accounts, unfavourable tax laws, or the inability of banks to take ownership of and export commodities. Once a financing is in place, banks remain exposed to changes in relevant laws and regulations. For instance, export licences for certain commodities could be suddenly revoked to foster local sales and consumption, say if there is a food shortage and risk of famine.

Although some of these risks can be addressed through adequate insurance cover, governments should aim to ensure that the tax, legal and regulatory environment is conducive to a wide offering of financing services by both the domestic and foreign financial markets. Lenders are sometimes still confronted with major impediments to structured pre-export financing transactions. For example, in the mid-1990s structured prepayments had not yet taken hold in Russia due to the obligation to pay a 20 per cent VAT on advance payments received by Russian companies from foreign entities against future exports of goods and services, with such VAT to be reimbursed only after the actual export of goods and services had taken place.

Regulations governing bank accounts in Russia have also played against structured finance deals. For a start, under Russian law a borrower had the right to close its bank account at any time, thus limiting the comfort given by escrow accounts. Also, there has been the onerous passporting requirement, whereby foreign exchange must first be repatriated in Russia before a portion of it can be re-exported to an offshore escrow account. Even if only for 24 hours, there is therefore an element of transfer risk that cannot be completely eliminated. In some cases, the Russian government has granted some exemptions to the passporting requirements, thus removing this additional risk element. This has been the case, for instance, for a US$40 million structured export finance transaction arranged at the beginning of 2003 for Sibneft with the support of Coface. Unfortunately, other emerging countries besides Russia still have in place regulations requiring repatriation of export proceeds, which directly impedes the ability to obtain foreign exchange financing on the back of structured commodity finance techniques.

Next, given that the widespread privatisation of the production and marketing of commodities in emerging countries has resulted in an increase in the level of due diligence required to put in place structured finance deals, due to the emergence of smaller producers and traders with limited track records, local governments and donors should carefully evaluate the impact of further privatisation and deregulation on the offer of financing to the commodity sector. They should also pay particular attention to the phasing out of commercial subsidies to producers and consumers, so as not to jeopardise the volume and quality of the commodities produced or the ability of commodity producers to profit from their trade.

Government monopolies can also have detrimental effects on the availability of hard-currency financing. In Russia again, the resumption of gold purchases by Gokhran, the Russian governmental precious metals agency, all but put an early end to the structured prepayment programme arranged in 1999 by the EBRD and Standard Bank London for small Russian gold producers. The situation fortunately eased rapidly and, at the beginning of 2002, the Russian government finally repealed a law that still restricted the right to export gold only to licensed banks. This decision should have a positive effect on the ability of gold producers to gain medium-term financing through structured deals.

Despite this bleak laundry list of headaches, government regulations have evolved in a way that fosters the use of structured commodity finance techniques: convertible currency is more easily available, the use of overseas escrow accounts has become more acceptable and government policies are generally more predictable. Some regions or countries are even taking major positive steps in this regard. For example, the so-called *acte unique* in French-speaking West Africa in the late 1990s is facilitating transactions relying on the transport of commodities in more than one country in the region. On the positive side, in the particular area of structured commodity finance, governments do have an important role to play by investing in the development of their country's infrastructure (such as port facilities, roads, warehouses, market intelligence, electricity and telecoms).

Note that a particular annoyance for arrangers of structured finance has been the negative pledge clauses imposed by the World Bank and other donor-supported institutions. To circumvent the limitations imposed by these clauses, some arrangers have ensured that negative pledge clause requirements are waived on an exceptional basis. In one particular structured export finance transaction arrangers drew sufficient comfort from a letter from the state-owned borrower making clear that the proposed financing did not conflict with their existing negative pledge requirements. Alternatively, the financing can be structured precisely to go around such clauses (for example, some forms of prepayments). In one benchmark financing for the government of Papua New Guinea (PNG), 'to avoid negative pledge restrictions, UBS [...] bought from the government the right to receive the corporation tax payable by the resource companies in PNG. Arrangements were made for the tax rights to be saleable and for the tax to be payable in US dollars. This involved UBS writing draft legislation for the PNG parliament to approve, and much negotiation with the resource companies to ensure proper payments'.[21]

Structural aspects

Whether or not a structured commodity finance transaction succeeds in providing attractive financing to the borrower, while minimising political and payment risks for lenders, depends on the effectiveness of the structure in meeting the objectives agreed by all parties. This in turn depends on the engineering capacity of the arranger of the financing transaction. Arrangers do not come cheap and borrowers should not hesitate to negotiate their fees down, but it is money well spent, especially if the same structure can be repeated in the future without incurring each time the same level of arrangement and legal fees. For example, a market specialist observed that recurring structured commodity finance deals arranged for Angola's Sonangol have: 'unique complexities, in particular the various intricate covenants that control crude oil allocations, that need a good strong lead arranger to cope with. Only a handful of banks seem capable of doing so'.[22]

A particular structural difficulty, for instance, may stem from the necessity for lenders to be able to put their hands on the commodities and/or related sales proceeds while circumventing onerous tax or regulatory provisions. In 2002, for example, Uralektromed, a Russian copper producer based in the Ural region, raised a US$35 million one-year syndicated loan secured by exports to Glencore (co-arranged by Standard Bank London and Moscow International Bank). The loan was made directly to the producing company and not to its parent company, the newly consolidated corporate group Urals Mining & Metallurgical Company. This gave lenders a more direct claim on the commodities being used as security for the financing.

Also, as already mentioned, arrangers should seek to design a structure that minimises the probability that the financing can be rescheduled. To this end, the transaction should resemble as much as possible a trade financing rather than a balance sheet or balance-of-payments financing. Doing so will also help the arranger to limit provisioning requirements.

With regard to international future flows securitisations backed by commodities, ratings can be improved by implementing the right credit enhancement features in the right place. Some of these features, such as those listed below, are also common in structured commodity bank finance.

- *Guaranteed export proceeds.* As mentioned, this can be achieved through a mixture of over-collateralisation, top-up clauses and hedging of commodity prices, foreign exchange or interest rates. If the transaction relies on a long-term contract, the financing should be fully repaid by the contract's maturity date.
- *Acceleration triggers.* Repayment should be accelerated in the event that certain covenants (such as performance measures or debt service coverage) have been breached.
- *Debt service reserve account.* As mentioned, a liquidity reserve could be established in addition to the escrow account into which payments are made by buyers that cover debt service for a period of time (typically six months) in the event of a disruption in production, or to cover the timing differences between receipt of payments from commodity buyers and required debt service payments. A large reserve account may support a medium-term loan to emerging markets without provisioning requirements.
- *Third-party guarantors.* Structured commodity finance transactions arranged for both banks and the capital markets increasingly rely on third-party guarantees of part (for example, surety bonds) or the whole (a wrapper) of the transaction. They are discussed in Part III.
- *Optimisation of fiscal aspects.* The structure should address tax-related issues in a relevant manner and adequately deal with issues such as withholding tax on interest, VAT on prepayments or stamp duties of pledged commodities.

In addition, some particular forms of countertrade, and some of the more complex structured commodity finance transactions, bring with them particular areas on which additional due diligence should be conducted: 'Banks active in the trade finance field have been showing more and more appetite for risks and for more ambitious deals in situations where their normal credit criteria cannot be met. This means that the demand for structured deals requiring the intervention of law firms has been rising as well . . . issues such as how the risks are divided between the different parties become crucial'.[23] With this perspective, the next chapter gives an overview of the legal documentation and advice required to support structured commodity finance transactions.

---

1 Director of AON Political Risk, James Brittain's presentation entitled *Analysing Transaction Risks* at a conference on 'Assessment & Mitigation of Risk in Structured Finance in Africa' organised by CWC in association with UNCTAD in Paris, April 2000.

2 'Reinforcing the structure', *Trade Finance,* March 2002.

3 'Performance risk deals' by John McNamara, *Trade Finance,* September 2001.

4 For instance, Dun & Bradstreet provides information on both public and private companies worldwide.

5 'Performance risk deals' by John McNamara, *Trade Finance,* September 2001.

6 Natasha Isakova, senior manager of Standard Bank London, quoted in 'Onwards and upwards' by Simon Pirani, *Trade Finance,* September 2001.

7 An agreement between a buyer and seller in which the buyer will still pay some amount even if the buyer refuses to take delivery of the commodities.

8 'Ashanti: The full story' by Emmanuelle Moors, *African Business,* December 1999.

[9] From a presentation by James Brittain of AON entitled 'Analyzing Transaction Risks', made at a conference on Assessment and Mitigation of Risk in Structured Finance in Africa, organised by CWC in association with UNCTAD in Paris, *April 2000.*

[10] A bonded warehouse is a designated area approved and licensed by the relevant customs authorities for storing imported non-dutiable goods. A bonded warehouse may be the whole premises, a designated part of the premises, a storage tank or any other approved place. The designated part is demarcated with lines, separating it from other areas. The non-designated area of the same warehouse premises may be used for other purposes.

[11] See the report by UNCTAD Secretariat, 1996.

[12] Christian Joerg of SGS, quoted in 'Securing the frontier supplies', *Trade Finance,* April 2002.

[13] Dan Day-Robinson, managing director of Day-Robinson International Consulting, quoted in 'A collateral advantage', *Trade Finance,* June 2001.

[14] Presentation entitled 'Warehousemen' made at a conference on Assessment and Mitigation of Risk in Structured Finance in Africa, organised by CWC in association with UNCTAD in Paris, April 2000.

[15] *Food Policy: The Role of Warehouse Receipt Systems in Enhanced Commodity Market and Rural Livelihoods in Africa* by Jonathan Coulter of the Enterprise, Trade and Finance Group of the Natural Resources Institute, January 2003.

[16] Christian Joerg of SGS, quoted in 'Securing the frontier supplies', *Trade Finance,* April 2002.

[17] Lamon Rutten of UNCTAD, quoted in 'Under-explored potential of SCF', *Trade Finance,* April 2002.

[18] 'A collateral advantage', *Trade Finance,* June 2001.

[19] *Food Policy: The Role of Warehouse Receipt Systems in Enhanced Commodity Market and Rural Livelihoods in Africa* by Jonathan Coulter of the Enterprise, Trade and Finance Group of the Natural Resources Institute, January 2003.

[20] James Brittain of AON, presentation entitled 'Analyzing Transaction Risks' made at a conference on Assessment and Mitigation of Risk in Structured Finance in Africa, organised by CWC in association with UNCTAD in Paris, April 2000.

[21] 'Missed opportunities', *Trade Finance*, May 2003.

[22] 'Working the dream', *Trade Finance,* March 2002.

[23] 'Lawyers win again', *Trade Finance,* March 2002.

Chapter 9

Legal aspects

With the expansion of structured commodity finance deals, demand for legal support for this financial product is increasing rapidly. To quote one adviser: 'There is a strong tendency on the customers' (borrowers') side to ask for individually tailored finance products. On the banks' side we see an increasing demand for security'.[1]

This chapter begins with a brief overview of the legal documentation typically supporting structured commodity finance transactions and of the salient legal aspects that arrangers should examine. There are no pro forma documents because the documents supporting structured commodity finance transactions should always be tailored to the needs and objectives of the parties involved, with, more often than not, the assistance of external legal advice.

Note that legal documentation and legal opinion should comply with the requirements established by the upcoming Basle II in order for a commodity loan to qualify as specialised (structured) lending, and thus attract significant provisioning requirements and related attractive borrowing costs.[2]

Legal documentation

The main documentation includes financial documents to which the bank (or banks) are party and the documents covering the supporting commercial transaction.

Financial documents

Structured commodity deals typically involve at least the documents detailed in the following subsections.

Facility agreement

In case of an export receivables financing or inventory financing where the owner of the commodities is also the borrower, there would be a facility agreement between one bank (acting for its own account or on behalf of other lending banks in a syndication) or several banks and the borrower, covering the general terms and conditions of the financing arrangement, including:

- standard representations and warranties on the part of the borrower; and
- usual clauses inserted in syndicated transactions, including cross-default, material adverse change and right of set-off.

With prepayment financing structures, there would typically be a limited recourse loan between the bank(s) and the commodity buyer, generally a trading company. As explained by one lawyer:

> One of the roles that we can play in situations of this type is to advise the trading house on the draft documentation provided by the lending bank. For instance, the trader will typically obtain an agreement from the bank that the trader's liability in case of non-repayment is limited to say 10 per cent or 20 per cent of the total amount, on the basis that the finance is being provided ultimately to the producer, even though the trader is the immediate borrower. The documentation will list circumstances in which this limitation of responsibility does not apply.[3]

Alternatively, the bank can also enter into a back-to-back sales contract with the commodity buyer mirroring the terms and conditions of the prepayment made by the borrower to the commodity buyer.

Security agreements

In an export receivables structured financing, the security agreements should include at least the following documents:

- assignment of commodities export sales contract or contract rights (primarily the right to sue the buyer for non-payment); and
- assignment of associated export sales receivables (proceeds).

Structured inventory financing relies primarily on the following security structure:

- pledge over commodities stored in the warehouse giving sale rights and generally supported by warehouse receipts; and
- progressively replaced by a new security such as the assignment of sales contract (s) rights and associated receivables.

In a prepayment, the security structure relies on the true sale of the commodities to the commodity buyer. As mentioned, the bank(s) can either lend to the commodity buyer or enter with the buyer into an equivalent purchase contract. In any case, the advance would also be supported by an assignment of the commercial contracts and export receivables.

Other financial documentation

Additional agreements necessary to support the financing transaction include:

- account management (collection and reserve accounts);
- agency agreement;
- (if relevant) documents supporting the establishment and operation of the special purpose vehicle (SPV); and
- (if relevant) a letter of credit (L/C) (for example, a green-clause L/C).

Supporting commercial documents

Sales contract

The benefit of the sales contract between the commodity owner and the dedicated buyer (or buyers) should be assigned to the bank(s). In addition, in a prepayment structure the bank may enter into a back-to-back sales contract with the offshore borrower making the prepayment to the commodity owner.

Insurance documents

Lenders should also obtain a copy of existing commercial insurance covering the commodities being financed and arrange to be named as loss payee or to be assigned the proceeds of such insurance. The same procedure applies to any additional commercial, credit or political risk insurance subscribed to by either the borrower, the commodity owner or the buyers (as relevant) in relation to the financing transaction. Note that policy risk remains with the insured.

Additional supporting documents

As discussed earlier, a wide array of additional features can reinforce the security of the proposed structured financing.

- In the case of inventory financing, the documentation would normally include a collateral management agreement with the inspection company or collateral manager, warehouse receipts and delivery orders. A typical warehouse agreement will contain the following clauses: (i) description of services; (ii) control of release of goods; (iii) insurance; (iv) fees and charges; (v) indemnity; (vi) duration; and (vii) governing law.[4]
- Acknowledgement by the buyers of the security agreements and payment instructions under the agreed payment mechanism (open account, letter of credit, and so on). In the absence of dedicated buyers, there should at least be a list of approved buyers.
- Any third-party guarantee (such as performance guarantees from a local bank) and documents supporting any other credit enhancement feature.
- Issuance of all necessary governmental and regulatory approvals (in relation to possible foreign exchange controls, need for export licences and so forth).

Legal advice and opinion

The lender should obtain a comprehensive legal opinion from both a local counsel based in the borrower's jurisdiction and from an international law firm typically based in the same country as the jurisdiction of the lending documents. Care must be taken to select independent, qualified lawyers providing expert advice.

For instance, while trading companies have traditionally acted simply as intermediaries between the exporter and the commodities end-buyer, they are now increasingly playing a role in trade finance. This has raised demand for legal services to help to structure the more complicated transactions that result.[5]

Legal opinions

Legal opinions should address three principal issues.

1. The transfer of the receivables and reserve fund from the commodity owner or exporter to the lender (as relevant). For instance, note that the assignment of sales contracts benefits

or foreign exchange receivables may be limited by negative pledge covenants included in other loan agreements signed by the borrower, in particular with regard to financing obtained from multilateral institutions and banks.

2. The perfection of the security interest of the lenders. On this issue, UNCTAD believes[6] that to 'perfect' its security interest in the commodities a lender with a mortgage would prefer warehouse receipts to be (i) documents of title and (ii) registered; for a lender with a pledge, 'perfection' would require (i) registration and (ii) physical or constructive possession. Unregistered pledges may be acceptable if registration is too expensive, or if it is common market practice and the borrower has a good track record, although the risk of loss from non-registration should be considered. The situation is different when the commodities are sold to the lender (directly or indirectly through the commodity buyer), as the lender becomes the beneficial owner of the commodity and not a secured lender.
3. The enforceability of this security interest – for instance, the rights of the lender to export the pledged or assigned commodities in case of a default from the borrower.

In the case of securitisation involving an SPV, the most important legal aspect is the 'true sale' transfer of the receivables, rather than a financing, to the effect that the underlying assets cannot become the property of the originator's estate in the event of a bankruptcy. The legal structure of the transaction should be sound and enforceable under both the laws of the applicable local jurisdiction and the laws governing the transaction.

Which law?

Local law will always be used for the security over inventory and receivables. The loan agreement will sometimes be governed by local law but, for large transactions, is more typically governed by English or New York law.

Although subjecting a financing contract to common law makes it easier for loan syndication purposes, this decision carries with it various risks, in particular regarding the ability to seize pledged assets in case of default. Especially as regards inventory financing, the majority of transactions are concluded under English law. However, the impact of the local law under which the transaction takes place should also be carefully examined. This risk is sometimes overcome by using a local bank as security agent.

In any case, much of the legal due diligence serves to clarify uncertainties regarding the interpretation and application of the law, as well as differences between legal systems and regulations in different countries involved in the proposed transaction.

Inside versus outside legal advice

Because of the downward pressure on lenders' and arrangers' fees and other remuneration due to increasing competition between banks, extra attention is being paid to the level of legal fees. As a result firms have to quote more or less fixed fees on most cases. However, lawyers point out that fixed or capped fees prevent them from devoting the time necessary to resolve complex issues relating to the taking or enforcing of security. As a result, only specialist firms that have a great deal of experience with the countries and commodities involved, having standard forms and in many cases local offices, can effectively compete for this work within the tight financial and time constraints imposed. Large law firms tend to work on complex structured trade or commodity deals, leaving the plain vanilla trade financing transactions to the smaller law firms, if any. According to one London-based lawyer, the fee for a characteristic US$100 million complex structured transaction would be around US$75,000.[7]

On the other hand, major banks maintain their own internal legal departments, which can act as intermediary between the arranger and external counsel when complex trade finance deals are involved. For instance, in 2002 BNP Paribas operated a specific division manned by six lawyers whose activities included participation in negotiations, optimisation of deal structures, assistance to account officers in presenting their case to the bank's credit committee, organisation of the taking of local security interests, instructing and monitoring local lawyers, and dispute management.

On a different level, an increasingly worrying legal issue for banks is the fact that, when they hold pledges over goods or foreclose on related security, they may be liable for environmental damage caused by the goods concerned under the principle of deemed possession: 'Proper environmental due diligence is required, and the documentation has to protect the bank against liability in these circumstances'.[8]

Regarding outside legal advice, the most common names in trade finance include Allen & Overy, Clifford Chance, Denton Wilde Sapte, Gide Loyrette Nouel, Lovells, Milbank Tweed and Norton Rose. In 2003, Denton Wilde Sapte was voted 'Best Trade Finance Law Firm' for the fourth consecutive year by the readers of *Trade Finance* magazine. The firm is well-known for the annual Ghana Cocoa Board financing but is also active elsewhere in Africa; for instance, it provided advice in 2001 on the US$60 million pre-export financing for the Konkola Copper Mines in Zambia, and also on the Anaconda Nickel structured commodity finance transaction in Australia, which included an SPV element.[9] According to Nicholas Budd, now with DWS and formerly with White & Case (Paris), the big law firms first began to get really involved in structured commodity trade financing after the break-up of the Soviet Union:

> This entailed the disappearance of state-backed trading mechanisms, triggering a tremendous demand for new sources and methods of financing commodity trade... trading companies involved in deals with Russia and neighbouring countries turned to their banks for new solutions. The banks in their turn started looking to legal advisers to help them reduce risks and build in guarantees on their trade finance operations in Russia and eastern Europe.[10]

---

1 Gabriele Fontane of Thümmel, Schütze & Partner, quoted in 'Lawyers win again', *Trade Finance,* February 2002.

2 See 'Operational requirements for specialised lending under Basle II' by Nicholas Budd, *Trade and Forfaiting Review,* April 2003.

3 David Lacey, a partner at law firm Lovells, quoted in 'Lawyers win again', *Trade Finance,* February 2002.

4 Presentation entitled 'Warehousemen' made at a conference on Assessment and Mitigation of Risk in Structured Finance in Africa, organised by CWC in association with UNCTAD in Paris, April 2000.

5 'Lawyers win again', *Trade Finance,* February 2002.

6 Report by UNCTAD Secretariat, 1996.

7 'Lawyers win again', *Trade Finance,* February 2002.

8 'A view from Paris', *Trade Finance,* April 2000.

9 'Awards for excellence', *Trade Finance,* June 2001 and June 2002.

10 'The law and the profits', *Trade Finance,* April 2000.

Chapter 10

Evaluation of structured commodity finance techniques

At the end of Chapters 4 and 5 some of the intrinsic benefits and limitations of structured inventory and pre-export financing were highlighted. To close this Part II an attempt at a broader evaluation of structured financing techniques is appropriate. Following a summary of how both inventory and pre-export finance can provide attractive financing in difficult situations, there is an explanation of the possible role of structured commodity finance in providing longer-term financing. Finally, the wider impact of these financing techniques on commercial trade relations and emerging markets economies is examined.

Providing attractive financing in difficult situations

Structured commodity finance provides access to financing in difficult situations and attracts better lending terms, which may or may not include lower interest rates. Borrowers who can choose between clean financing and structured finance will generally find interest rates on structured loans cheaper, although a portion of these savings will be eaten up by larger arrangement fees. If a borrower does not have the credit standing to obtain a clean loan, then structured finance is generally less onerous than loans secured on other forms of collateral (such as mortgages or cash deposits), although the interest rate would still reflect the poor credit risk. What is general to all structured commodity finance transactions is the capacity they give commodity owners to borrow in excess of what would have been available under a clean or traditionally secured loan. In the end, these techniques may even enable companies with a poor credit risk to obtain financing that otherwise would have not been granted, and thus to maintain or expand their commodity-related business.

Structured commodity finance also helps to identify commercial, commodity price and financial risks. Moreover, the repayment schedule can be designed to match the cash flows from the sale of the commodities (self-liquidation). Financing terms can be further improved by integrating a commodity price risk-hedging programme. For instance, the purchase of put options generally permits higher financing ratios. Hedging programmes also improve budget forecasting. Of course, the hedging component would require additional due diligence. This type of credit enhancement feature is discussed in Part III.

Structured commodity financing is also useful in countries where accounting standards are poor. This is because the lending decision is mainly based on an analysis of the underlying commercial transaction, and thus puts less weight on companies' financial statements and shareholding structure than conventional loans. As a corollary, one could argue that pervasive reliance on inventory financing could preclude emerging market companies from the efforts necessary to have a strong balance sheet and to publish financial statements according to recognised accounting standards, a practice that is key to obtaining medium- and long-term

Exhibit 10.1

Anecdotal evidence of the cost of structured versus non-structured finance

In 1996 the interest margin on Ghana's Cocoa Board (Cocobod) structured export receivables financing (then US$260 million) was at an almost all-time low of 50 basis points (bp). The same year, a margin of 70bp was paid by Ghana National Petroleum Corporation (GNPC), another state-owned company, on a US$80 million oil import financing transaction. Both transactions were syndicated to a large number of international banks. The former was a tightly structured pre-export financing transaction, while the latter was mainly secured by local currency deposits. Participation fees were also somewhat higher for the import financing, resulting in sensibly higher overall earnings for banks participating in the oil import transaction. However, both financings were still cheap for a high-risk country and had to do with the fact that, thanks to a series of structured commodity finance deals supported by impeccable performance on the part of Ghanaian borrowers, Ghana's risk had become familiar and acceptable at this price to commercial banks, which were also actively competing among themselves to obtain financing mandates in Ghana.

In fact, a few months earlier, in Kenya, a syndicated US$12.2 million letter of credit import facility arranged by Standard Bank London for Stanbic Kenya to onlend the funds to the Kenya Tea Development Association (KTDA) attracted an interest margin of 200bp (even excluding arrangement, participation and L/C fees). The transaction was secured by the payment of the proceeds of tea exports into an offshore evidence account controlled by Standard Bank and by the strict conditions precedent to the disbursement of funds included in the letter of credit.

At the time, Kenya's country risk was not significantly higher than Ghana's. Moreover, the Kenyan facility was extended not directly to a company doing business in the commodities sector but to an arguably more creditworthy local bank (actually a subsidiary of Standard Bank London's own parent company). Finally, although the offshore account was simply an evidence account on which the lenders had no rights, it was arguably more representative of the ability of the borrower to repay a hard-currency loan than the cedi-denominated deposit that secured that Ghanaian oil import financing. It is clear that the status of Ghana as a 'prime' borrower was perhaps deemed more important than the underlying structure in pushing down the cost of the financing.

The evolution of the pricing of Ghana cocoa deals could actually support the argument that syndicated transactions for emerging country borrowers are sometimes underpriced. Ghana first returned (after a 10-year absence) to the Euroloan market in May 1991 with a US$75 million facility bearing an interest margin over Libor of 1.25 per cent pa, a 150 per cent receivables cover and a government guarantee. Two years later, the transaction had risen to US$140 million, the margin was down to 0.75 per cent pa and the receivables cover was down to 125 per cent. The government guarantee had also disappeared. In 1996, the interest margin was, as mentioned, only 0.50 per cent pa, while the receivables cover was a mere 100 per cent. One could argue that the improvement in the fundamentals of Ghana cocoa exports and Ghana sovereign risk during this period did not fully justify the lower interest margin and the reduced security. In fact, in 1996 a US$75 million structured facility was arranged for the Société Internationale de Cacao et Café of neighbouring Côte d'Ivoire, a country which is an even bigger cocoa exporter, with a margin of 1.75 per cent and a security cover of 125 per cent.

The pricing of the Cocobod deal continued its fall into absurdity to reach a margin of just 35bp over Libor for the 1999–2000 season. After that syndication ran into trouble, the market eventually realised the inadequacy of the Cocobod pricing and in 2001 the syndication was arranged at the highest margin in six years – still a mere 52.5bp. As noted by a market specialist:* 'The health of the Cocobod loan received a definite boost [in 2000] with a revised bidding process. The competitive bidding process used until then had meant that banks associated with losing bids ended up not participating in the deal at all ...'. For the 2001–2002 season, the arranging group was made up of 11 banks.

*'Cocobod reborn', *Trade Finance,* October 2001.
Source: Author's own research.

financing in the international capital markets. In reality, as will be discussed later, structured commodity financing arranged by banks tends to pave the way for longer-term financing. These techniques also lead to asset-backed securitisations, thus opening the door to straight bond issues.

Finally, transactions can be repeated, which provides some sort of amortisation of large up-front arrangement fees paid out to banks. See Exhibit 10.1 for a comparison of the costs of structured versus less structured pre-export financing deals for otherwise comparable borrowers and countries.

Supporting access to longer-term financing

As noted by a leading arranger of structured commodity finance transactions, they can have maturities of 'anything between 60 days and five years (longer if you count gas as a commodity)'.[1] The record to date is a US$1.5 billion seven-year deal arranged for Luhoil in June 2003, collateralised on oil exports.

Back in the late 1990s it seemed that prepayment structures were the most conducive for emerging markets borrowers to obtain medium-term financing. One of the first medium-term structured commodity finance transactions was actually the prepayment arranged in 1995 by BP and UBS for Sonangol (Angola), discussed earlier. It was supposedly easier for prepayment structures to support claims made to credit committees and bank regulators that a transaction was essentially trade-related, hence that it was less likely to be caught in an external rescheduling and that it should not attract provisioning requirements. In fact, many times thereafter, Sonangol returned to the market with a similar structure.[2] However, the old export receivables financing structure showed its versatility and, thanks to a new lease of life in Russia and other former Soviet Union countries, proved over and over its capacity to provide medium-term financing.

The principle behind these medium-term structured commodity financing transactions is that the maturity of each disbursement and/or of the facility is initially less than 365 days – and hence does not attract provisioning requirements – but the maturity can be extended automatically on specific dates, provided that certain pre-agreed conditions are met. What is important is to convince bank regulators that the financing (i) can always be repaid within one year, if necessary; and (ii) is essentially trade related. As explained by John McNamara with regard to point (i): 'The aim of the acceleration mechanism is to give the lenders an exit within an accelerated time, typically 12 months. The advantage is that it allows the lenders to present the deal as more obviously short-term trade, and therefore non-provisionable . . . . This acceleration is achieved either by retaining a larger percentage of the cash flow running through the collection account, or by escalating the export contract on which the transaction is based'.[3]

Since conditions of extension are generally limited to good performance on the underlying trade transaction, and ongoing validity of initial sets of representations and warranties, any borrower who is confident that these conditions will be met can also be virtually certain to have locked-in medium-term financing. In practice, there could be a simple option mechanism to extend the maturity automatically if these conditions are met. In certain instances, however, the extension of the maturity may be conditional upon an additional set of criteria, which are not within the power of the borrower: 'A "subjective" material adverse change will allow lenders to declare material adverse change on any grounds they like, from deteriorating market conditions to poor weather, and thus extract themselves from the facility early'.[4] In some cases, the maturity of a syndicated financing transaction may not be extended if a majority of banks does not want to extend their participation. In cases where a medium-term maturity is achieved through a rollover mechanism, whereby the loan must be repaid before it can be drawn again for a new period, some bank regulators may insist that a bank should be individually in a position to opt out on any rollover date for the deal not to attract provisioning requirements.

Structuring commodity financing around shorter-term revolving periods may serve not only to minimise the incidence of provisioning requirements or rescheduling, but also to maintain a relatively low pricing when there is too much uncertainty regarding the longer-term situation of the borrower or that of its business or political environment.

Improving commercial operations and international trade

Sometimes a tightly structured financing is the only way for a company in the commodity sector to obtain financing for working capital purposes or the purchase of commodities, or even to grant financing in turn to a commodity buyer for commercial reasons. Even in less drastic cases, structured commodity financing has indirect benefits for the underlying commercial transaction, such as encouraging longer-term sales contracts and, more generally, a stronger relationship between all the parties involved. By extrapolation, structured commodity finance helps to maximise domestic and international trade flows.

Inversely, companies that are dependent upon their commodity buyers or suppliers for financing can investigate the possibility of obtaining separate bank financing and have cash payments for their trade contracts. For instance, in the mid-1990s the Malawi Petroleum Control Commission (PCC) had in place a petroleum import contract with the trading subsidiary of a major oil company. This contract had clearly unattractive commercial terms, in part because of the PCC's insistence on 90-day payment terms. This unwillingness of the PCC to seek better commercial terms continued for years, despite the fact that PCC was receiving various structured finance proposals from first-class international banks for longer-term financing at much better all-in terms. A bank financing would also have enabled the PCC to be in a better negotiating position *vis-à-vis* its suppliers of petroleum products. Unfortunately, lack of proper incentives, combined with a limited understanding of structured finance, deprived Malawi of the opportunity to pay less for, and finance more cheaply, its petroleum imports. Fortunately, under pressure from the Bretton Woods institutions, the government of Malawi finally decided in 1999 to liberalise the import of petroleum products, turning the PCC into a mere monitoring institution. Needless to say that, until this decision was taken, the PCC's exclusive reliance on oil suppliers for its financing needs cost Malawi dearly in foreign currency terms.

Improving emerging market economies

Over recent years the components of structured pre-export financing have dramatically evolved, in line with the liberalisation and deregulation of commodity markets, and in particular with the disappearance of governments as commercial and financial intermediaries.

Thanks to structured commodity finance techniques, large hard-currency financing can now be arranged without government guarantees. This is in line with the requirements of the Bretton Woods institutions and frees external public accounts of emerging countries from undue involvement in commercial transactions. Moreover, new structured pre-export financing loans do not put unnecessary pressure on the balance of payments because they are generally self-liquidating and strictly linked to actual export flows.

For its part, inventory financing reduces the pressure for immediate sale of the commodities and thus has a smoothing effect on price volatilities. Moreover, the required logistics also encourages the development of warehouses and warehouse grading systems, which in turn will further foster exports from emerging markets. In the emerging market economies, structured commodity financing has become an essential tool for developing and supporting trade and investment opportunities.

[1] 'Performance risk deals' by John McNamara, *Trade Finance,* April 2002.

[2] For instance, a US$600 million prepayment financing with a tenor of four years that was voted 'Deal of the Year 2001' by *Trade Finance* magazine (arranged by BNP Paribas with Glencore International as international oil lifter).

[3] *Structured Trade and Commodity Finance in Emerging Markets* by John McNamara, Woodhead Publishing Limited, 2001.

[4] Ibid.

Part III

Third-party credit enhancement: insurance and guarantees

Introduction to Part III

Structured finance can render certain risks palatable that otherwise would have to be insured if unacceptable to lenders. Paradoxically, insurance and guarantees are also becoming valuable or necessary elements of structured finance transactions.

When part of structured finance transactions, insurance and guarantees help to transfer whatever risks may be left after the collateral elements have been put into place. One of the reasons for the attractiveness of third-party credit enhancement is that foreclosure or realisation of collateral is very time-consuming and costly in case of default. Lenders also do not like to liquidate collateral because it generates bad publicity. Companies providing insurance or guarantees are both more adept at it and are less concerned with the consequences.

With appropriate insurance cover and third-party guarantees, a structured commodity finance transaction is closer to being 'watertight', and thus more attractive to both the borrower (in terms of cost, tenor and so on) and the lender (in terms of security). Moreover, lenders are not always willing or able to increase the cost of financing to the level theoretically required for higher-risk loans. Regardless of the potential fees and interest income, a loan may simply not be approved by a bank credit committee. However, the financing may proceed on the back of the insurance of part of the unwanted risk, or with an acceptable third-party guarantee. Also, while insurance and guarantees rarely allow banks to reduce their provisioning requirements, they still make the underlying loan easier to syndicate.

By insuring certain risks (commercial, political, market) that they do not want to keep, lenders are in a position to offer financing to higher-risk borrowers and better all-in lending terms to all borrowers. Insurance cover is discussed in Chapter 11, while Chapter 12 presents some useful means of incorporating commodity price risk management into structured commodity finance transactions. Third-party guarantees, which operate at different levels to mitigate credit risk, are examined in Chapter 13. Chapter 14 discusses providers of insurance and guarantees, and compares private operators with non-commercial providers. Finally, in Chapter 15, some key conclusions on insurance and guarantees are summarised.

Chapter 11

Insurance

The insurance market offers a comprehensive range of potential risk transfer solutions for companies with credit and political risk exposures linked to international trade and overseas projects. Potential beneficiaries of such insurance cover include manufacturers and exporters, international traders and investors, banks, and issuers of securities. In this area, political risk insurance has been widely available for years and is steadily being complemented by credit risk insurance. Although the latter is commonly referred to as 'commercial risk', it should not be confused with commercial insurance (against fire, theft and so on), which is not a financial credit enhancement tool.

Political risk insurance

History of political risk insurance

Political risk insurance (PRI) developed out of marine insurance provided by Lloyds at the beginning of the 20th century. The range of covers available remained limited until the 1970s, when contract frustration cover was first placed in the marine markets at Lloyd's. A capacity crunch first occurred in the 1980s following a high level of claims. Until the mid-1990s, private political risk insurance remained a niche market and was only used as a last-resort alternative to export credit agencies (ECAs), which had developed after World War II to compensate for a lack of interest, at that time, from the private insurance market.

Thereafter, the PRI market grew rapidly and overall capacity rose from a mere US$70 million in 1995 to about US$700 million in 2002, down from a peak of about US$900 million in 2000. More capacity and new products have now turned political risk insurance into a fully fledged market. Notably, the private PRI market steadily encroached upon the territory of ECAs and this tendency has gained further momentum in recent years due to the increasing number of countries that are 'blacklisted' by ECAs.

Unfortunately, the World Trade Center and Pentagon terrorist attacks of 11 September 2001 exacerbated the already fragile conditions in emerging markets for borrowers and investors (in particular in Argentina) by pushing demand up. As observed shortly thereafter by a market specialist: 'The bank markets have gone back to political risk insurance, and structures that externalise transferability and convertibility risk are enjoying a new vogue for emerging market transactions'.[1] At the same time, there is less capacity in the insurance markets. The private PRI market for contract frustration and unfair calling of bonds is expected to contract to about US$600 million in 2003; and the PRI market for non-repayment of loans and non-honouring of government guarantees is expected to drop even more significantly, from about US$880 million in 2002 to US$690 million in 2003.[2]

Meanwhile, given that the huge amount of Argentinean claims has not always been recognised by insurers as being caused by political risk events, banks now often seek so-called 'comprehensive cover' that includes not only PRI but also credit risk.

Users of political risk insurance

Contracts eligible for political risk cover include export contracts with public buyers, that is, foreign governments or government-owned or controlled companies. For such trade contracts, political risk cover is provided under the general heading of 'contract frustration cover'. In the case of direct foreign investment assets, political risk cover is provided under the general heading of 'investment cover'.

Other contracts eligible for political risk cover include supplier credits with public borrowers or public guarantors, import contracts with public suppliers or guarantors and, finally, bank loans and capital market issues.

Today the political risk market is used by:

- exporters of industrial and consumer goods to emerging countries;
- importers of goods (including commodities) from emerging countries;
- investors in emerging countries;
- banks involved in trade finance, structured finance and project financing; and
- leasing companies.

Political risk cover

Political risks are generally equated with cross-border or civil wars, military coups or dramatic debt crises in emerging countries. Yet political risks are not always the result of events in emerging countries, as they can also be prompted by decisions taken by OECD-based nations (for example, embargoes placed by the United States on some countries). Political risks can also affect exclusively industrialised countries, a recent example being the lengthy embargo introduced by France against meat imports from the United Kingdom at the height of the 'mad cow' crisis.

A typical contract frustration policy would cover losses arising from the following events:[3]

- government law, order, decree;
- non-payment by a public buyer;
- wrongful calling of bonds;
- non-certification (of shipment documents or invoices);
- war (occasionally excluded);
- import or export restrictions;
- currency inconvertibility and non-transfer;
- arbitration award default;
- non-respect of contractual obligations; and
- unilateral termination of the contract (public buyer).

In the past, political risk insurance was mainly requested by exporters and foreign investors. Following the emerging market crises of East Asia (1997), Russia (1998) and Argentina (2001) this type of insurance is increasingly requested by lenders to support trade and project finance deals in volatile emerging countries. Another recent change that took place in the early 2000s is the fact that political risk insurance has entered the capital markets. Zurich Emerging Markets Solutions (ZEMS), for example, provides PRI to cover corporate bond issues, thus improving issue marketability. As explained by Daniel Riordan, Managing

Director of ZEMS, with regard to PRI cover for a recent US$450 million Petrobras deal: 'By providing 18 months cover for the transfer and convertibility risks it was possible to lift the bond rating by four notches to Baa1'.[4] This particular bond issue was used to finance the import of petroleum products.

Credit risk insurance

History of credit insurance

The market for credit risk insurance[5] is almost as old as that for political risk insurance, but it has evolved more slowly. In the 1970s the credit insurance market was made up essentially of export credit agencies (ECAs), which eventually bore large claims linked to losses on trade financing bank loans. In the 1990s ECAs were joined by Lloyds, which returned to the credit markets after an absence of more than 50 years. However, Lloyds loss ratios thereafter grew to such levels that its main syndicates withdrew again in 2000. Today, only three out of four Lloyds syndicate members have good capacity for credit risks. This has prompted the emergence of new private market specialists in this type of commercial risk, such as Zurich.

Credit insurance underwritten by ECAs initially provided cover exclusively on a whole-turnover basis. At first Lloyds tried to copy these whole-turnover (portfolio) covers, but they rapidly realised they did not know how to underwrite this type of risk and, after an initial withdrawal, Lloyds now underwrites credit insurance cover on a case-by-case basis.

Users of credit risk insurance

Trade, investment and financing contracts with private counterparties are eligible for credit risk insurance. Many underwriters, such as Chubb, still underwrite credit risk on a portfolio basis. As noted by Wayne Bayer, vice president of Chubb and co-manager of trade credit insurance: 'The advantage of such trade credit policies over forms of repayment like letters of credit lie in their flexibility. Chubb's policy allows policyholders to tailor their cover insuring their domestic or their foreign sales, or both. Further refinement allows them to include all credit customers or just key clients with sales above a set volume'.[6] Obtaining insurance for non-payment is also generally much cheaper than getting an L/C confirmed.

By removing payment risk, credit risk insurance cover is a perfect complement to performance-based structured commodity finance transactions. As explained by one market specialist: 'An assurance of payment policy not only provides peace of mind but can also strengthen an organisation's balance sheet from the viewpoint of lenders, investors and shareholders. Increasingly, companies are integrating trade credit insurance into their overall financial credit and risk management strategies and are, in effect, unleashing the power of their account receivables'.[7]

Credit risk covers

Credit insurance covers the risk of insolvency or of bankruptcy of industrial or commercial companies. For simplicity, we have broken down credit insurance cover between trade-related credit insurance cover and investment cover.

Trade contracts made with private buyers can be insured through credit insurance cover for losses arising from the following events:[8]

- government law, order or decree;
- insolvency or protracted default of private buyer;
- war (sometimes excluded);
- import or export restrictions;
- calling of bonds following declared insolvency or political events;
- currency inconvertibility and non-transfer; and
- arbitration award default.

Investment insurance
Although less relevant to the area of structured commodity finance, note that foreign direct investments and projects finance can be similarly insured for the following risks:[9]

- confiscation, expropriation, nationalisation;
- selective discrimination;
- currency inconvertibility and non-transfer (of dividends, royalties, fees and so on);
- political violence (that is, property damage following events such as war, strikes, riots or civil commotion);
- other risks such as forced divestiture and forced abandonment; and
- loss of revenues (or business interruption) following the above-mentioned perils can be added, but as an extension only.

Evaluation of political and credit risk insurance

Insurance of commodity-related trade contracts is typically short-term, as insurance policies cover only pre-shipment and post-shipment export phases. In turn, insurance cover for exports of capital goods or services can extend into the medium term. Actually, political and commercial risk insurance for trade contracts can easily extend to EPC (engineer, procurement and construction) contracts, with a significant portion of the contract, in terms of risk period and share of overall contract price, involving home-office services or overseas construction. As such, medium-term insurance cover is instrumental to the financing of new investments in emerging countries, in particular in the commodity sector. Exporters and project finance lenders can even obtain insurance cover for periods extending beyond 36 months (the typical time limit accepted by the private insurance market) by binding a policy for an initial period of three years and then, six or 12 months on, extending the policy in order to cover the entire period required to complete the investment. For longer-term covers, market providers of political and commercial risk insurance are in direct competition with export credit agencies and other donor-supported providers of insurance.

Political and commercial risks can be insured separately or together. In the field of commodities, it should be noted that the privatisation of the means of production and of the trading of commodities in the 1990s reduced the need for certain types of political risk insurance. At the same time, new forms of commercial risk insurance emerged that can be extremely useful to support structured commodity finance transactions. For instance, a few years ago the first cover for private supplier default was introduced, to provide insurance against losses of prepayments (made in cash or in kind) to private sector exporters of commodities and other goods from emerging countries, due to supplier insolvency and financial default.[10] (In this particular policy, one condition was for the underlying contract to place an unconditional obligation on the exporter to repay the prepayment in cash if, for any reason, the debt was not discharged by the delivery of the goods.)

For cash contracts, exporters use political and commercial risk insurance to cover their contract termination and payment risks, while for financed contracts banks seek insurance in order to reduce the risks to acceptable levels and/or provide better financing terms to borrowers. According to one trade finance lawyer:

> In a number of transactions, we have become aware of a move to secure financing not only by obtaining collateral but also by minimising the bank's lending risks. In forfaiting transactions, for instance, banks prefer more than ever to limit what they purchase to accounts receivables that are covered by export insurance or bad debt insurance.[11]

Finally, arrangers of securitisations secured by trade receivables can use political and credit risk insurance to enhance the portfolio of trade receivables to the level necessary to achieve the desired rating. The insurance structure can also be in line with debt servicing requirements so that payments received from insurers in case of events of default on the trade debts can match the financial commitments of the obligor.

While demand for political and credit risk insurance is increasing, availability has been constrained after 11 September 2001, given its consequences in terms of political instability and actual or potential conflicts worldwide. In this respect, a leading political risk broker noted the following changes in the political risk market after 11 September 2001:[12]

- country exclusions;
- periods tightened;
- capacity squeezed;
- reinsurers imposing constraints;
- refocus of capital providers to application of capital for highest return (that is, property and liability);
- rates increasing; and
- review of products.

Exporters and lenders are now facing a 'hard market', and this analysis has confirmed an earlier assessment made by Daniel Riordan, senior vice president and managing director at Zurich Emerging Markets Solutions: 'This is the first real hard market in insurance in 15 years . . . capacity is now two-thirds of what it was six months ago . . . Rates are up 20–30 per cent on average. Certain markets, such as Brazil, are even more extreme. That's a market where there is virtually no capacity . . . . There is also a major flight to quality . . . . Tenors will be shorter'.[13] However, things need to be put in perspective: if we compare today's market with the market in the early 1990s, capacity has multiplied by 10 and, where there was absolutely no solution for risks over 36 months, these solutions exist today.

[1] Valentino Gallo, global head of structured trade at Citigroup, quoted in 'Keeping the deals flowing', *Trade Finance,* November 2001.

[2] *Private Political Risk Insurance Market: BPL Global Capacity Survey,* February 2003.

[3] Presentation entitled 'The Private Market' made by Laure Reboul of Gras Savoye at the 'Séminaire Risques Politiques' conference, organised by Willis and Gras Savoye, London, November 2002.

[4] 'Dodging the bullets' by Alex Cox, *Trade Finance,* July/August 2001.

[5] Note that the term 'credit insurance' is used interchangeably with 'commercial risk insurance'.

[6] 'Dodging the bullets' by Alex Cox, *Trade Finance,* July/August 2001.

[7] Peter Aitken, vice president and co-manager of trade credit insurance at Chubb, quoted in 'Dodging the bullets' by Alex Cox, *Trade Finance,* July/August 2001.

[8] Presentation entitled 'The Private Market' made by Laure Reboul of Gras Savoye at the 'Séminaire Risques Politiques' conference, organised by Willis and Gras Savoye, London, November 2002.

[9] Ibid.

[10] Presentation made by Charles Berry, Managing Director of Berry Palmer & Lyle Ltd, entitled 'Insuring Against Non-delivery and Non-performance: Commercial and Political Risk Insurance', made at a conference organised by IBC in London, December 1995.

[11] Gabriele Fontane of law firm Thümmel, Schütze & Partner, quoted in 'Lawyers win again', *Trade Finance,* February 2002.

[12] Contribution to the 'Séminaire Risques Politiques' conference, organised by Willis and Gras Savoye, London, November 2002.

[13] 'Protective layers' by Jonathan Bell, *Trade Finance,* February 2002.

Chapter 12

Commodity price risk management

The discussion so far has covered the extent to which commercial and political risks can be insured, and the benefits of doing so in order to obtain better financing terms. However, companies operating in the commodity sector face another major risk that also affects access to financing, and this is market risk.

A commodity exporter, for example, is exposed to the risk that the price of the commodities to be sold throughout the financing period falls to levels that could compromise a timely service of its debt obligations. To varying degrees, this commodity exporter may also be exposed to foreign exchange and interest rate risks. Price volatility in these markets has increased in recent years, making it important for participants in the commodity sector to properly manage (that is, hedge) their market risk.

Hedging can be accomplished either over the counter (OTC), generally with banks but also increasingly with other hedge providers such as insurance companies, or through a commodities exchange or internet-based commodities market-place. The same principle applies to the hedging of interest rate and foreign exchange risks. A discussion of foreign exchange and interest rate hedging techniques and applications is beyond the scope of this book, but it may be useful to discuss the benefits of hedging commodity price risk and the ways of incorporating such hedging into structured finance transactions.

As regards the risks of failing to manage commodity price risk adequately, the experience of Ashanti Goldfields in the lead-up to its commodity derivatives crisis at the end of 1999 provides some useful lessons (see Exhibit 12.1[1]). Besides avoiding similar disasters, the proper hedging of commodity price plays a vital role in structured commodity finance by enabling better lending terms and/or providing attractive features to lenders and borrowers. Once a commodity derivative element is incorporated into such a financing, the timing and volume of export cash flows can be relied upon to provide security and support for both the debt service and the hedging programme.

Commodity derivatives can be incorporated into a financing transaction in a variety of ways, in particular by (i) fixing prices or establishing floors in a structured prepayment or export receivables financing, (ii) linking interest rates or principal repayments to prices and (iii) selling options to subsidise interest rates. The first two examples have a hedging component, in that the borrower is protected against the consequences of adverse commodity price movements. In the third structure, the borrower is willing to forgo this protection and give up its entitlement to any upside move in commodity prices to reduce the level of its debt service charges

These three basic structures are examined in the following sections. Of course, many added features can be embroidered onto these most common forms of commodity-linked financing structures in order to design structured financing transactions that meet, to the extent possible, the needs and requirements of both lenders and borrowers. Finally, note that it is cheaper and easier to hedge an exposure at times when market conditions are relatively

Exhibit 12.1

Ashanti Goldfields commodity derivatives crisis (1999)

Since the mid-1990s or so, Ashanti had systematically hedged through forward sales not only most of its ongoing production, but also much of its gold reserves still in the ground, at levels much above its production costs, thus locking in considerable future profits. In total, as of mid-1999, the company had a hedge position of 11 million ounces, or 50 per cent of its gold reserves.

For several years the prices at which it had hedged were also considerably above market prices, giving the company in mid-1999 a paper profit of over US$250 million. However, the company's hedging strategy ran into problems when gold prices started to increase markedly in the third quarter of 1999, following an announcement by key central banks and the IMF that they would not sell any more gold on the open market in the next few years. At that time, many of Ashanti's hedges consisted of 'zero cost' options: purchases of put options financed by the sale of call options. When prices increased, the banks that had bought the call options from Ashanti started asking for margin calls (cash deposits). While Ashanti had more than enough gold in the ground to cover its future financial obligations, it did not have easy access to cash, nor, given the sovereign risk problems related to its location in Ghana, could it borrow funds at short notice against the (increased) value of its reserves. Ashanti, in effect, had not hedged itself against this 'cash flow risk'. This could have been done, for example, by adding the purchase of out-of-the-money call options to its position.

In the end, the liquidity crisis forced Ashanti to accept very restrictive conditions and sell some of its best assets to banks in order to rapidly obtain a much-needed foreign exchange loan. The mistake made by Ashanti was to use commodity price derivatives to generate income, rather than simply to hedge its exposure to price volatility.

Source: Author's own research.

favourable – that is, when commodity prices are relatively high and upward-sloping for commodity exporters, and vice versa for importers.

Fixing export prices or establishing floors

As explained in Chapter 5, in a structured prepayment a commodity exporter would sell forward its production against an up-front payment by the commodity buyer. If the forward price curve is favourable, this commodity exporter could elect to enter into fixed price swaps to lock in the forward price curve. Commodity sale prices can be fixed directly with the commercial buyer. However, if the commodity exporter prefers to sell in the spot market to one or more dedicated buyers, a price swap could be arranged by the lending bank or another hedge provider, or even directly with a commodity futures exchange. These fixed prices would in turn determine the value of the prepayment. When the prepayment is a disguised loan, fixed prices ensure that export proceeds will be sufficient to meet capital repayments, interest payments, and other fees and costs associated with the loan.

Alternatively, where an exporter using a prepayment structure to raise finance is also eager to retain part or the whole of the upside potential if prices rise, this exporter can use put options to establish a floor price to future export revenues. The characteristics of the option transaction (number of put options, reference periods, exercise prices and so forth) would be set to coincide with the volume, timing and reliability of the anticipated export cash flows supporting the amortisation of the prepayment.

Fixed prices and price floors can support better lending terms to exporters, in particular a higher financing ratio. Likewise, commodity price swaps and put options can be incorporated into structured export receivables financing.

In some of the early pre-shipment financing transactions arranged by Bankers Trust for Sonangol (Angola) a string of put options ensured that the aggregate of the contractual price of the monthly cargo pre-financed and of the monthly put option settlement amount (if any) would be sufficient to cover the debt service. Thus Sonangol was able to borrow up to 85 per cent of the expected value of cargoes due for future shipment. The remaining 15 per cent covered the fact that hedging is never 100 per cent perfect due to a variety of factors, among which are the unpredictability of shipment dates and volumes, the basis risk if benchmark prices or formulas differ between the physical and the paper market, and so on. Without the put options, however, Sonangol would have been able to borrow only perhaps about two-thirds of the anticipated value of a cargo scheduled for delivery during the first year, and probably even less for a cargo scheduled for shipment in the second and third years.

Linking interest rates to commodity prices

Often, the borrower can pay for these put options by selling a certain number of call options at a higher price, in effect buying a 'collar'. Depending on the level of the strike prices and on other factors, the collar can be either at a zero cost or result in a cash inlay or outlay for the exporter.

For example, to support a revolving tolling facility arranged at the beginning of 2002 for RusAl, Société Générale designed a zero-cost hedging structure secured by a cash deposit form the borrower. Both the potential cash payments to be made by the hedge providers (in case of lower aluminium prices) and the cash deposit were assigned as security to the lenders under the facility.[2] Over the life of the hedging transaction, the exporter agreed to pay a settlement amount when commodity prices increased above the call strike price and receive a settlement payment when commodity prices fell below the put strike price.

Such a collar could be embedded in a structured financing by linking settlement payments to interest payments. The important aspect of this structure is that, when commodity prices rise, the settlement amount due from the exporter is typically added to the interest payment (not always in a transparent way), but this cost is balanced by higher export proceeds. Hence the exporter pays more interest (net of settlement amounts) when commodity prices are high, and vice versa. For example, in May 1996, Merrill Lynch arranged for Slovnaft, the Slovak Republic's oil company, a US$50 million three-year loan with interest payments linked to crude oil prices.

There are a number of possible variations on this theme to tailor the derivative component to the financing needs and market views of the borrower. For example, the transaction can include a cap (in the case of an exporter) or a floor (in the case of an importer) above or below which the interest rate is no longer subsidised. The subsidy can also be limited to specific quantities of commodities or periods of time. More rarely, it is not the interest rate but the principal amount itself that is linked to commodity prices. For example, in February 1995, Merrill Lynch closed a US$250 million five-year aluminium-linked transaction for a smelter expansion project to be undertaken by Dubal, an aluminium smelter based in Dubai, whereby the principal repayment of the five-year notes was linked to aluminium prices.

Subsidising interest rates

This is a variation of the previous structure, whereby the only option entered into by the commodity exporter is the sale of call options. The key aspect of this structure lies in the cash provided up-front by the option premium, which can be used to subsidise the interest rate payable on the loan. Of course, if commodity prices rise above the strike price, the call option is exercised and a settlement payment is due from the exporter. However, as in the previous example, higher prices would then be received on future exports as well. Again, one should note that, for companies based in emerging countries, the sale of call options can lead to serious liquidity problems in cases of sudden margin calls (or shortfalls or delays in actual exports), as illustrated in 1999 by the Ashanti Goldfields crisis.

A significant difference from the previous structure lies in the fact that any borrower can subsidise interest rates by selling any type of option on the price of any commodity – or on the price of any other asset for that matter. If the options are exercised, the amount of the settlement payments due from the borrower can markedly increase the overall cost of the financing, to the point of putting at risk the financial situation of the borrower. Thus, to be on the safe side, borrowers should sell options only under strict conditions. Ideally, these options should be covered, meaning that a borrower selling call options on a certain volume of commodities during a certain period of time should expect to export at least the same volume of the same commodities during the same period of time.

In 1991 the Ghana National Petroleum Corporation (GNPC) sold call options on the price of crude oil to earn additional income (the call premium) and subsidise the interest rate on a commercial loan granted by Bankers Trust Company to finance the import by GNPC of petroleum products.[3] This sale of call options was risky because these call options were not covered, since GNPC did not export crude oil but oil products, the prices of which do not correlate perfectly with crude oil prices. Actually, GNPC was importing crude oil for refining and subsequent export of oil products, and thus was doubly exposed to rising crude oil prices, first in the physical markets and secondly in the paper markets.

Likewise, selling put options is safer if the seller is also importing the underlying commodity. However, this importer/put option seller combination remains more risky than an exporter/call option seller combination, whereby a loss in the paper markets is compensated by an actual gain in the physical market and not just by lower disbursements. Finally, to limit potential losses in the paper markets, the sale of call or put options should ideally be capped in such a way that the maximum amount to be paid over the life of the transaction as settlement amounts is known and acceptable. This last condition becomes crucial if the hedging programme is to be sustained in the long term in a politically sensitive environment.

In short, companies selling options on commodity prices should trade in these commodities, have strong views on the direction and intensity of future prices, and be able to withstand worst-case scenarios. Similarly, exporters and project contractors should preferably not sell foreign exchange options during a contract offer phase, as they may be left with an unlimited, uncovered, negative foreign exchange exposure.

Evaluation of commodity price risk management

To reduce lending risks and make extra profits, banks increasingly ask borrowers to hedge their commodity price risk exposure or otherwise link the financing to the price of the commodity. Commodity-linked financing is also encouraged by non-commercial fund providers. For example, many World Bank loans to Pemex, the Mexican national oil company, were supported by a hedging programme on Pemex oil exports.

In the majority of cases, it is the bank and not the borrower that suggests integrating commodity price derivatives with the financing transaction. As observed by one market participant with regard to medium-term structured deals to prime Russian names: 'It is very difficult to convince a producer that hedging programmes, reasonably applied, serve in the first place the interests of the producer and only in the second place that of the bank'.[4] Hopefully, the situation will change in the future, with more borrowers in the commodity sector realising the potential benefits of hedging their price risk, whether or not a financial transaction is involved.[5]

When banks suggest or require that some commodity price derivative elements be included in the financing structure, they generally prefer to act as hedge provider themselves. Banks argue that financing is easier to arrange (in terms of documentation, credit limits and so forth) when the hedging element is also provided by them (or by an affiliated company). In large syndicated bank financings, this role can be taken by one of the syndicate participants. Note that this generally means additional credit exposure for the hedging bank, which most banks are nevertheless glad to bear given the thick margins obtained on hedging compared with lending.

The hedge provider can also be a multilateral development bank (such as the World Bank or the IFC), an insurance company or a commodities exchange. Building on their capacity to manage risks, hedge providers are actually moving into banks' territory by arranging structured finance deals. A few years ago, for instance, the large insurance company AIG created a new subsidiary (AIG International Inc) to engage not only in hedging and trading, but also in financing activities related to the metals, energy and other commodities markets.

---

1 From 'Ashanti: The Full Story' by Emmanuelle Moors, *African Business*, December 1999.

2 'Hedge laying provides string base', *Trade Finance*, March 2002.

3 Presentation by Tsatsu Tsikata of GNPC at the Commodity Price Risk Hedging conference organised by UNCTAD, Harare, 1998.

4 Carla Jakoby of WestLB, quoted in 'Onwards and upwards', *Trade Finance*, April 2002.

5 For some practical tips on introducing a risk management programme, refer to the article 'Getting to know commodity price risk management: Into a brave new world' by Lamon Rutten, published in the report *New Strategies for a Changing Commodity Economy*, UNCTAD, 1999.

Chapter 13

Guarantees

Guarantees discussed in this chapter include the most common types of guarantees used to support straight or structured commodity loans, namely, contractual guarantees, credit guarantees and wrapping guarantees, as well as other useful tools such as credit derivatives.

Guarantees can be either 'on demand' (clean and unconditional guarantees), or payable upon submission of one or more documents, for instance a termination notice or an arbitration award, evidencing that the conditions stipulated in the underlying commercial contract for calling the guarantee have been met (conditional guarantee). There are numerous possibilities as to the wording of guarantees and the nature of the risks covered. With the exception of wrapping guarantees, guarantees are typically put in place for a fraction of the value of the underlying commercial contract, ranging from 5 per cent to 25 per cent.

In the United States, guarantees are often issued by insurance companies. In the rest of the world, guarantees are typically issued by commercial banks, either as 'bank guarantees' or as 'standby letters of credit'.

Contractual guarantees

Contractual guarantees are commitments to pay sums of money to the beneficiary of the guarantee or perform certain undertakings on demand or upon non-fulfilment or breach of contractual terms by the party on whose account the contractual guarantee was issued.

Most unconditional performance guarantees are issued by banks, while most conditional performance guarantees are issued by insurance and other specialised companies as 'surety bonds'. Nevertheless, the scope and text of both instruments is negotiable, and, in the context of contractual bank guarantees, the terms 'guarantee' and 'bond' can be used interchangeably.

Types and scope of contractual guarantees

Performance guarantees are the most common form of contractual guarantee. They give the holder of the guarantee the right to receive payment of a certain sum, typically 10 per cent of the contract price, in case of failure by the party on whose account the guarantee was issued (the contractor) to perform as per the terms of the contract. More rarely, the issuer of the guarantee would commit to enable performance of the contract in case of failure by the contractor. When this is the case, performance guarantees can be equated to parent company guarantees, sometimes requested in their stead when the contractor is not deemed strong enough on its own.

Other fairly common contractual guarantees – in effect also guaranteeing the due performance of the contractor – are bid bonds, performance bonds, advance payment bonds, retention bonds and maintenance bonds. Each of these contractual guarantees provides security for the due performance of the contractor at various stages of a contract. In the case of engineering, procurement and construction (EPC) contracts, a contractor can be required to provide three or four different types of contractual guarantees.

Performance guarantees are traditionally used in project finance because they offer financial compensation for the failure to perform by key contractors and thus guarantee project completion. For the same reasons, performance guarantees can bring added value to performance-based structured commodity finance transactions by minimising the financial impact of any default on the underlying performance risk.

Bank guarantees

Performance guarantees supporting structured commodity finance transactions are typically provided by local banks. Compared with foreign banks or insurance companies, local banks have both a better knowledge of the commodity owner and the capacity to influence some of the local factors instrumental in the due performance of the underlying commercial contract. In most cases the all-in cost of the financing, net of bank guarantee fees, would be lower for the commodity owner. In other cases, however, performance guarantees can become expensive for borrowers. In addition, when performance guarantees are granted by local banks, international lenders remain exposed to the credit risk of this local bank and thus need to weigh the benefits of receiving a performance bank guarantee against the impact of such additional credit risk on country limits and provisioning requirements.

Unconditional bank guarantees perform an important role in many export sales and projects because they separate the right to require payment under the guarantee from the necessity to prove default by the other party. However, they can also cause conflict and controversy by providing scope for fraudulent and abusive claims. This is why banks are allowed to refuse payment or performance in cases where the demand is plainly fraudulent or groundless. In other cases, contractors can negotiate to replace contractual bank guarantees by surety bonds, which typically are payable only upon presentation of documents evidencing failure by the contractor under the contract.

Surety bonds

Surety bonds are commonly used in the United States, and then extended to both North and South America. They are contractual guarantees but instead of being issued by banks they are issued by insurance companies. They cost less than those offered by banks because of the more constraining capital risk weighting ratios applied by banks.

This type of guarantee can be extremely valuable to support structured commodity finance transactions. As an example of the successful use of a surety bond to enhance a structured commodity finance transaction, note the facility arranged for Companhia Siderurgica Paulista (Cosipa), a major Brazilian steel producer. In this transaction, a surety bond was provided by Liberty Mutual Insurance of the United States to guarantee that deliveries of minimum quantities of steel by Cosipa would be sufficient to support the debt service: 'Because of the bond (which cost 2.35 per cent a year), it was possible to issue notes at a rate almost 5 per cent below the rates on Brazil's benchmark Treasury bonds'.[1]

Credit guarantees

Credit guarantees can be called in cases of payment default by an obligor. Credit guarantees issued by commercial banks are often structured as standby letters of credit whereby the issuing bank commits to pay the beneficiary upon presentation of agreed documents. In certain cases the scope of such standby letters of credit can be extended, for instance to cover termination payments due under an EPC contract.

Credit guarantees of medium- and long-term tenors are typically issued by export credit agencies to support buyers' or suppliers' credit arranged by commercial banks in a context of project finance. Traditionally, ECAs have added their credit guarantees to loan obligations already guaranteed by either a local bank or the government of the borrower. However, ECAs increasingly prefer to put in place structured finance transactions instead of relying on such local guarantees.

Performance and credit guarantees are clear credit enhancements, and thus can facilitate access to both straight and structured commodity loans of all tenors.

Wrapping guarantees

In the 1980s so-called monoline guarantee companies ('monoline insurers' or 'monoliners') emerged in the United States. The provision of wrapping guarantees is the main business of these companies. Their volume of operations is very large (about US$2 billion per year in premium income in the late 1990s) and profitable, and their range of products is expanding rapidly as they seek out new markets.

History of wrapping guarantees

Monoline insurers initially developed to guarantee timely payment of principal and interest to mutual bond investors in the United States. These bond guarantees were also called wrapping guarantees because they covered all financial obligations due by the issuer. In the United States, wrapping guarantees enabled municipalities with weaker credit ratings, as well as agencies and project authorities with no credit history, to buy third-party guarantees enabling their debt issues to reach 'investment grade' status. To price their wrapping guarantees, monoline insurers assess the default risk of the underlying transaction in a systematic manner, more or less in the same way as credit rating agencies do.

A wrapping guarantee thus results in issuers paying a lower interest rate than would have been the case based on their own credit rating alone. Without the guarantee, second-rate issuers would have to sell their debt in the 'junk' debt market, pay a much higher interest rate and perhaps not fully place their debt issue. Fees paid to these monoliners are typically half of the improvement in the all-in interest rate brought about by their guarantee. Bond or wrapping guarantees have thus enabled poorer municipalities to enter credit markets on better terms, and have permitted new and unseasoned agencies to find a ready market for their debt. Beginning in about 1993, there has been a slowdown in the rate of municipal bond issuance to the benefit of a broader spectrum of non-municipal bond issues. Since then, wrapping guarantees have been used for hospitals, housing, transport, roads, schools, parks and recreation facilities, sewer and water facilities, investor-owned utilities, and environmental projects.

In recent years, US monoline guarantee companies have actively diversified into structured corporate debt and asset-backed securities. They have also successfully expanded internationally, in particular in Europe and in Asia.

Extension of wrapping guarantees to Structured Commodity Finance

To what extent are wrapping guarantees relevant to structured commodity finance? Already, there is evidence that securitisations find better market conditions with a monoliner guarantee than they would without. Moreover, third-party wrapping guarantees have clearly supported access to the capital markets by non-traditional forms of corporate debt and asset-backed securities. The volume of such introductions has grown enormously. It now appears that the types of guaranteed products that can be placed in the capital markets are more a function of the imagination of those creating the structured financing than of any inherent limit in the guarantee industry, which by most measures has had excess capital for many years.

More recently, monoline insurers have become involved in the commodity sector. High risk is not a problem. On the contrary, their expertise lies precisely in assessing the risks involved in a transaction and pricing them correctly. For example, in 1998 a joint venture was formed by MBIA and AMBAC, two leading monoline guarantee companies, to guarantee a US$1.5 billion oil-backed, export receivables-backed securitisation for Pemex Finance Ltd, a Cayman Islands SPV established to raise finance for Pemex, Mexico's state oil company. The notes were issued in two tranches, in December 1998 and February 1999, and were backed by Pemex's crude oil exports to the United States. Similarly with soft commodities, in November 1998 MBIA guaranteed on its own a US$230 million asset-backed securitisation for CoBank, a Denver-based cooperative bank, secured by inventories of maize, wheat and soya beans. This transaction gave farmers and processing companies access to capital market finance through a US$200 million commercial paper programme and a US$30 million revolving fund facility. Likewise, in February 2002 Citibank successfully closed a US$250 million offering of senior secured notes for Arcel Finance, the export securitisation vehicle of Aracruz Celulose, Brazil's largest pulp exporter. As explained by one of the arrangers: 'The transaction achieved investment grade ratings from all three rating agencies, and benefited from a AAA-rated financial guarantee insurance policy that allowed the issue to achieve a coupon below 6 per cent, in spite of volatile market conditions'.[2] In terms of wrapped structured commodity finance transactions, the landmark deal was certainly the PF export receivables master trust signed in December 2001 for Brazil's Petrobras. The deal was based on a prepayment structure, where three initial AAA-rated senior trust certificates worth US$450 million were wrapped by, respectively, XL Capital Assurance, MBIA and AMBAC.[3]

Credit derivatives

The discussion so far has centred on forms of insurance and guarantees that can reduce the risks involved in lending, and thus facilitate access to financing. In addition to using such intrinsic tools, a bank that no longer wants to remain exposed to payment risk on a loan can also assign or sell this loan to another bank, on a primary or secondary basis, in the credit derivatives market. Indeed, since the early 1990s, the range of alternatives available to shed credit risk exposure has dramatically expanded thanks to the development of credit derivatives. These allow banks to trade their credit risk exposure and so to reduce the risk involved in a particular loan, or in their overall loan portfolio.

Credit derivatives enable one party to buy credit risk insurance by paying a premium to, or entering into a swap with, the other party. The concept is similar to that of hedging commodity price risk. There are several basic structures available. For example, the hedge provider can sell to the loan holder an option against a fall in the market value of an asset. If the option is exercised, the hedge provider would pay an amount equal to the difference between the initial value of the asset and the market value on the exercise date. Unfortunately, for certain types of assets (such as loans) market value is difficult to assess. In such cases, the structure could stipulate that, if the option is exercised, the hedge provider would take delivery of the deteriorated asset and pay to the loan holder its initial value. Hedging could also be structured as a swap whereby a company would swap the cash flow from its asset for an agreed interest rate stream (for example, Libor plus a spread) and final settlement could be in cash as above.

Credit derivatives enable banks to hedge the credit risk on an asset that may be desirable to hold for various specific reasons – say for tax reasons (eg, so as to use withholding tax credits) or for relationship reasons (eg, to participate in syndicated loans). Alternatively, lenders may not be comfortable with a credit risk for the entire maturity and may be willing to buy short-term protection for a long-term asset, or inversely. In short, credit derivatives enable borrowers to free up credit lines and expand and/or diversify their lending portfolios. As such they may encourage banks to lend more to high-risk companies, such as borrowers operating in the commodity sector.

Under Basle I, the use of a credit derivative would in most cases actually increase the amount of capital that a bank has to set aside, as the bank would receive no benefit for hedging its credit risk but would need additional capital to cover additional potential losses on the derivatives. However, based on the current draft of Basle II, it appears that this disincentive will be corrected to permit banks to effectively use credit derivatives as credit risk mitigants, thus enabling banks to increase their loans to high-risk commodity companies located in emerging countries.

On the other side of the transaction, hedge providers are willing to take the credit risk and make an income commensurate with that risk, and with their own portfolio composition and strategic outlook. In practice, the use of credit derivatives has been hampered by difficulty in deciding when default should be declared and settlement effected.

Evaluation of guarantees

Third-party guarantees provide clear credit enhancement to a wide range of straight and structured financings. When guarantees are used to support structured finance deals, the fine line between guarantees and insurance cover becomes even thinner (except for the aspect of conditionality that is the 'essence' of insurance). Traditionally, insurance cover is contracted by exporters while guarantees are sought by lending banks, but this is not always the case. A financing transaction, for instance, could be supported by a third-party guarantee in respect of the due performance of the contractor, or by insurance cover against certain events equally affecting the performance of such contractor but not within its control.

The insurance broker BPL Global, for example, some time ago proposed 'performance risk insurance' cover for prepaid purchase and tolling contracts. In effect, such 'non-delivery' cover closely resembled a performance guarantee, in that it covered failure by the supplier/obligor to perform under the contract, but it was specifically linked to the occurrence of the following events, most of which were outside the control of the supplier/obligor:

- *force majeure* frustration of contract;
- breach of contract by the supplier/obligor;

- import/export embargo or licence cancellation;
- other government action; and
- trade disruption.

A major difference between the two instruments is that payments made by an insurance company after a claim do not have to be reimbursed by the insurance holder, since its financial obligations are limited to payment of the insurance premium. Guarantees, on the other hand, must generally be reimbursed to the paying bank (or insurance company) by the party on whose account they have been called.

[1] 'Under-explored potential of SCF' by Lamon Rutten, *Trade Finance,* April 2002.

[2] Valentino Gallo of Citigroup, quoted in 'Market Update', *Trade Finance,* March 2002.

[3] 'Setting new standards', *Trade Finance,* March 2002.

Chapter 14

Providers of insurance and guarantees

As discussed in previous chapters, a vast array of insurance, guarantees and price risk management products are available to support and complement structured finance transactions in the commodity sector. These products are offered by the private insurance market, commercial banks (as described in Chapter 13), and non-commercial providers of insurance and guarantees, in particular export credit agencies (ECAs). Note that even this simple division has become somewhat arbitrary because non-commercial providers are increasingly working on a commercial basis and forming alliances with the private sector.

Private insurance market

Arrangers of structured commodity finance transactions sometimes request third-party performance or payment guarantees, especially from local banks deemed more knowledgeable about the borrower and willing to take local risks. However, borrowers and lenders alike will find a wider range of products available from private insurance companies – not only payment and performance guarantees, but also trade, credit and political risk insurance.

In practice, the political and credit risk insurance market is divided between short-term insurance on the one hand, and medium- and long-term insurance on the other. The private insurance market has traditionally focused on the short-term market.

While insurance cover is ultimately underwritten by insurance companies, its components are increasingly designed and put in place by insurance brokers that specialise in the field of trade, credit and political risk insurance.

Insurance companies

The private insurance market for short-term political and credit risk has grown considerably over the past decade or so, and has become well-diversified and mature. In the 1980s private companies were clearly only a complement to ECAs. However, the private insurance market expanded from only four main players in the late 1980s to a dozen today, with capacities over the same period multiplying by 10.

Main types of commercial insurers

According to Cauri, a leading insurance broker, private credit insurers may be grouped into three broad categories:[1]

- specialised groups;
- independent specialised companies; and
- specialised departments of large generalist companies.

Specialised groups (credit risk)

Over the past decade or so, several independent specialised companies have emerged in Europe, generally as a result of mergers, to provide short-term export credit insurance. This trend began in 1991 with the privatisation and sale by the British government of the short-term operations of ECGD to NCM, the Dutch export credit agency. As later observed by Steen Parsholt, CEO of NCM Netherlands: 'The [purchase] by NCM of ECGD short-term business . . . was the real kick-off for the consolidation in credit risk capacity. And the consolidation which has taken place has helped capacity'.[2] Although NCM is primarily involved in private export credit insurance, it still retains its role as the Dutch export credit agency and, through its subsidiary EKR, as the Danish export credit agency. NCM is located in a dozen countries including, through MNCIC, the United States. Finally, in 2001 NCM merged with the German insurer and export credit agency Gerling to become Gerling NCM (51 per cent owned by Gerling, followed by Swiss Re with 25 per cent plus one share). Gerling's main subsidiaries include Gerling-Speziale, Gerling-Namur and Gerling-Nordic.

Besides Gerling NCM, the Euler group has emerged as the world's leading credit insurance group in terms of premium income. Its main subsidiaries are Euler-Sfac (France), Euler-Cobac (Belgium and The Netherlands), Euler-Trade Indemnity (United Kingdom, Australia and South-East Asia), Euler-SIAC (Italy), and Euler-ACI (North America). Euler is the only major private credit insurer not active in the field of public export credit. In 1998, through the French insurance group AGF, Euler became a subsidiary of the German insurance group Allianz, which is also the main shareholder in Hermes.

After NCM and Euler, the Coface group in just a few years grew to become a major player in international private credit insurance. Its principal subsidiaries are Coface LBF (United Kingdom), Allgemeine Kredit (Germany), Viscontea (Italy) and Österreichische Kreditversicherung (Austria). Coface is also directly active in other countries, including Spain, Singapore, Japan, Chile and Brazil. Coface also operates through the Creditalliance network, which organises credit insurance operators worldwide, including CNA in the United States. Besides its involvement in the private credit insurance market, Coface retains its role as the French export credit agency.

These companies provide cover on a whole-turnover (portfolio) basis.

Independent specialised companies (credit risk)

These operators are sometimes part of an insurance group, or are underwriting agents acting for the account of generalist insurance companies that do not want to support a specialised department. Independent specialised companies include the already mentioned CNA, FCIA and TUA (United States); Assurcrédit, a subsidiary of the Winterthur and AXA insurance groups (France); Credito y Caucion and Maptfre Caucion y Credito (Spain); and Hermes (Germany), which is also very active as export credit agency for the government of Germany.

This category should also probably include the monoline guarantee companies discussed in Chapter 13, such as MBIA in the United States.

Specialised departments of large insurance groups (political and credit risk)

Several major companies have put in place specialised credit insurance departments, for example AIG, Zurich, and Royal and Sun Alliance. Lloyds has also developed credit insurance skills to complement its traditional capacity to underwrite political risk insurance.

Leading commercial insurers

A non-comprehensive list of leading commercial insurers was put together by Willis (United Kingdom) and Gras Savoye (France), two leading insurance brokers.[3]

Lloyds syndicates

Lloyds syndicates include ACE, Ascot, Beazley, Catlin, Faraday, Goshawk, Harrington, Hayward, Hiscox, Kiln, Liberty Mutual, MAP, MK Wheeler, Talbot, Wellington and XL London Markets. Among the most active syndicates for political risk are ACE, Hiscox and Liberty, but actually most of the Lloyd's syndicates are owned by private insurance companies. For instance, Chubb owns 30 per cent of Hiscox. Other syndicates (ACE, Ascot and so on) have US shareholders.

Other companies

Other leading commercial insurers are AIG, ACE Global Markets, Axis, Chubb, Euler, Exporters, FCIA, Generali, Gerling NCM, Hannover Re, Sovereign, Unistrat/Coface and Zurich. A large majority of these insurers are members of the International Credit Insurance Association (ICIA).

In terms of overall quality of services provided by private insurers, Zurich Emerging Markets Solutions (ZEMS) was voted Best Private Insurer in 2002 and 2003 by *Trade Finance* magazine. ZEMS is a subsidiary of Zurich Financial Services Group and began its operations only a few years ago: it has taken the lead from AIG, which held this top position from 1999 to 2001. As explained by Daniel Riordan, MD of ZEMS: 'Our group's political risk policy offers pre-project limits of US$80 million with maximum term of 15 years, while our credit risk insurance provides per-project limits of US$25 million with maximum term of seven years'.[4]

Evaluation of private insurance market

Market providers of insurance and guarantees compete with export credit agencies and other non-commercial providers of insurance and guarantees in supporting financing for emerging market countries, in particular for the commodity sector.

Private insurers have become increasingly active, and have been at the forefront of new initiatives launched in the political and credit risk insurance markets to better adapt their products to the needs of their customers. They have also been encroaching upon the traditional territory of ECAs by slowly moving into medium-term credit cover. Compared with ECAs, private market operators have the advantage of offering a speedy response and a flexible approach, without the restrictions imposed by ECAs in terms of national content criteria and political interest for or against particular countries. In addition, private insurers have a long tradition of cooperation and syndication of capacity. More generally, the private insurance market is very volatile, and new forms of cover can appear and disappear fairly quickly.

Before the terrorist attacks of September 2001, and the Enron and WorldCom bankruptcies a few months later, the private insurance market was highly flexible and had significant capacity. However, with political claims and bankruptcy losses increasing in 2001 and 2002, the private insurance market has now become much tighter.

This cyclical nature of the private market is actually one of its main drawbacks compared with export credit agencies. The recent hardening of the private insurance market has been compounded by reinsurance restrictions, and has resulted in higher premiums, lower capacity and, more importantly, in less flexibility, notably in terms of tenor. As a result, insurance cover provided by export credit agencies starts to look attractive again.

Insurance brokers

Credit and political risk insurance is generally arranged through insurance brokers acting as authorised agents for their policyholders. Such insurance brokers typically offer a comprehensive range of risk transfer solutions for companies with trade, credit and political risk exposures, including exporters, international traders and banks or issuers of securities. The main tasks of trade, credit and political risk insurance brokers are as follows:

- to assist customers in assessing their needs and to devise the most appropriate insurance package;
- to approach the insurers that are best able to respond to these needs and can demonstrate (i) financial and technical capacity to indemnify losses rapidly, (ii) sound technical capability and (iii) product and service flexibility;
- to negotiate the best possible terms for customers (coverage and pricing);
- to monitor the insurance policy and conduct administrative services within its area of responsibility; and
- to assist its policyholders in periods during which risks of loss emerge and, if the loss is confirmed, to help policyholders to obtain fair indemnification from private credit insurer(s), export credit agencies or other providers of insurance cover.

To carry out their role efficiently, insurance brokers should offer a combination of technical skills and thorough market knowledge. One other aspect of the role of insurance brokers is 'market security'. All insurance counterparties are studied and monitored, not only for their financial strength, but also for specific insurance aspects such as payment of claims.

A non-exclusive list of insurance brokers specialising in trade credit and political risk insurance and consultancy would include UK-based BPL Global[5] and Willis;[5] France-based Gras Savoye,[7] Cauri[8] and Platus; Export Insurance Agency (US); and international brokers such as Marsh[9] and AON,[10] which, in recent years, have grown dramatically by acquiring local independent brokers.

Market participants in the commodity sector can also provide coverage of their insurance needs to their collateral management companies or other third parties involved in arranging a structured finance transaction. As explained by Christian Joerg of SGS: 'Our collateral management insurance has been carefully designed, in consultation with our brokers and underwriters, to provide comprehensive coverage, including, at the option of our clients, war risk on land, and confiscation/expropriation, nationalisation and deprivation coverage. Underwriters accept declarations based on our expertise and ability to safeguard the financed goods'.[11]

Although their costs are not transparent, and thus it is difficult to properly evaluate their added value, insurance brokers certainly have a greater role to play in the arrangement of insurance and other credit enhancement features. This is due to the increased variety and complexity of insurance products, combined with the extended network of reinsurance and co-insurance agreements now in place between providers of insurance and guarantees. As observed by one insurance provider: 'What we are seeing is an active market for tailor-made solutions. Sellers want money, buyers want credit and banks want things to be risk-free. The role of the broker therefore is a strong one because a client may not know exactly what they need, just that they have a problem, and an underwriter may not have the time to come up with a solution. It is up to us to respond'.[12]

Export credit agencies

ECAs were originally established by governments to promote exports and foreign investment by their national companies through the removal of part or all of the non-payment risk faced by

Exhibit 14.1

OECD members' export credit agencies[13]

Country	*ECA*
Australia	Export Finance and Insurance Corporation (EFIC)
Austria	Österreichische Kontrollbank AG (OeKB)
Belgium	Office National du Ducroire/Nationale Delcrederedienst (OND)
Canada	Export Development Corporation (EDC)
Czech Republic	Export Guarantees Development Corporation (EGAP)
	Czech Export Bank
Denmark	Eksport Kredit Fonden (EKF)
Finland	Finnvera Oyj
	FIDE Ltd.
France	Compagnie française d'assurance pour le commerce extérieur (Coface)
	Direction des Relations Economiques Extérieures (Ministère de l'Economie) (DREE)
Germany	Hermes Kreditversicherungs-AG (Hermes)
Greece	Export Credit Insurance Organization (ECIO)
Hungary	Hungarian Export Credit Insurance Ltd (MEHIB)
	Hungarian Export–Import Bank
Italy	Sezione Speciale per l'Assicurazione del Credito all'Esportazione (SACE)
Japan	Nippon Export and Investment Insurance (NEXI)
	Japan Bank for International Cooperation (JBIC)
Korea	Korea Export Insurance Corporation (KEIC)
	Export–Import Bank of Korea (KEXIM)
Luxembourg	Office du Ducroire (ODD)
Mexico	Banco National de Comercio Exterior, SNC (Bancomext)
Netherlands	Nederlandsche Credietverzekering Maatschappij NV (NCM)
New Zealand	Export Credit Office (ECO)
Norway	Norwegian Guarantee Institute for Export Credits (GIEK)
Poland	Korporacja Ubezpieczén Kredytów (KUKE)
Portugal	Companhia de Seguro de Créditos, SA (COSEC)
Slovak Republic	Export–Import Bank of the Slovak Republic (Eximbank SR)
Spain	Compañía Española de Seguros de Crédito a la Exportación, S.A (CESCE)
	Secretaría de Estado de Comercio (Ministerio de Economía)
Sweden	Exportkreditnämnden (EKN)
Switzerland	Export Risk Guarantee (ERG)
Turkey	Export Credit Bank of Turkey (Türk Eximbank)
United Kingdom	Export Credits Guarantee Department (ECGD)
United States	Export–Import Bank of the United States (Ex–Im Bank)

exporters. The range of products, eligible countries and conditions differs between ECAs. Their involvement is generally via buyer credits, through which ECAs lend or provide guarantees to banks lending to the buyer, directly or through a local bank. These loans are generally on attractive terms with long maturities and fixed interest rates, usually better than commercial rates.

The calculation of the premium payable on guarantees issued by ECAs is based on complex formulas linked, among other things, to the risk rating attached to the particular country. Coface, for instance, has put in place its '@rating' grading system using seven criteria to assess indicators in 140 countries. The first three are: political factors likely to interrupt payment or performance of contracts in progress, risk of a currency shortage and the state's ability to meet its commitments abroad. Another three are inspired by recent market difficulties: risk of a sudden devaluation, risk of a systemic crisis in the banking sector and cyclical risk. The final criterion is based on Coface's experience with existing or past guarantees and looks at payment behaviour for short-term transactions.[14]

ECAs are also active providers of medium- and long-term commercial (credit) and political risk insurance for exports and foreign investment.

Overview of export credit agencies

The Organisation for Economic Cooperation and Development (OECD) provides a list of the official export credit agencies of both OECD member countries (see Exhibit 14.1) and non-OECD member countries (see Exhibit 14.2).[15] Note that Iceland and Ireland[16] do not have official export credit agencies.

Some ECAs are tied directly to a government ministry, such as Canada's EDC, the United Kingdom's ECGD and India's ECGC, but most are independent companies. A couple of ECAs, NCM in The Netherlands and OND in Belgium, serve as export credit agencies for two countries (Denmark for NCM and Luxembourg for OND). To illustrate the range of products typically offered by ECAs, a summary of the activities of ECGD[17] is provided in Exhibit 14.3.

Many ECAs have their own commercial activities in addition to acting as their country's official export credit agency. This is especially the case for NCM, as well as for Belgium's OND, France's Coface, Germany's Hermes and Singapore's ECICS. Most ECAs now focus

Exhibit 14.2

Non-OECD members' export credit agencies[18]

Country	ECA
Argentina	Compañia Argentina de Seguros de Crédito a la Exportación SA (CASC)
Hong Kong, China	Hong Kong Credit Insurance Corporation (HKEC)
India	Export Credit Guarantee Corporation of India (ECGC) Export–Import Bank of India
Israel	Israel Foreign Trade Risks Insurance Corporation (FTRIC)
Malaysia	Malaysia Export Credit Insurance Berhad (MECIB)
Singapore	ECICS Credit Insurance Ltd (ECICS)
Slovenia	Slovene Export Corporation (SEC)
South Africa	Export Credit Insurance Corporation of South Africa (ECIC)
Taiwan	Export–Import Bank of the Republic of China

Note: This listing is not exhaustive. Mention can also be made of other non-OECD members' active ECAs, such as Indonesia's ASEI or Egypt's EDBE.

Source: OECD.

on medium- and long-term tenors, and have left short-term political risk and credit insurance cover to the private sector.

In general, ECAs provide both finance and guarantees. This is the case, for instance, for most 'eximbanks', such as Australia's EFIC, Austria's OeKB and the US Ex-Im. Some ECAs operate through dual systems, such as in South Korea (KEIC and the Export–Import Bank of Korea), Japan (NEXI and JBIC), and Sweden (EKN and SEK).

OECD supervision

The OECD has developed certain rules, referred to as the Export Credit Arrangement, governing the financial terms and conditions of the support provided by ECAs. The main purpose of the Export Credit Arrangement is therefore to provide a framework for the orderly use of officially supported export credits. In practice, this means providing for a level playing field whereby exporters compete on the basis of commercial factors rather than financial terms. The Export Credit Arrangement also seeks to reduce subsidies and trade distortions related to officially supported export credits.

Exhibit 14.3
ECGD activities

ECGD, the Export Credits Guarantee Department, is the United Kingdom's official export credit agency. ECGD is actually a separate government department reporting to the Secretary of State for Trade and industry. The ECGD supports UK exports by arranging finance facilities and credit insurance for contracts ranging from around £20,000 up to hundreds of millions of pounds. There is special help for smaller exporters and the ECGD also provides overseas investment insurance for UK-based companies investing overseas. On average, ECGD underwrites business worth over £4 billion a year. As with other ECAs, ECGD provides a wide range of products and services relevant to the commodity sector. The main areas of activity are summarised as follows.

Finance facilities

Buyer credits enable banks to extend loans with the backing of ECGD at favourable fixed or floating rates to overseas buyers or their local bank. The UK exporter is paid cash. Buyer credits can be used to support export of goods as well as construction or service contracts. ECGD can also unconditionally provide a 100 per cent guarantee for local currency financing funded from the local financial markets. In this area, ECGD tends to concentrate on 'pure cover', financing thus providing no interest rate support unless the buyer's country has a sufficiently well-developed swap market where ECGD can hedge its interest rate risk.

Supplier credit finance facilities enable exporters to access non-recourse finance for the ultimate benefit of buyers whose payment risk is borne by the lending bank and, ultimately, by ECGD.

Credit insurance

ECGD's export insurance policy provides insurance against political and commercial risks affecting the capacity of the buyer to pay the exporter. This insurance is suitable for transactions that involve capital goods, major services and construction projects. ECGD recommends that insurance for export contracts involving the sale of consumer goods or commodities on short payment terms be obtained from the private insurance market.

ECGD's bond insurance policy provides cover against undue call of bonds or guarantees issued by banks or insurance companies to support the exporter's obligations under the contract.

Through the overseas investment insurance scheme, ECGD also provides insurance against political risk on the equity or loan investments that UK companies may make in overseas companies and for any related guarantees.

In the area of commodities, most of ECGD's involvement appears to be in the oil and gas sectors.

Source: ECGD.

The OECD's work related to official export credit policies and practices also takes place under the auspices of the Export Credit Group,[19] an official OECD body. All OECD-member ECAs, with the exception of the Slovak Republic's, are also members of the ECG. The European Commission participates fully in ECG meetings, which are also attended by the International Union of Credit and Investment Insurers (the Berne Union). As an example of its focus, the Export Credit Group has adopted a statement of principles to ensure that export credits to HIPC (heavily indebted poor countries) are not provided for unproductive use. Finally, the OECD provides a forum for discussion and coordination of national export credit policies.

Under the OECD's Arrangement on Guidelines for Officially Supported Export Credits (the Consensus), an exporter is entitled to receive a minimum interest rate based on an official interest rate matrix. If the commercial rate charged on the buyer's loan is higher than this minimum rate, the ECA enters into an interest rate swap with the lending bank, in effect giving it a subsidy to be passed on to the exporter. As an example of such an interest rate matrix, the basic commercial interest reference rates (CIRRs) for two- to five-year credits for the period from 15 March 2003 to 14 April 2003 for some of the main currencies were as follows:

- euros = 3.68 per cent;
- sterling = 4.62 per cent;
- US dollars = 3.05 per cent;
- yen = 1.13 per cent;
- Australian dollars = 5.62 per cent;
- Canadian dollars = 4.78 per cent; and
- Swiss francs = 1.93 per cent.

Evaluation of export credit agencies

Compared with those offered by the private sector, insurance and guarantees provided by ECAs bring specific benefits, such as 'gilt-edged' security, with the added advantages of making the underlying financing zero-weighted for capital adequacy purposes, government-to-government problem resolution, a longer policy period and attractive premiums.

In the area of political and credit risk insurance, ECAs have also made tremendous progress over recent years as regards entering into co-insurance or reinsurance agreements with both other ECAs and private insurers, resulting in more capacity and flexibility for customers worldwide. Moreover, the integration of European countries has resulted in many European ECAs now agreeing to cover content from other European countries, typically 15 per cent of the contract price. Also on the positive side, the range of products offered by ECAs is expanding, for instance with new insurance cover being developed for foreign exchange risks in so-called weak currencies.

However, the outlook for ECAs is not clear-cut: 'Up to now ECAs have been able to be very flexible, but a potential threat to this comes from new guidelines requiring them to stick more closely to standards set by multinational organisations. One area this will affect is environmental impact assessment. By making these requirements more stringent, transaction times will increase as will their expense as a result of the consultant work . . . . The effect may be to force some ECAs to pull out of deals'.[20] Besides their comprehensive analysis of the environmental impact of the underlying project, a number of other factors have combined to limit the ability of ECAs to meet the needs of their potential customers, in particular the 'politicisation' of export credit programmes, often used as foreign policy tools. Moreover, the need to promote exports to preserve or generate employment is a reality at a time when widespread globalisation is resulting in big job losses at home. In terms of volumes, note that ECAs are now facing national budgetary constraints, especially in Europe. Finally, despite allowances for local content and, increasingly, regional content (for example, other European countries in the case of a European ECA), support from a particular ECA (ie, before any co-insurance or reinsurance agreement) is still tied to national sourcing, potentially forcing a borrower to enter into less attractive commercial transactions in order to obtain the necessary financing or insurance cover.

Despite all this, the recent hardening of the private insurance market has given a new lease of life to export credit agencies, placing them increasingly in the role of insurers of last resort. In terms of supporting financing to the commodity sector, ECAs have a clear role to play where medium- or long-term financing is required and the underlying commercial transaction is initiated by exporters or investors from OECD countries. Yet even in such cases ECA cover may be unavailable. This is the case, for instance, when there is no cover for the country where the buyer is located. ECGD, for example, is on cover for only half the world's countries and maintains restrictions in terms of capacity or otherwise for most of the other half. ECA cover may also be unavailable where the buyer is unable to obtain the government or local bank guarantee that is traditionally required as security by ECAs. In this respect, however, it should be noted that some ECAs are increasingly willing to consider extending their support in the absence of such traditional local guarantees, or for countries officially off-cover, provided that the transaction is structured in a way that mitigates payment risks – which is exactly what structured finance does. As observed by one market specialist: 'One outcome of the various [emerging market] crises . . . has been renewed interest from the ECAs in countertrade, and indeed in any transaction where there is a clear concept from the

Exhibit 14.4

Structured ECA financing for the Tukmenbashi Refinery

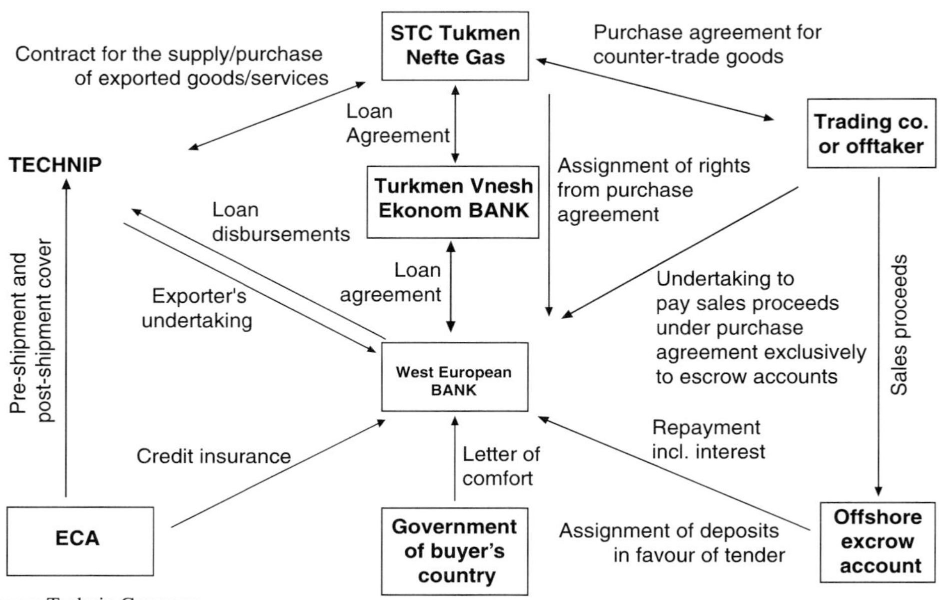

Source: Technip Germany.

beginning as to how the ECA will get repaid in the event of a claim . . . . Some sign that this is coming may be seen in the merger of structured commodity finance/structured trade and commodity finance teams with the structured export finance teams in a number of banks'.[21] Likewise, France's Natexis Banque Populaires recently announced its intention to acquire a controlling interest in Coface with a view to 'further development of factoring services, structured financing, securitisation and credit enhancement operations'.[22]

Just like commercial lenders, ECAs are starting to realise that they may be better off in difficult countries with a good structure where repayment is guaranteed by dedicated export proceeds than from the government, the central bank or a local commercial bank. This new attitude can be illustrated by the structure put in place with the support of Hermes for the financing of a diesel-hydrotreater at the Turkmenbashi Refinery in Turkmenistan (see Exhibit 14.4[23] and 14.5).

Exhibit 14.5

Turkmenbashi Refinery structured ECA financing

Technip,* an international engineering and construction company, in 2002 signed an engineering, procurement and construction (EPC) contract to build a diesel-hydrotreater at the Turkmenbashi Refinery in Turkmenistan. The financing was both structured around the sale of fuel products and supported by Hermes, the German ECA. The financing structure was built as follows (see also Exhibit 14.4).

- 15 per cent of the contract value was paid in cash in advance (condition precedent of the coming into force of the EPC contract), and 85 per cent of the contract value (and ECA premium) was financed under a buyer's credit arranged with a cover from the German ECA (15 per cent of the ECA premium was paid in cash as a condition precedent to the disbursement of the loan). The loan was provided by a consortium of German banks under the leadership of Deutsche Bank.
- Disbursement under the loan was effected directly to the exporter (Technip) pro rata supplies and services.
- The euro-denominated, ECA-covered loan was repayable in 20 half-yearly instalments (with the first repayment falling due six months after commissioning of the project), but the structure did not provide financing for interest during construction.
- The borrower had the alternative of fixing the interest rate upon full disbursement (scheduled for mid-2005) at the then-prevailing market rate for the duration of the repayment period.
- Repayment was secured by a long-term product offtake agreement for commodities and/or refined products with a reliable and experienced western European offtaker acceptable to the ECA and to the lenders for the total lifetime of the loan, supported by an offshore escrow account to receive the proceeds from the offtake with funds assigned to the lending banks as collateral for the debt service. (As an alternative, the arrangers agreed to accept a CIS-based offtaker registered in western Europe with a back-to-back offtake agreement with a western-based offtaker and an assignment of the proceeds to the escrow account.)
- Initially, the structure envisaged that additional security would come from a long-term feedstock supply agreement for the total lifetime of the loan, but this was eventually deemed not necessary because the refinery was also the owner of the crude oil.
- Loan servicing was further secured by a debt service reserve account to build up at least one repayment instalment plus related interest prior to the due date of the subsequent instalment.
- Instead of a sovereign guarantee, the government of Turkmenistan provided a letter of comfort for the undisturbed and unhindered performance of the contract and related financing arrangements. In particular, the government undertook that the supply of feedstock and the export licence would be available throughout the contract period and the repayment period of the loan, and consented to maintain a foreign currency account outside Turkmenistan where all export proceeds would be deposited.

* Then Technip-Coflexip.
Source: Technip Germany.

Other non-commercial providers

This section covers credit and political risk insurance, guarantees and other forms of credit enhancement provided on a bilateral, regional or multilateral basis by governments and related or affiliated institutions to support trade and overseas investment.[24]

As already discussed, governments provide such support on a bilateral basis through their export credit agency, but some market participants tend to prefer other types of government-supported institutions. For instance, one legal adviser claims with regard to insurance products in Latin America that 'in addition to private sector insurers we also make use of guarantees from bodies such as the American Development Bank and the International Finance Corporation'.[25]

In this section the evolving role of governments in providing loan guarantees is reviewed, as well as the range of cover provided by the World Bank group and other multilateral development banks and financial institutions.

Government-supported insurance and guarantees

Governments can provide credit enhancement through a wide range of instruments, including public insurance companies, development finance institutions and local government guarantees. In this area of insurance and guarantees, governments have also increasingly collaborated with the private sector.

Public insurance companies

Besides supporting national exporters and foreign investment through export credit agencies, governments have sometimes established separate public insurance companies. For example, the Overseas Private Insurance Corporation (OPIC) insures investments made in emerging countries by companies based in the United States.

Development finance institutions

Governments also provide guarantees through bilateral development finance institutions (DFIs), for instance DEG in Germany or USAID in the United States. Not all DFIs operate in the same way. A few have specific geographical criteria, either due to their mandate (such as the CDC Group of the United Kingdom) or de facto (like France's Agence Française de Développement), but the majority of DFIs are active worldwide.

These institutions used to be exclusively focused on emerging countries' developmental needs, supporting increasingly, and sometimes exclusively, the private sector. However, led by the United Kingdom's Commonwealth Development Corporation, DFIs are now seeking to operate on a profitable basis, at the expense sometimes of their initial and exclusive focus on economic development.

Local government guarantees

Until the mid-1990s, most large commodity trade financing transactions arranged for borrowers in emerging countries, especially in sub-Saharan Africa, were supported by a government guarantee. At that time, these countries' main commodity imports or exports were typically controlled by a marketing board or a state-owned company. Even where a particular financing transaction was well-structured to mitigate the risks involved, and thus making it more attractive to lenders, the transaction was often 'sweetened' with a government guarantee.

Even if the country had defaulted in the past, or was having balance-of-payments difficulties, it was hoped that governments would not want to default on their large and highly visible trade financing.

Over the past few years, however, government guarantees to support large-scale trade financing transactions have all but disappeared. This trend began with the market liberalisation programmes prescribed by the Bretton Woods institutions after the world debt crisis of 1982 and dramatically accelerated after the fall of the Berlin Wall in 1989. Under the new orthodoxy, governments had to withdraw from strictly commercial activities and commodity marketing boards were progressively dismantled as emerging countries were encouraged to become full market economies.

In the opinion of some lenders, government guarantees would have been useful during this transitional period until other sizeable players had emerged and banks were happy to lend to them on a stand-alone basis. This lingering involvement on the part of governments, however, was not favoured by the IMF and the World Bank. In the end the progressive disappearance of government guarantees had the effect of accelerating the acceptance of new and innovative structures in an effort to keep the cost of funds as low as possible, thus giving a boost to the development of structured commodity finance.

Despite this general trend of fading government backing, however, some emerging country governments have found new ways of rejuvenating their support for trade finance. Lesotho, for instance, launched at the end of 2001 a new scheme whereby its central bank provided commercial and political risk covers to banks lending to the country's exporters for their working capital needs.[26] Besides the provision of insurance cover, local governments can invest in, or otherwise support, private companies providing insurance and/or guarantees to trade or project finance transactions in the commodity sector. By doing so governments can open certain markets that will eventually be taken over by the private sector. To help to evaluate this strategy, one simply needs to remember that it was through specific government guarantees that the securitisation market was initially developed in the United States.

Stretching the concept of guarantees to areas that lie outside the financial realm, what governments can do to support the commodity sector is to guarantee the backbone of a market economy. In particular, this includes guaranteeing the availability and transparency of information, most particularly price information; guaranteeing the adequacy and reliability of government regulations to the needs of the commodity sector, particularly in the area of liquidation and bankruptcy laws; and so on.[27]

The World Bank group

The World Bank is mainly active in the area of investment insurance and guarantee through the Multilateral Investment Guarantee Agency (MIGA).[28] Moreover, the group's poor countries arm, the International Development Association (IDA), and its private sector arm, the International Finance Corporation (IFC), have also added insurance and guarantees to their range of product offerings, such as the Partial Risk Guarantee programme.

MIGA

MIGA was established as a subsidiary of the World Bank in 1988. MIGA provides political risk insurance to private lenders and investors in developing member countries, and thus helps emerging countries to attract and retain foreign investment. With respect to qualified investment, MIGA insures the following risks:

- currency transfer;
- expropriation;
- breach of contract; and
- war and civil disturbance.

MIGA provide a standard coverage of 15 years, which may be extended to 20 years under certain circumstances. MIGA can insure new cross-border investments originating in any MIGA member country, destined for any developing member country. Under certain conditions, investments made by nationals of the host country are also eligible. New investment contributions associated with the expansion, modernisation or financial restructuring of existing projects are also eligible, as are acquisitions that involve privatisation of state-owned companies.

In keeping with MIGA's objective of promoting economic growth and development, investment projects must be financially, economically and environmentally sound, and contribute to the development of the host country. Types of foreign investments that can be covered include equity, shareholder loans and shareholder loan guarantees, provided that the loans have a minimum maturity of three years. Loans to unrelated borrowers can be insured, provided that a shareholder investment in the project is insured concurrently or has already been insured. Other forms of investment, such as technical assistance and management contracts, and franchising and licensing agreements, may also be eligible for MIGA guarantees.

Since its creation in 1988, MIGA has facilitated an estimated US$2 billion in foreign direct investment by covering investment projects in 79 countries and providing more than US$9.0 billion in guarantees, up from US$3.4 billion in 1997.

MIGA insures investments in a wide range of industries. In the late 1990s, mining represented 15 per cent of the outstanding liabilities of MIGA. In Africa, where the portfolio of guarantees is more geared to hard and soft commodities than in other regions, MIGA's outstanding guarantees portfolio at the end of 2001 was composed of 35 per cent in mining, 21 per cent in manufacturing, 18 per cent in agribusiness and 17 per cent in infrastructure, with the remainder in tourism, finance and related industries.

MIGA's involvement in the commodity sector declined in 2002 compared with previous years. Back in 1997 alone, MIGA had insured investment in a gas-fuelled power plant (China), a steel slag processing plant (Egypt), a gold and copper mine (Argentina), the expansion of a coal mine (Colombia), and a secondary aluminium alloy processing plant (Russia). In the area of soft commodities, where from the start MIGA was not very much involved, the same year MIGA extended a US$8.3 million overall cover for the construction and operation of a modern flour mill in Dubreka, Guinea (Africa). In 2001 MIGA provided US$23.9 million in guarantees for an onshore bulk-liquid terminal for a liquefied petroleum gas and diesel fuel project in the Dominican Republic, US$39.1 million for a fertiliser and animal feed supplement project in Jordan, US$9 million for a shareholder loan for a flour mill in Guinea (following the above-mentioned guarantee), US$56.3 million for an underground gold, silver, and copper mine in Tanzania, and US$7.4 million for a new cotton ginning facility in Togo.

MIGA argues that it plays a major role in diffusing the flow of foreign direct investment by guaranteeing projects in many countries that do not rank among the major recipients of foreign direct investment or are not covered by export credit agencies. MIGA is keen to promote a 'developmental impact [by] striving to improve the lives of people in emerging economies, consistent with the goals of host countries and sound business, environmental and social principles'. At the same time, MIGA ensures 'financial soundness [by] balancing developmental goals and financial objectives through prudent underwriting and sound risk management'.

Other World Bank programmes

One of the historical goals of the World Bank, as set out in its articles of agreement (Article 1), is 'to promote private foreign investment by means of guarantees or participations in loans and other investments made by private investors'. This initial focus on guarantees and leveraging private sector investments was mostly overlooked until MIGA was created in the late 1980s. Over the past decade or so, the various arms of the World Bank group have launched other guarantee or insurance programmes in line with the strategic reorientation of the group towards a more highly leveraged form of intervention.

The most important instruments in this respect are the partial risk guarantees (PRGs) and partial credit guarantees (PCGs) created in 1994. PRGs are mainly used for private sector projects and cover all private debt (loans and bonds) against specific political risks. PRGs can be used in the following situations: (i) sectors in the early stages of reform, (ii) large size/riskier operations and (iii) operations highly dependent upon the support/undertakings of governments. Between 1994 and 2001, a total of 24 PRGs were issued, supporting the mobilisation of US$2.3 billion of project cost and the capitalisation of US$10 billion in private finance.[29] PCGs for their part are mainly used for public sector projects and cover part of the debt against general debt service defaults.

An example of a PRG was the US$30 million IDA guarantee issued in 1999 in support of the US$223 million Azito Power Project in Côte d'Ivoire. Using locally produced natural gas, the project was structured on a build-own-operate-transfer (BOOT) basis, with the government of Côte d'Ivoire committing to purchase the electricity generated by the plant on a take-or-pay basis. The PRG guaranteed commercial lenders against default in debt service payments resulting from a government failure to meet its payment or purchase obligations, as well as a range of other risks, including availability and convertibility of the local currency, and political and natural *force majeure* events. Most PRGs in effect have been issued for energy projects. In the commodity sector, the World Bank expected to issue its first PRG for the Prirazlomnoye Oil Field in Russia, but the project was eventually developed by Wintershall of Germany based on another project financing scheme. In terms of PRGs for the commodity sector, there seems to be a natural gas project planned for South Africa's Sasol.

An example of a PCG was the major US$600 million guarantee issued in 1999 in support of the US$4.9 billion investment programme of the Electricity Generating Authority of Thailand (EGAT). This enabled EGAT to issue two series of 10-year bonds, each for US$300 million, and rated A- by Standard & Poor's. This rating was considerably better than that of the Thai sovereign ceiling. The PCG guaranteed bondholders payment of the principal, as well as a first default by the government of Thailand on interest payments. In the end, the first commodities project supported by this scheme was a US$180 million PCG to support the future Bolivia–Brazil 3,000-kilometre natural gas pipeline, approved in 2000 with financial closure scheduled for 2003.[30]

The World Bank has also started providing sovereign risk insurance for trade-related transactions through its Trade Insurance Facility. This facility basically provides private sector lenders with insurance against political risks and covers financial exposures such as prepayments, deferred payment sales, leases, imports of goods to warehouses for local sale or processing and re-export, plus obligations of confirming banks with respect to letters of credit. At the beginning the Trade Insurance Facility was restricted to transactions for Bosnia–Herzegovina, Albania and Ukraine. Later, Russia, Azerbaijan, and a group of eastern and southern African countries were added. A similar short-term trade insurance facility was also put in place by the International Finance Corporation (IFC), the private arm of the World Bank group. For example, in 1999, under a US$140 million programme, the IFC issued a guarantee to pre-selected companies to cover imports of raw materials paid through L/Cs, as well as for pre-export finance for processing and other pre-shipment expenses.

Besides specific programmes, the World Bank has been supporting insurance companies and guarantee funds on an ad hoc basis. For instance, in 2001, the World Bank provided US$5 million as a start-up loan to the African Trade Insurance Agency (ATIA). The ATIA is co-funded by the Common Market for Eastern and Southern Africa (Comesa), and aims to encourage private insurers to offer political risk insurance (including cancellation of export and import licences) for trade transactions. One of its first agreements was with the private German insurer Gerling Namur (now part of Gerling NCM). To support the ATIA, the World Bank also provided US$105 million-worth of credit to the seven participating countries, placed in offshore trust accounts and to be used by political insurers to pay for valid claims.[31]

Regional development banks

Regional development banks are also active in the field of insurance and guarantees, including the Asian Development Bank (ADB), the Inter-American Development Bank (IADB), the African Development Bank (AfDB), and the European Bank for Reconstruction and Development (EBRD).

The ADB, for example, put in place a programme for small- and medium-sized companies in Pakistan guaranteeing L/C-confirming international banks against a default on the part of the Pakistani importer or the local bank due to certain political events. As noted by Werner Liepach of the ADB: 'An innovative aspect of this facility is that we are stripping out country risk from the L/C and transferring this risk to ADB. Thus, ADB assumes the political risk while the banks carry the commercial risk. This makes best use of ADB's and the banks' respective strengths'.[32]

Apart from these emerging countries' regional development banks, in the EU the European Investment Bank (EIB) has developed a wide range of guarantee products, notably through the European Investment Fund. However, while the EIB provides financing to borrowers in emerging countries, its guarantee programme seems to be confined to European counterparties.

Evaluation of non-commercial providers of insurance and guarantees

Governments worldwide provide various forms of support to encourage investment in specific sectors of the economy (eg, infrastructure), to particular borrowers (eg, small companies) and to specific regions (eg, Italy's Mezzogiorno). In turn, insurance and guarantees form part of numerous government aid instruments, including direct subsidies plus grant and concessional lending. Non-commercial providers of insurance and guarantees certainly have a role to play in supporting the commodity sector, mostly through the provision of insurance and guarantees to exporters and foreign investors, and to banks arranging trade or project financing.

The World Bank, in particular, has developed numerous insurance and guarantee products in the past decade or so in an attempt to leverage its intervention in emerging countries. However, as noted by Vivian Brown, Chief Executive of ECGD: 'It's still a greater amount that is coming out of the ECAs compared to regional development banks and the World Bank'.[33] For their part, donor-supported investment insurance and guarantee companies have provided effective credit enhancement to traditional commercial financing.

In practice, with the exception of the oil and gas sectors, most of these new initiatives have been supporting infrastructure projects. The level of government support to the commodity sector has actually fallen in recent years, in line with the disappearance of commodity marketing boards and local government guarantees to trade and project finance deals.

Cooperation between providers of insurance and guarantees

If one notable development in the insurance market has been the development of private insurers, another has been the increased collaboration among the various providers of insurance products through co-insurance or reinsurance agreements. At the same time, providers of third-party guarantees have also increasingly joined efforts with other institutions. In effect, co-insurance and reinsurance are the insurance market's equivalent to syndicated bank loans.

Public–private cooperation

Governments worldwide are providing insurance and guarantees to support exports and foreign projects, as well as local and cross-border insurance companies and guarantee funds, either directly or through development finance institutions or multilateral development banks.

Donor-supported private guarantee funds

Governments are investing in, or otherwise supporting, private or semi-private insurance companies and guarantee funds to support trade with, or investment in, emerging countries. Some funds are focusing on specific regions.

For example, France's Proparco, the private arm of the French DFI, has invested in the Aria Fund, which covers investments made in countries that are within the scope of the CFD (that is, mainly French-speaking West Africa). Similarly, with more or less the same regional scope, the Guarantee Fund for Private Investment in West Africa (GARI) was created in 1994 by bilateral and multilateral development institutions and private banks. Most insurance companies and guarantee funds cover political risk, but some do not. For example, the Aria and GARI funds cover 'every economic risk with the exception of political risk'.

In recent years, donors have increasingly teamed up with the private sector to provide guarantees to projects meeting both developmental and commercial objectives. One such creative initiative was the establishment of Asian Securitisation and Infrastructure Assurance, a regional donor-supported institution providing guarantees on asset-backed securities and infrastructure debt issued by Asian companies (see Exhibit 14.6).

Infrastructure is one of the more promising areas for credit enhancement due to its strategic and commercial importance to economic development. Arguably, the efficient development and trade of hard and soft commodities could be of similar interest to both governments and private investors. Commodities are the backbone of all economies, although less visible and permanent

Exhibit 14.6

Asian Securitisation and Infrastructure Assurance

Asian Securitisation and Infrastructure Assurance, Ltd (ASIA), based in Singapore, started operations in 1995. Its shareholders are private investors, local and international financial institutions, and development finance institutions such as the Asian Development Bank. It was initially rated AA by Duff & Phelps.

The company's principal business is to provide financial guarantees on asset-backed securities and infrastructure debt to be placed in primary and secondary Asian fixed-income capital markets. This company was set up to support the development of infrastructure project finance and asset-backed securities. At the request of the Asian Development Bank (a shareholder in ASIA), no more than 20 per cent of the guarantees should be issued in 'strong' countries such as Singapore, Korea, Hong Kong and Taiwan. The remaining 80 per cent of the guarantees must be placed in The Philippines, India, Indonesia and China, as well as unrated countries that have substantial political and currency risks.

By the end of 1997 ASIA had written over US$1 billion of guarantees. However, following difficulties brought about by financial crisis in 1998, its management was taken over by a US monoline insurer.

Source: Euromoney/SFI News 1998.

than infrastructure. They also provide foreign exchange revenues, which infrastructure projects do not. With the right political impetus, there is nothing in principle that should prevent a company such as ASIA from providing guarantees to debt issued by the commodity sector.

The list of donor-supported insurance companies or guarantee funds covering emerging market countries is actually virtually endless. Such support is typically provided through bilateral or multilateral development finance institutions.

Cooperation between ECAs and the private sector

The first cooperation between private insurers and ECAs goes back to the 1980s, with successful claim payment and recovery experiences.

In the past decade, ECAs have refocused their activities on medium- and long-term tenors. Most export credit agencies have realised that they are better off not being directly involved in short-term business, and have sold or delegated these activities to private insurers. As already mentioned, the kick-off was given by the sale of ECGD's short-term business to NCM. For instance, the Australian Export Finance and Insurance Company (EFIC) contracted a preferred alliance with NCM for its short-term business, worth about A$3.5 billion annually. As explained by Mark Vaile, Australia's trade minister: 'NCM's alliance with EFIC will bring together two corporations with complementary skills and experience to provide an improved range of services to Australian exporters, particularly small- to medium-sized enterprises. NCM has a proven and successful experience in servicing exporters through this kind of transition'.[34]

The increased cooperation has been driven by factors such as the need to reduce administrative costs for exporters, banks and insurers, and a search for efficient portfolio management and leverage of insurance capacity.

Cooperation between multilateral development banks and the private sector

Multilateral development banks have also been stepping up their cooperation with the private sector. For its part, MIGA underwrites directly and also enters into partnerships with other political risk insurers through co-insurance and reinsurance arrangements. MIGA reckons that such collaboration provides investors with more comprehensive investment insurance coverage worldwide. In 1995 MIGA also introduced a brokerage programme, encouraging investment brokers to cooperate with MIGA.

Other public–private sector cooperation

Zurich Emerging Markets Solutions (ZEMS), one of the leading private insurers, entered into cooperation agreements with several public agencies and public sector insurers, in particular with the above-mentioned African Trade insurance agency. As noted by Dan Riordan, ZEMS's EVP and managing director: 'we expect cooperation in the form of co-insurance and facultative reinsurance between public and private insurers will increase significantly in 2003 to 2004'.[35] Collaboration with the private sector enables non-commercial providers of insurance and guarantees to select projects that have a developmental mission. OPIC's president and CEO Peter Watson, for instance, believes that OPIC should 'focus more closely on companies and countries that cannot access private financing or insurance and complement, not compete with, the private sector'.[36]

Public–public cooperation

As much as non-commercial providers of insurance and guarantees are increasingly collaborating with the private sector, in recent years they have also been able to overlook their political and cultural differences and reach out to one another.

Cooperation among multilateral development banks, DFIs and ECAs

The Azito Power Project (discussed earlier), supported by a PRG, is an example of cooperation between the World Bank group and bilateral development finance institutions. The US$140 million senior debt included not only the US$30 million PRG-guaranteed commercial bank debt (12 years), but also a US$32 million IFC 'A' loan (14 years), a US$30 million IFC 'B' loan (10 years) and a US$48 million CDC club loan (12 years).

Likewise, as part of OPIC's increased focus on economic and social development, it has decided to 'cooperate more closely with other institutions that support private lending and investment in developing countries, including the Ex-Im Bank, the US Trade and Development Agency, the International Finance Corporation and the Multilateral Investment Guarantee Agency'.[37]

In recent years ECAs have been signing cooperation agreements with multilateral development banks and other public institutions supporting cross-border trade through insurance and guarantees. For example, MIGA's first project in Jordan was also the first reinsurance of a MIGA contract by Finnvera, Finland's investment insurance agency. This collaboration was the result of an October 2000 agreement between the two agencies to work together to co-insure and reinsure projects.

Cooperation among export credit agencies

Cooperation among export credit agencies is also rife. Co-insurance and reinsurance agreements among ECAs enable the provision of a single export package combining the support of several ECAs, thereby improving the competitive merits of a bid and simplifying procedures for all parties concerned. The attractiveness of such cooperation also stems from the fact that exports for large projects are no longer sourced in a single country but increasingly sourced regionally, or even internationally.

Regional reinsurance or co-insurance agreements are still the most frequent types of cooperation. For instance, in 2001 four Nordic export credit agencies signed reciprocal reinsurance agreements: EKF of Denmark, EKN of Sweden, Finnvera of Finland and GIEK of Norway. As noted by Lars Kolte, managing director at EKF: 'Many state ECAs are looking to diversify their portfolio. In order to develop a more even spread of risk countries we have, for example, done swaps with EKN of Sweden, exchanging Vietnamese for Indian commitments. With risk management techniques becoming more sophisticated, this latest agreement just takes things one important stage further'.[38]

Likewise, in 2001 ECGD already had 16 reinsurance cooperation agreements. As explained by Vivian Brown, its chief executive: 'We've got £20 billion-worth of guarantees on our books and around £6 billion of that has gone through those various cooperation agreements that we have in place with other ECAs . . . . There is much more collaboration now in projects where procurement involves global sourcing. But there is equally pressure for collaboration in markets where there is limited risk capacity and there are opportunities to share capacity'.[39]

To some extent, reinsurance agreements among ECAs are turning multi-sourcing financing transactions into plain vanilla deals, forcing banks to add value in other ways for their borrowers.

---

1 For more information refer to www.cauri.fr/us.

2 'Protective layers' by Jonathan Bell, *Trade Finance,* February 2002.

3 'Séminaire Risques Politiques' conference, organised by Willis and Gras Savoye, London, November 2002.

4 'Awards for excellence', *Trade Finance,* February 2002.

5 For more information on BPL Global and Berry Palmer & Lyle Ltd see www.bpl-global.com.

6 For more information refer to www.willis.com.

7 For more information refer to www.grassavoye.com.

8 For more information refer to www.cauri.fr/us/.

9 For more information refer to www.marsh.com.

10 For more information refer to www.aon.com.

11 'Securing the frontier supplies', *Trade Finance,* April 2002.

12 Harvey Hine, Director of Miller Special Risks, quoted in 'Dodging the bullets' by Alex Cox, *Trade Finance,* July/August 2001.

13 *Source:* http://www.oecd.org/EN/countrylist/0,,EN-countrylist-347-nodirectorate-no-no-140-24,00.html.

14 'Payment defaults force ratings watch', *Trade Finance,* October 2001.

15 *Source:* www.oecd.org.

16 Ireland does not have a government-backed ECA. Political and commercial risk is covered by a commercial entity called Church & General Corporate Insurance (C&G) in Dublin. This entity, however, does not provide any interest support or abide by consensus rates.

17 For more information refer to www.ecgd.gov.uk.

18 *Source:* http://www.oecd.org/EN/countrylist/0,,EN-countrylist-347-nodirectorate-no-no-178-24,00.html.

19 The full title of the ECG is the Working Party on Export Credits and Credit Guarantees.

20 Angelo Rizzuti, deputy general manager, multinational corporates and products at Bank Austria Creditanstalt, quoted in 'Reinforcing the line', *Trade Finance,* September 2001.

21 *Structured Trade and Commodity Finance in Emerging Markets* by John McNamara, Woodhead Publishing Limited, 2001.

22 'Natexis moves to acquire Coface', *Trade Finance,* April 2002.

23 Presentation by Rolf Hilker, Head of Project Finance, Technip Germany, December 2002.

24 See *Credit Guarantees: An Assessment of the State of Knowledge and New Avenues of Research* by Michael Gudger, FAO, November 1997.

25 Conrado Tenaglia, a partner with law firm Linklaters, quoted in 'Lawyers win again', *Trade Finance,* February 2002.

26 'Export finance', *Trade Finance,* December 2001.

[27] For more information on how government can support structured commodity finance and commodities price risk management see UNCTAD publications on the subject.

[28] For more information see www.miga.org.

[29] *Source:* Presentation entitled 'The Role of the World Bank in Mitigating Risk' by Michel Wormser, the Energy Forum, June 2002.

[30] *Source:* www.worldbank.org/guarantees.

[31] 'Taming African risks', *Trade Finance,* July/August 2001.

[32] 'ADB provides political risk guarantees in Pakistan', *Trade Finance,* October 2001.

[33] 'Agencies reach out', *Trade Finance,* March 2001.

[34] 'EFIC selects NCM to handle short-term business', *Trade Finance,* October 2001.

[35] 'Ride the wave', *Trade Finance*, June 2003.

[36] 'OPIC reveals new focus', *Trade Finance,* November 2001.

[37] Ibid.

[38] 'Nordic ECAs lead the way', *Trade Finance,* September 2001.

[39] 'Agencies reach out', *Trade Finance,* March 2001.

Chapter 15

Insurance and guarantees: conclusions

Insurance and guarantees provide attractive ways of mitigating risks, and exporters, investors, lenders, insurance companies and insurance brokers are becoming more sophisticated and innovative in their use of risk management tools. So if straight loans can be insured or guaranteed, could this be an alternative to structured commodity finance? The answer is 'it depends'. On the one hand, insurance of specific risks may give sufficient comfort to lenders to take the remaining risks and grant the loan. On the other hand, the risks involved in a particular transaction are very complex and insuring or guaranteeing each risk would probably not be possible. Even if it were, the costs involved in credit-enhanced commodity financing would probably exceed those of a well-structured commodity-backed financing. Banks may also find it difficult to insure certain types of risks in certain countries.

Some forms of insurance and guarantees bring about the problem of moral hazard, that is, that banks become more lenient in their credit assessment as a result. This would be the case, for instance, with wrapping guarantees callable upon first demand. Most insurance policies (some ECAs provide exceptions) deal with moral hazard by providing policyholders with cover for less than 100 per cent of the actual exposure and placing some restrictions on the risks covered. This strategy, however, may fail to force lenders to pay more attention to risks inherent in export credit deals, since the residual risk on long-term loans may be fully covered by profits. Credit insurance, for its part, still has ample opportunities for growth. As noted by one market professional:

> [Companies] have a number of alternatives [to properly manage their credit risk]. First, they could do nothing – in which case they would have a serious problem. Second, they can become more risk averse – thus they become much less accommodating to new business opportunities. Third, companies take it on board that they need to manage risk more extensively, and pay more for their premiums . . . . At the end of the day, the trade finance market is better served by insurers saying 'we will support the market, but it will cost more', rather than total withdrawal.[1]

In any case, banks can also use insurance or guarantees to remove the risk in some of the debt they originate, for instance to free their balance sheet and originate more debt. This way banks have a larger credit market for the financing they originate, in effect becoming the marketing agents for the credit markets.

Meanwhile, companies providing insurance and guarantees are increasingly promoting structured finance. Export credit agencies, for example, increasingly require a certain type and level of security, similar to that for a structured commodity finance transaction. Some private insurers (for example, monoliners) are clearly diversifying into structured finance transactions and asset-backed securitisations. The language and product barriers between structured finance and risk management are becoming blurred. The UK insurance broker

Willis actually refers to its activities as 'structured financial solutions', a combination of operations in the areas of mortgage and contingency, structured financial risks, political risk, and project finance. This new umbrella group was formed in January 2001 to take advantage of synergies among these different products and capabilities.[2] Likewise, after the merger of NCM and Gerling, the group declared its intention to 'develop further its operations in credit insurance and trade receivables services such as debt collection, factoring and guarantees as well as financial solutions like securitisation'.[3]

Finally, while structured finance can be extremely competitive in meeting short-term and, under certain conditions, medium-term financing needs, this form of financing is not appropriate for long-term financing requirements in the commodity sector. In this area insurance and guarantees have a definite role to play to support both debt and equity investment. The advantage of structured commodity finance is that financing does not depend on the availability of insurance or guarantees. In fact, as summed up by John McNamara: 'The Enron effect is good for trade financiers . . . . You try getting a surety bond structure through a credit committee today. And while credit derivatives are still going strong, post-Enron they will go through much more examination before being accepted. And anything that smacks of Enronesque accounting is going to be under pressure . . . . By comparison, structured trade finance remains intact'.[4]

---

1 Steen Parsholt of NCM Netherlands, quoted in 'Protective layers' by Jonathan Bell, *Trade Finance,* February 2002.

2 'Séminaire Risques Politiques' conference, organised by Willis and Gras Savoye, London, November 2002.

3 'ECAs eye global strategies', *Trade Finance,* September 2001.

4 *Structured Trade and Commodity Finance in Emerging Markets* by John McNamara, Woodhead Publishing Limited, 2001.

Part IV

Applications

Introduction to Part IV

In Parts II and III some of the techniques underpinning structured commodity finance transactions were discussed, with particular emphasis on the increasing use of third-party credit enhancement mechanisms. Part IV focuses on the application of structured commodity finance within the realm of financing alternatives available to the commodity sector.

The discussion starts with an overview of the financing needs of companies operating in the commodity sector and how structured commodity finance has evolved to satisfy these needs (Chapter 16). From there, the discussion moves on to specific applications of structured finance techniques as regards commodities (Chapter 17). Subsequent chapters examine the increasing provision of structured commodity financing by commercial partners (Chapter 18), as well as its impact on bank loans and capital market debt (Chapter 19). Next come discussions of the role of equity (Chapter 20) and of multilateral banks and other donor-supported organisations (Chapter 21) in funding the commodity sector, and of their growing use of structured commodity finance. Finally, we look at regional differences in the application of structured commodity finance techniques (Chapter 22) and at their relevance to Islamic banking (Chapter 23).

The thread underlying the analysis is the observation that changing economic paradigms (after the fall of the Berlin Wall) plus changing trade and foreign investment patterns (globalisation), combined with recurrent emerging market economic crises (in recent years notably East Asia, Russia, Turkey and Argentina), have fostered the development and growth of structured commodity finance techniques.

Chapter 16

Financing needs of the commodity sector

Companies operating in the commodity sector have widely differing balance sheets and investment and earnings patterns. This means that their financing needs are not comparable between one another. Their needs also vary dramatically in line with the production and marketing cycle. The financing needs of a gold producer contemplating a new investment, for instance, differ substantially from those of a small cotton trading company. Where does structured finance fit within the range of financing tools available to companies operating in the commodity sector? To help to answer this question, the issues of capital structure and financing strategy of commodity sector companies must briefly be addressed, followed by an analysis of how structured commodity finance has steadily evolved to meet their financing needs in terms of maturity and use of funds.

Debt versus equity funding

Devising an optimum capital structure has kept many academics and finance managers awake at night. To simplify, companies should seek a balanced ratio of debt versus equity and should meet new financing needs with the source of funds that is currently being underutilised, in both their opinion and that of the market. Compared with equity, debt is more risky for a company because debt servicing can become onerous when business is bad. On the positive side, debt financing brings tax benefits because interest payments, unlike dividends, are deductible from taxable income. Debt is also cheaper than equity because equity investors want a risk premium for being last on the list of creditors.

Optimum debt/equity ratios vary from one company to another. There are no simple answers to the capital structure decision, and companies should take into account the following factors as an indication of the relative levels of debt and equity that they should seek to achieve:

- taxes (companies with an expected stream of high earnings should have more debt[1]);
- business risk (companies with a high business risk should have more equity);
- asset type (companies with intangible assets relying on high growth opportunities should have more equity); and
- need for financial slack (companies likely to face good investment opportunities at short notice should have more equity or other reliable sources of debt).

For instance, companies with safe, tangible assets and plenty of taxable income to shield should have high debt ratios. Unprofitable companies with risky, intangible assets should rely primarily on equity finance.

Companies in the commodity sector operate in a risky environment, which calls for a sizeable level of equity funding. Hard commodity producers have more tangible assets and thus can probably support higher debt ratios than soft commodity producers. Trading companies were traditionally highly leveraged too until they began to strengthen their capital base in the mid-1980s after several medium-sized trading companies en masse defaulted on their debt.

Having said that, most emerging market companies remain undercapitalised simply because of capital flight. Their owners are not inclined to leave retained earnings in the business (subject to taxation, currency devaluation, expropriation, civil unrest and so on), but would rather export them through various transfer pricing strategies, so that the 'equity' of the company sits in bank accounts in London or Miami, well away from local risks.

Short-term versus longer-term financing

Traditionally, companies have tried to match the duration of their assets with that of their liabilities, financing short-term transactions with internal funds or short-term suppliers' credit or short-term loans, and long-term fixed investment with long-term debt or equity. This asset–liability match is less rigid today thanks to the development of sophisticated financing and risk management techniques.

As a corollary to the above, a company's working capital requirements are determined not only by the relative size of its short-term assets, but also by its level of medium- and long-term capital. A well-capitalised company (low debt/equity ratio and mostly long-term debt) that retains in the country a large portion of its earnings is likely to have permanent excess cash and little short-term financing needs. This financing strategy, for instance, is appropriate for companies that can encounter attractive trade or investment opportunities at short notice.

In the commodity sector, short-term financing is appropriate for trade activities, and is typically met by small- and medium-sized bank facilities (loans, deferred payments under letters of credit and so on). Medium- and long-term financing supports general-purpose expenses and new capital investments. This traditional separation, however, is being blurred, not only by new techniques to manage maturity mismatches, but also by the development of structured commodity finance, which gives borrowers more opportunities with regard to their longer-term financing needs.

Indeed, while structured commodity finance belongs to the short- and medium-term debt category, over the past years its techniques have evolved to provide attractive medium-term financing, for instance by incorporating automatic rollover mechanisms or stronger political and credit risk mitigants. The techniques of structured commodity finance can thus transform short-term assets (inventories and sales receivables) into medium-term financing, in particular to finance new capital-intensive projects. For example, in 2001 KBC Bank completed a US$14.25 million 19-month financing for Bwana Mkubwa Mining, the copper mining subsidiary of First Quantum Minerals, located in Ndola (Zambia). Proceeds under the facility were used in part to refinance existing debt and in part to expand the Bwana Mkubwa processing plant, and to exploit and develop the nearby Lonshi copper deposit in the Democratic Republic of Congo. Repayment came from revenues generated through copper cathode exports and the transaction was also secured with the assets of Bwana Mkubwa. As a result, the KBC facility attracted an interest rate of just 2.5 per cent per annum over Libor. As explained by one of the arrangers: 'The tailings at Bwana Mkubwa had a remaining life of around 27 months at the time of the financing. In order to ensure a sufficient reserve post repayment of the transaction we agreed with the borrower a 19-month tenor for the facility . . . . Developing Lonshi changes the whole ball game for Bwana Mkubwa'.[2]

Some market participants, however, criticise this type of prestigious medium-term structured commodity financing transactions because of the opportunity cost borne by the borrower due to over-collateralisation. Since in theory the deal can be repaid in one year (despite the apparently longer tenor), the commodity pledged as collateral is not available for other borrowing, which is wasteful from an economic standpoint.

Such forms of medium-term structured commodity financing nevertheless remain attractive because the alternative of unsecured hard-currency medium- and long-term financing is generally not available to high-risk commodity players located in emerging countries, unless the onerous provisioning requirements faced by banks can be alleviated by co-financing arrangements, whereby the main lender is a multilateral or regional bank,[3] or by an export credit agency (ECA) guarantee. These medium-term loans are typically used to fund the critical earlier years of a project (for example, the construction and initial operating stages), and are often straightforward (as opposed to structured), with banks having full recourse to sponsors or third-party guarantors until repayment or until the obligations of the borrowers are taken over by longer-term lenders. For their part, long-term creditors find comfort in the fact that default on their loan would trigger a series of cross-defaults with other donor-supported facilities, which project sponsors and governments would normally want to avoid. Nevertheless, loans forming part of project finance still contribute regularly to the market for distressed loans, and experience shows that banks may be more likely to suffer from debt rescheduling, restructuring or outward default as co-lender in a project finance loan than under structured finance deals – although, to be fair, this has also to do with the nature of project loans in terms of their importance and impact on the local political scene and economy.

Nevertheless, medium-term loans remain more difficult to raise than short-term loans, even on a tightly structured basis, especially when the regional economic and financial situation is unstable. For example, in 2002, when the Latin American environment was difficult for new foreign exchange financing, Standard Chartered Bank arranged a one-year US$70 million pre-export finance facility for Amaggi Exportaçao e Importaçao, a Brazilian soybean merchant. As observed by one of the arranging team: 'At one year, the deal is opened up to a much wider investor base. In particular, Brazilian banks are much more likely to do short-term transactions as opposed to medium-term deals'.[4]

Corporate versus transaction-based financing

Within the range of financing alternatives, structured commodity finance began as way of providing trade financing. Soon, however, its techniques were used for general purpose financing, and even to finance new projects and capital investments, even before its techniques had evolved to provide medium-term financing. For example, as far back as 1993 an oilfield in Angola (offshore Block 4/26), in which Sonangol was first-time operator, was developed on the back of a short-term structured transaction (arranged by Bankers Trust Company) backed by crude oil exports. Likewise, in 2001 WestLB arranged a US$30 million facility for Nidera (Argentina) secured by an assignment of futures export sales of Nidera's soyabean, sunflower, wheat, corn and other agricultural products to its affiliate in The Netherlands. With only a nine-month tenor the deal was nevertheless earmarked for capital expenditures.

A more recent trend, as observed by Clemens Falkhauser, head of commodity and trade finance for eastern Europe at HypoVereinsbank, is for longer-term loan structures to 'increasingly mix typical commodity finance structures with elements of standard corporate loans. Financial covenants are being incorporated into the documentation. Account is taken of the levels of total indebtedness, the ratio of total foreign exchange revenues to foreign exchange debt profile, and other such factors'.[5] For example, in 2001 Standard Bank London (SBL) and Glencore arranged an 18-month US$25 million oil-backed structured loan for Russia's Severnaya Neft (Nord Oil). The transaction was considered by SBL a hybrid between a limited recourse project finance transaction (due diligence and emphasis on underlying cash flow) and a pre-export facility (offtake contract): 'The key distinguishing feature between the two is start-up risk'.[6]

In short, structured finance techniques have proved their versatility and are now successfully applied to finance a wide range of trade and investment needs in the commodity sector, and also increasingly to provide general purpose financing.

Type of borrowers

Most examples of structured commodity finance presented in this book involve large commodity exporters. Indeed, their characteristics enable structures that are more cost-effective (for the borrower) and profitable (for the lender) than under other conditions. Yet the techniques described in Part II can be applied, with the qualifications already identified, to other users in terms of their size and role in the production and marketing cycle.

Arranging structured commodity finance transactions is labour-intensive and thus expensive. Deals need to reach a certain size in order to make it attractive for both parties to enter into them. Having said that, inventory financing (as defined in Part II) can be applied to smaller, higher-risk borrowers for amounts as low as just a few million US dollars. Financing requirements of small borrowers can also be bundled up under a common structured inventory financing. With some exceptions, large companies would find it more attractive to use the less onerous (in terms of commercial autonomy) pre-export financing structure as opposed to inventory financing. Large borrowers are also in a better position to do so because they are more likely than small borrowers to export the commodities produced or sell them to first-class buyers. In many countries small companies have nevertheless been able to benefit from structured pre-export techniques by forming cooperatives to make up for their lack of critical size that resulted from the dismantling of most marketing boards.

As structured commodity finance techniques become familiar to a region or countries, applications tend to trickle down to smaller borrowers. In many emerging countries, notably in Russia, structured commodity finance techniques are now enabling second-tier commodity producers to obtain foreign exchange financing under acceptable terms and conditions. Obviously, these medium-sized companies typically first approach the market with small tightly structured, short-term deals.

Structured commodity finance techniques can be used by producers (such as mining companies or agricultural estates), processing companies (eg, edible oil refiners), manufacturers (eg, steel mills) and traders. As mentioned, exporters are the prime targets of structured commodity finance deals. Even when the financing is used to pay for imports, the structured element is typically provided through not only a pledge over the imported commodity but also an assignment of the sales proceeds, preferably derived from exports. In turn, the sales proceeds can relate to either the very commodity being financed (for example, petroleum products being re-marketed locally) or the product resulting from the refining or processing of the commodity. Export sales proceeds can also finance the imports of unrelated commodities (such as the large coffee pre-export/oil import structured loans arranged in the mid-1980s for Tanzania) or even the import of other inputs for the commodity sector. For example, in 2001 South Africa's ABSA Bank lent US$29 million to the Zambian Food Reserve Agency to finance the import of fertiliser for Sasol and Omnia in South Africa. The financing was collateralised and repaid from the sale of maize at harvest time.

Structured finance can even be used to finance the whole production and marketing chain of a particular commodity. For example, in 2001 WestLB arranged a structured facility for a Brazilian soybean trading and logistics company to enable it to prepay its domestic supplier of fertiliser (Phase I). The domestic fertiliser trading company used the prepayment to buy the fertiliser from an international fertiliser trading company (Phase II). The fertiliser was in turn sold to local farmers and paid for through delivery of beans to the local fertiliser trading company. To increase control over the transaction, the funds were actually disbursed by the lender against unloading certificates of fertiliser bought by the local fertiliser trading company. Soybeans were subsequently stored in a warehouse (and pledged to the lenders) and subsequently exported to an international trading company (via documentary collection). Export proceeds were used to repay the facility. The arranger combined the facility in Phase II with a pre-export facility for the Ukrainian company supplying the fertiliser, repaid through export delivery of fertiliser. As explained by one of the arrangers: 'The advantages of such a deal are close control over the goods, usage of funds, as well as building upon the existing track record between the parties involved and extending business along the chain of goods. We did this deal in Brazil the first time, and moved forward to finance the fertiliser in Ukraine to supply soybean producers. Now we finance the whole commodity chain'.[7]

---

1 Tax incentives are used in some countries to encourage US dollar finance related to exports. In Brazil and Turkey, for example, exporters are entitled to substantial tax subsidies for US dollar borrowings that are not available to borrowers not engaged in exports.

2 Andrew Robinson, assistant vice president of KBC's African structured trade finance desk in London, quoted in 'KBC arranges finance for African copper producer', *Trade Finance,* November 2001.

3 Note that this approach will not work under Basle II, where the deal will have to stand on its own on the basis of the individual bank's status, as a standard or IRB bank, and the status of the primary lender is irrelevant.

4 Cameron Letters, senior vice-president, structured trade and commodity finance at StanChart in New York.

5 'Cash cows step it up' by Simon Pirani, *Trade Finance,* September 2001.

6 'Eyes on the new producers' by Jonathan Bell, *Trade Finance,* September 2001.

7 Markus Fuchs, head of the soft commodity desk of WestLB in Dusseldorf

Chapter 17

Applicable commodities

Not all commodities are good collateral for structured commodity finance transactions. For example, with some notable exceptions, it would be extremely difficult to structure a deal on the back of rapidly perishable commodities. Likewise, commodities with highly volatile prices can only be considered if their price risk can be adequately hedged.

Since the first half of 2002, many hard and soft commodity prices have risen in US dollar terms. Such a rise would tend to reduce short-term working capital needs and increase capital investment financing needs. As we know, structured commodity finance techniques can address both needs.

This analysis assumes that the reasons for high commodity prices are structural rather than temporary. However, this has clearly not been the case for all recent commodity price increases, in particular for crude oil, where steep price rises at the beginning of 2003 resulted mainly from the crisis over Iraq. Nevertheless, regardless of the resilience of high commodity prices, they allow borrowers to raise more money against a given volume of commodities pledged as collateral and also to hedge their commodity price risk under relatively good price conditions.

Hard commodities (natural resources)

The expansion of structured commodity finance in the 1990s largely occurred on the back of natural resources. Indeed, hard commodities have intrinsic qualities (such as their durability), as well as a liquid and transparent market, that make related collateral more valuable than in the case of soft commodities. Moreover, amounts involved in hard commodities trading are typically larger, and thus provide more incentives for arranging and lending banks to get involved. Finally, companies operating in the natural resources sector generally tend to access the capital markets as soon as possible in order to fund their capital investment, often on the back of export receivables structures already tested with bank loans.

Initially, the discussion in this chapter focuses on a commodity that has a unique potential in terms of supporting structured financing arrangements – gold. This is followed by an overview of the application of structured commodity finance techniques to borrowers operating in other extractive industries, including the oil and gas sector.

Gold

Gold is special in the realm of structured commodity finance due to its monetary value and lingering use as an international reserve. Therefore, attractive financing can be obtained on the back of gold using structures that would not always be applicable to other commodities. The following subsections cover the basic structures of gold loans, gold sale repurchases, gold-backed loans and prepaid forward gold sales.

Gold loan

Under this structure a company would borrow gold from a bank for an agreed time. To raise funds, this company would sell the gold at spot prices either in the market or directly to the same bank. The 'repayment' of the gold could take place either progressively or via a bullet repayment at maturity. The rate covering the 'repayment' of gold would normally be a function of (i) the gold lease rate; and (ii) whether or not future gold deliveries ('repayments') are hedged through forward contracts or otherwise. This structure is particularly suitable for producers, as they are naturally hedged through their future gold production and sale.

Gold loans have been very actively used in Australia, and to a lesser extent in the United States and in sub-Saharan Africa. For example, in January 1996 Standard Bank London provided a US$16 million gold loan to PTA Bank, a small regional development bank, to refinance a gold loan previously extended by PTA Bank to Cluff Resources to finance a gold mining project in Zimbabwe. Using the same structure, a gold producer could also raise finance in the capital markets. For example, back in 1994, the Australian gold producer PosGold financed the acquisition of a gold mine with a US$200 million gold-denominated Eurobond (arranged by Merrill Lynch).

Gold sale repurchase

Under this structure a company would raise funds by selling gold to a bank with an agreement to buy it back at an agreed future date and at an agreed price. To limit credit risk, the bank could require this company to make regular payments to an interest-bearing sinking fund that would eventually be used to repurchase the gold. Interest earned on such an account would in turn reduce the implied interest rate paid by the company, otherwise a function of the gold sale price (based on gold spot prices) and the gold repurchase price (based on the forward gold curve).

This structure is particularly suited to central banks, which can use gold sale repurchases to raise medium-term financing without losing title to their gold reserves. In 1992 Bankers Trust Company entered into a five-year US$18.5 million gold sale repurchase agreement with the Bank of Tanzania that funded the purchase of a Fokker 50 aircraft by the government of Tanzania.

Gold-backed loan (with floor)

Under this structure a company would make a gold deposit with a bank for an agreed time to serve as collateral for a loan granted by the same bank. The gold deposit would be remunerated at the gold lease rate, and the accrued gold could be either capitalised with the initial gold deposit or delivered to the company and sold by it to reduce its interest payment amounts. The ratio of the loan to the value of the gold deposit would be higher if the company hedged the gold deposit against a fall in gold prices, for example by buying a put option at a strike price equal to the spot price. To finance the put option premium, and further reduce interest payments, the company could also sell one or more call options to the bank, thus capping the effective price at which the company would eventually realise the gold deposit at maturity.

This structure is also well-adapted to central banks. For instance, in 1991 Bankers Trust Company granted a four-year US$7.2 million gold-backed loan to the Bank of Zambia, supported by the collar structure just described.

Prepaid forward sale of gold

Under this structure a company would sell gold to a bank for future deliveries at a price equal to the discounted value of future payments. In practice, gold would be sold at market prices on these forward dates, with the bulk of the proceeds used to effect principal and interest repayments to the lenders that funded the sale. As with the previous structure, the company could also buy a string of put options to hedge its exposure against a fall in gold prices. This structure is very similar to the prepayment structure discussed in Part II, with the difference being that the lender makes a loan without recourse.

Backed by its own gold production, Ashanti Goldfields in 1996 signed a prepaid forward gold sale with Dresdner Bank and Union Bank of Switzerland, and raised US$40 million to refinance US$28 million of high-yield debt and to expand the Freda Rebecca mine in Zimbabwe.

A similar transaction was arranged in 1999 by the EBRD and Standard Bank London whereby prepayment was made to Russian gold producers through Bank Zenit, a local Russian bank, to be repaid by gold deliveries. As noted by Oleg Yenukov, head of trade finance at Bank Zenit in Russia: 'For Russian banks, gold is one of the most reliable sectors to work in. They usually provide one-year financing equal to one-third of the year's production collateralised by the entire output. The alluvial producers are mostly very small companies that produce only during the summer months, and need financing during the winter to take equipment and other supplies to remote sites'.[1]

Other metals

Steel

Steel is not as attractive a collateral as gold but can still efficiently support structured deals, as was the case with the facility arranged in the summer of 2001 for Siderar, Argentina's main integrated steel producer. At that time, the economic situation in Argentina was already in a dire state, although the real had not yet been devalued. Jointly arranged by Beal and WestLB, the three-year yen-denominated (worth US$35 million) facility was supported by payments from OECD offtakers of steel export proceeds into a collection account.

Because their financing needs are mainly related to new long-term capital investments, large steel producers have turned to the capital markets to obtain long-term financing on the back of their export sales. At the end of 2000, for instance, the Brazilian steel producer Cosipa issued US$175 million senior secured seven-year export-backed A-rated notes through Cosipa Overseas (Cayman Islands). The proceeds were used to fund Cosipa's capital expenditure programme. The transaction was supported by, among other things, a financial guarantee from Cosipa, a performance guarantee from a US-based insurance company and letters of credit from first-class international banks on the steel exports. This bond issue was actually followed by a structured bank loan of a similar tenor.

Since 2001 banks have felt less comfortable lending short-term money to the steel industry, especially in the light of the difficulties created by renewed US steel tariffs and worldwide economic slowdown. In the near future, medium-term structured finance deals will probably be limited to the most reliable steel producers in terms of quality and market. There is also a fundamental problem with steel deals, in that steel cannot be hedged: there are no forward or futures markets.

Non-ferrous mining sector

Aluminium and copper (nickel) have been widely used to support structured commodity finance deals, both inventory financing and pre-export financing structures.

For example, in 2002 Russia's Norilsk Nickel raised a three-year financing on the back of an inventory of 60,000 tonnes of nickel to be warehoused outside Russia. At the time the transaction was being arranged (jointly by ING, Credit Suisse First Boston and Standard Bank London) the inventory had a value of about US$400 million, but the loan was expected to range between US$100 and US$200 million. The opportunity cost of storing nickel for such a long period was apparently largely outweighed by the benefits to the borrower in terms of pricing and maturity.

As regards aluminium, RusAl financed many of its operations on the back of structured commodity finance techniques, often as part of tolling arrangements.

There is a good potential for the application of structured commodity finance techniques to move further into the copper (nickel) and aluminium markets. As noted by one market specialist with regard to the Russian market: 'After the 1998 crisis, all the banks jumped into oil. There is now a feeling that portfolios must be diversified. Norilsk Nickel and RusAl have the clear advantage of producing LME-deliverable material'.[2]

Precious metals

Structured finance techniques have been used to finance the expansion of platinum and diamond mines, and to provide general purpose financing to large producers in the precious metals sector.

For example, in 2002 Almazy Rossii Sakha (Alrosa), Russia's largest diamond producer, raised medium-term financing around a new five-year trade agreement entered into with De Beers. The deal was arranged by Société Générale, which at the time was also contemplating a securitised bond issue to be secured by export receipts of diamond sales.

Oil and gas

Oil helped to contribute to the expansion of structured commodity finance techniques in the 1990s, supporting financing to both medium-sized and large producers on the back of their existing production. Oil was also one of the first commodities for which structured commodity finance techniques were introduced into securitisation deals.

Given the large number of gas production projects sprouting in every corner of the world, gas sales can be expected to increasingly serve as collateral for many structured commodity finance deals in the future. One of the longest-maturity structured finance deals seen so far in the market in the gas sector was the US$300 million, six-year syndicated loan arranged for Russia's Gazprom in the spring of 2002. As noted by HypoVereinsbank, co-arranger of the transaction: 'The facility is secured by receivables on a long-term gas purchase agreement with a European offtaker. It will help to fund the development of gas fields . . . and to expand throughput capacity of Gazprom's transport network'.[3] A few months earlier, Russian oil company Lukoil and metal company MMK had obtained, respectively, a four-and-a-half-year and a three-year structured loan, then benchmark deals in their respective sectors.

Upstream

Crude oil is probably the best collateral to support structured commodity finance deals. The market for crude oil is highly liquid and transparent. Medium-term financing can thus be arranged on the back of short-term export contracts. For example, the record-breaking seven-year US$500 million deal arranged in 2003 for Lukoil was collateralised on oil exports supported by a one-year term contract with LitasCo, a Swiss-based trader controlled by Lukoil.[4] On the minus side, however, its excessive volatility means that arrangers have to be extremely careful in order to properly hedge the price risk element.

Downstream

Petroleum products also provide acceptable collateral. However, they also require more work on the part of arrangers in terms of due diligence because of a generally large basket of petroleum products pledged as collateral and the bigger basis risks on the price risk management side. Moreover, many petroleum products are sold to domestic markets, hence adding another risk element to structured commodity finance deals.

Soft commodities (agricultural products)

Soft commodities often used as collateral in structured finance deals include sugar, cotton, coffee, cocoa and, to a lesser extent, soybeans. For example, in 2002 Sucden obtained from BNP Paribas a US$15 million revolving loan facility to finance the importation of raw sugar into Russia for processing and sale on the Russian market. The deal was secured against certain cash flows and against sugar assets owned by one of Sucden's Russian subsidiaries. As explained by one of the legal advisers on the transaction: 'This was an interesting cross-border financing, which required us to structure the deal so as to comply with relevant laws from exporting countries, Russian raw sugar import rules and recently liberalised hard currency regulations'.[5]

Financing of certain soft commodities is tightly linked to the trading of these commodities, even more so perhaps for structured deals. Also, a particular difficulty involved in using soft commodities as collateral is their greater vulnerability to damage during storage and transport. Soft commodities are also less conducive to medium-term financing than hard commodities.

In fact, the soft commodity sector finds it difficult to fund its working capital needs or new investment, even on a structured basis. This is where multilateral development banks and other non-commercial lenders can intervene to add value, especially for small producers and traders. For instance, in 2001 the EBRD supported Rabo Invest (a specialised commodity financing arm of Rabobank International) in a US$143 million structured loan to 20 or so Russian processing and trading companies to import sugar, wheat and other commodities. In this transaction, Rabo Invest purchased the commodities and sold them back to customers, which was instrumental in circumventing a legal and regulatory environment deemed too unreliable by the arrangers. As noted by Hans Christian Jacobsen, director of the EBRD's agribusiness team: 'The scheme has been a way of providing structured financing products for Russia's agribusiness sector pending approval of legislation to set up a fully fledged warehouse receipt programme'.[6]

---

1 'Gold sector refines future finance', *Trade Finance,* May 2001.

2 Siobhan Walker, head of structured and general lending at ING in Moscow, quoted in 'Expanding the portfolio' by Simon Pirani, *Trade Finance,* April 2002.

3 'Lenders race to Gazprom' by Simon Pirani, *Trade Finance,* April 2002.

4 'A new era for Russian oil', *Trade Finance*, July 2003.

5 Chris Viner, a partner with law firm Norton Rose in Moscow, quoted in 'Norton Rose advises BNPP on Russian sugar financing', *Trade Finance,* April 2002.

6 'EBRD and Rabobank extend Russian scheme', *Trade Finance,* September 2001.

Chapter 18

Commercial partners

This chapter discusses financing provided by commercial partners, mainly suppliers of capital goods and services, and commodities trading counterparties.

Suppliers of capital goods and services

Financing extended by suppliers is commonly referred to as suppliers' credit. Under such arrangements the importer would typically make an up-front payment to the supplier and issue promissory notes, or accept term drafts, for the balance of payments due. Deferred payments can also be supported by a letter of credit. In turn, the supplier can obtain immediate funds by discounting or negotiating the trade paper, as discussed in Part I. Suppliers can also take payment in the form of goods through countertrade arrangements, as discussed in Part II.

If longer-term financing is required to pay for purchases of capital goods, suppliers are rarely able or willing to provide such financing on their own. They would need to obtain medium- or long-term financing from banks, typically with the support of export credit agencies (ECAs), and in turn extend such financing to importers. In practice, however, most ECA-backed loans are structured as buyers' credits and not as suppliers' credits. Even when structured as buyers' credits, ECA-backed financing is generally initiated at the request of suppliers and, in any case, cannot be set up without the full collaboration of suppliers. In this regard, it has already been noted in Part III that ECAs increasingly use structured finance arrangements as payment security, at the expense of their traditional reliance on government or bank guarantees.

Thanks to their relative clout with commercial banks, suppliers can obtain attractive financing terms for their importers. Some suppliers go one step further and arrange financing transactions on their own. This would typically be the case for large supply contracts and financing would then be arranged on a structured basis. For instance, the Swiss-Swedish engineering group ABB once had a highly regarded structured finance group. More enduring in this field, GE Capital, the structured finance group of General Electric, now operates on its own, even for projects in which its parent company is no longer involved, providing advice and capital to clients in the energy, infrastructure, communications and industrial development sectors worldwide. In particular, GE Capital is very active in arranging financing for gas-fuelled power plants and petrochemical plants. Of course, the example of Enron proves that companies should act carefully before relying on suppliers of capital goods and services for their financing or advisory needs.

Although suppliers and contractors can take the driving seat for corporate export credits, whether structured or not, they have a much more passive role when a proposed investment is to be funded through a project financing structure. In such cases, the financing is typically designed by the project sponsors, relying on the selected advising bank, whose role spans negotiation of financial and commercial documents through to the choice of the lead arranging bank(s).

Another source of financing falling into this category could be transport and logistics companies. For example, UPS Capital, a subsidiary of United Parcel Services, at the beginning of 2002 signed a financial services and logistics agreement with Eurofrut, one of Europe's largest fruit importers and distributors, under which UPS Capital agreed to factor invoices issued by Eurofrut to the supermarket chains. Under this structure, UPS Capital advanced up to 85 per cent of the value of invoices within one day of receipt of the documents. This integrated financial solution, combining the flow of goods, funds and information, illustrates the variety of financing alternatives now available to the commodity sector.

Finally, instead of being imported, capital goods can be leased from suppliers, as discussed in Part II.

Commodity trading counterparties

Commodity buyers based in industrialised countries can provide attractive financing under certain circumstances – for instance when securing supplies of raw materials or energy is essential to their operations – and such commodity buyers can obtain attractive financing from their banks. This would be the case, for example, for a large steel company based in an industrial country. In this case, financing can be arranged in the form of a cash prepayment to the commodity exporter or, alternatively, through the supply of raw materials within a countertrade arrangement. As mentioned in Part II, aluminium production is typically arranged and financed through tolling arrangements, which is a form of structured commodity finance.

Sellers of commodities, for their part, can provide financing to importers through extended payment terms. In practice, the principal commodities imported by emerging countries are petroleum products, and petroleum product suppliers can easily provide financing, if so requested, through deferred payment terms. How does their financing compare with other alternatives available to importers of petroleum products? For a start, deferred payments are a simple way for importers to access short-term finance without the need to obtain bank credit lines. Local banks are often reluctant to extend foreign exchange financing without commensurate cash collateral in local currency, which is expensive in terms of opportunity cost. Foreign banks, for their part, are not much interested in financing local importers on a clean basis. However, extended payment terms are rarely the cheapest way of obtaining finance because petroleum product suppliers will rightfully reflect their own financing costs in the price of the supply contract. This cost can usually be assessed by comparing the contractual price with the price net of any discount offered by the supplier for prompt payment. Even if the financing cost thus calculated looks attractive, its real cost is generally hidden somewhere in the terms of the commercial agreement and is virtually impossible to detect unless the terms of the contract are compared with those possibly offered by another supplier on a cash basis. A typical example of such hidden costs was provided by Malawi's unattractive petroleum procurement arrangements in the early 1990s (discussed in Part II). Structured commodity finance provides petroleum importers with an alternative to obtaining financing from their trading counterparties, for instance by securing the financing with the proceeds of the re-marketing of petroleum products to first-class buyers, possibly with the support of a local bank guarantee.

As far as trading companies are concerned, they operate on both sides of the commodity trade and are increasingly involved in arranging financing for their clients. As observed by one market specialist: 'In order to have a competitive advantage, traders progressively extend their services to their clients. Among their traditional functions, they provide for example pre-export financing to their sellers or provide credit to their buyers at the country of destination. Therefore, traders become part of the industrial chain, hence the requirement for external financing'.[1] The Noble Group, for example, expanded its operations from the simple trading of commodities into a wider range of services for its clients in the commodity sector, through its divisions spanning agriculture, energy, finance, minerals and ores, logistics and technology. In particular, Noble Group's finance division claims that it is able to offer complete structured trade and commodity finance, investment and insurance solutions.[2] This rise of large trading companies is creating a challenge for the commodities business of commercial banks.

The effective price realised by a commodity exporter, and the effective price paid by a commodity importer, depend not only on the terms of their commercial contract and financing arrangements but also on how their exposure to adverse commodity price movements is handled. The simplest way to hedge commodity prices is to fix them with trade counterparties. However, commodities trade counterparties are rarely the best hedge providers. The alternative is for commodity sector companies to base their commercial contracts on publicly available floating prices, plus or minus a fixed margin, and to hedge their commodity price risk separately in the paper markets. In this regard, the presence of a structured commodity finance deal encourages exporters and importers to analyse and eventually hedge their exposure to adverse price movements.

Finally, examples abound to show that the role of trading companies in structured commodity finance has evolved from that of being simple participants (structured export receivables) to acting as principals (structured prepayments) through to becoming arrangers themselves.

Evaluation of commercial partners as financiers

Too often, suppliers of capital goods and commodities can only bid for a particular contract if they can provide financing as well. This may be convenient for importers of capital goods but, as we saw, it is not always the cheapest way for them to obtain financing. Companies operating in the commodity sector should not force their commercial partners to offer financing but instead should give them the opportunity to bid with and without a financing package attached. In parallel, they should take the initiative to approach the financing markets themselves and negotiate the best possible financing terms for the proposed commercial contract.

Having said that, commercial partners sometimes open trade routes long before banks – and *a fortiori* the capital market – and can sometimes develop attractive financing offers. They also have a much more intimate knowledge of local commodity sector companies. As noted by one legal adviser: 'Many trading houses are now becoming involved much higher up the purchasing chain than they used to be . . . . This applies in particular to oil and metal mining in which the trading house typically enters into a long-term contract and may then become involved in pre-financing the supply arrangements. Thus the trading house becomes the first buyer in the chain, and often may take an equity stake in the producer'.[3]

Trading companies have also realised that increasingly transparent pricing environments limit the profit they can make on buying and selling. Thus a simple way to discreetly increase their overall margin is to provide financing, especially by paying in advance against future deliveries of commodities. As we saw in Part II, such prepayment arrangements are increasingly conducted on a structured basis.

[1] Christian Joerg of SGS, quoted in 'Securing the frontier supplies', Trade Finance, April 2002.

[2] 'Noble: A driving force in raw materials supply', *Trade Finance,* April 2002.

[3] Sara Kay of law firm Clifford Chance, quoted in 'Lawyers win again', *Trade Finance,* February 2002.

Chapter 19

Debt from banks and the capital markets

For simplicity this chapter is divided between (a) bank loans and facilities; and (b) capital market debt. Like the traditional trade financing instruments presented in Part I, structured commodity finance (SCF) techniques discussed so far generally support bank loans, disbursed either on a bilateral or on a syndicated basis.

SCF bank loans and facilities

Most companies operating in the commodity sector are either high-risk credits themselves, trading with high-risk counterparties and/or operating in high-risk environments, so banks are generally reluctant to lend to them on an unsecured or loosely secured basis. In the absence of tightly structured finance, banks would typically request either cash collateral (for example, to confirm a letter of credit) or other security requirements (such as a mortgage on the borrower's fixed assets). Such onerous security requirements would obviously not be necessary for first-class borrowers in a position to repay the bank on the back of their balance sheet – say a large importer in an OECD country.

The amounts that can be lent are also limited by the credit limits established by international banks. These limits are often set for exposure to a particular country, industry or company, or even for varying types of exposure (such as hedging versus a general purpose line of credit). Increasingly, banks distinguish between pure credit risk (for example, providing a confirmation of a local bank letter of credit) and loans that depend for repayment upon the performance of a commercial operation. When the latter are tightly structured, some banks may be prepared to reconsider their country limits and set up special credit lines for performance-related risk. This approach is more progressive than that of bank regulators, which under Basle I do not take into account the risk mitigation factor of structured finance to calculate their risk capital and related provisioning requirements.

Structured commodity finance transactions are very labour-intensive and are normally not worth the trouble for small amounts. However, since local banks can structure transactions and conduct the underlying due diligence at a much lower cost than international banks, the recent liberalisation of financial markets in emerging countries should give a boost to small SCF deals. Yet the main impetus for the dramatic development of structured finance bank loans has come from international banks.

Lamon Rutten of UNCTAD has identified the following 'push' factors for structured commodity finance over recent years:[1]

- consolidation in the commodity trading/processing industry;
- bank mergers, with, as one result, the disappearance of country risk capacity from the market;
- increasing competition from institutional investors;
- severe lack of appetite for traditional (unsecured) commodity financing;

- increased country risk awareness on the part of banks; and
- increased demand for risk capital.

These 'push' factors could be regarded as constraints faced by banks that forced them to reassess their lending strategy in order to improve the risk/return profile of their assets. This favoured structured commodity finance deals, in that they enable lenders to take the payment risk of OECD buyers on loans made to emerging country borrowers. This core feature of structured commodity finance brings about many positive consequences for banks operating with emerging countries, in terms of lower default risk, bigger loan amounts and syndication potential, higher profitability, and stronger relationships with emerging market borrowers. A summary of these characteristics is provided in the following subsections; then an overview is attempted of the impact of the upcoming Basle II Accord on structured commodity finance and of the tendency of large banking groups to integrate their commodities, trade and export finance operations.

Lower default risk

Borrowers benefit from structured loans in terms of attractive financing terms mainly because lenders face less default risks than under comparable clean loans. This is achieved by putting in place a good structure – not just a semblance of structure. Default risk is minimised if the structured commodity loan is self-liquidating and if proper incentives are in place to enable the borrower to perform on the underlying commercial operations, even in times of cash flow constraints.

Before structured finance techniques were properly implemented (see Part II), lenders had some expensive experiences with loosely structured commodity finance deals. An historical case of fraud quoted in many finance books relates to the US$200 million loan made some 30 years ago to Allied Crude Vegetable Oil Refining Corporation (USA). Warehouse receipts issued by a field warehousing company were taken as security. Unfortunately, the inspection company had failed to uncover the fact that, instead of containing salad oil, Allied's storage tanks were mainly filled with soap, seawater and unidentifiable sludge. After the fraud was discovered, the president of Allied went to jail, and the field warehousing company, which was owned by American Express, was rendered insolvent, but it was not adjudicated bankrupt because American Express paid off all the 50 or so warehouse receipt holders.

Frauds in the area of commodity financing have not stopped with the development of sophisticated SCF techniques. On the contrary, it seems that fraudsters are often one step ahead of lenders. Some of the most common frauds seen in structured commodity financing deals have been reported and analysed by UNCTAD in a recent publication.[2] In another book, John McNamara of Deutsche Bank presented an overview of 'Dos' and 'Don'ts' required for structures to effectively ensure timely service of debt obligations, plus some striking examples of deals that went sour.[3]

Nevertheless, structured commodity finance deals have proved their resilience, not only when private borrowers face cash flow constraints, but also in times of external financial crises. This was the case, for example, when the government of Zambia began to run into external payment difficulties in the mid-1990s and – reluctantly – continued to effect payments to lenders into a particular structured copper finance deal to the detriment of other external creditors. As explained by John McNamara,

Lenders to (then) state-owned Zambia Consolidated Copper Mines (ZCCM) based on the latter's exports of copper found their lending rationale tested when a third-party creditor of the Zambian government slapped a Mareva injunction on the agent bank to block reimbursements from the agent's dedicated collection account via the English High Court. The claim was that the revenues flowing through the said account were allegedly the property of the Zambian government, and the creditor sought to attach them. However, appeal by the agent successfully evidenced that the lenders had, via the offtaker, prepaid ZCCM for the copper, they also had an assignment of the underlying export contract, and that therefore the monies on the collection account belonged not to the Zambian government but to the lenders to ZCCM. The structural ring-fencing of the export cash flow worked and put the 'structured' lenders in a superior position to unsecured sovereign creditors.[4]

Bigger loan amounts and syndication potential

Tight structures enable banks to lend larger amounts than they would on an unsecured basis, especially if the structure involves a mechanism for hedging commodity price risk. Moreover, thanks to their attractive risk profile, well-structured commodity loans are easier to syndicate than traditional commodity finance loans, especially during economic slowdowns or when lending capacity is constrained. Syndicated structured commodity finance deals are also deemed prestigious for both the arranger and the borrower.

In turn, banks participating in large syndicated structured finance deals enjoy having their name associated with such prestigious transactions, gain exposure to otherwise remote borrowers and improve their knowledge of structured finance techniques.

Higher profitability

Arranging structured commodity finance deals is generally a highly profitable business for arranging banks, at least until the structured transaction becomes so successful that competition between arranging banks begins to eat into returns (as with, for example, the Cocobod deal). In fact, banks are so keen to market their skills as arrangers of structured deals that it is becoming increasingly difficult for companies operating in the commodity sector to rely on them for more mundane operations, such as the issuance of bank guarantees or letters of credit.

In the case of syndicated structured deals, mere participants will often find that their risk-adjusted return is not very attractive. Most of the fees paid by borrowers typically wind up in the pockets of arrangers or lead managers as arrangement fees, agency fees or 'skim' on participation fees. Moreover, as mentioned earlier, arrangers of structured commodity finance deals can also make substantial profits by acting as hedge provider. (Again, this does not mean that borrowers should not hedge their commodity price risk.)

Nonetheless, in these times of economic slowdown and emerging market crises, syndicated structured deals have proved to be good value for both deal arrangers and simple participants.

Stronger relationship with emerging countries' borrowers

The preparation and execution of structured commodity finance deals have enabled international banks to develop direct relations with the ultimate beneficiary of the loan, at the expense of local banks and international traders. This is turn has enabled them to offer other banking products to their emerging market clients.

Under traditional trade finance structures international banks tend to rely more on their local banking correspondent, whether subsidiaries or indigenous banks, for all aspects of the overseas bank facilities, from the origination of the deal to the credit analysis, disbursement and its subsequent administration. International banks that have branches or subsidiaries in emerging countries have even found it attractive to make clean loans to their branches or subsidiaries, and let them deal with the payment and performance risk of borrowers. Consequently, international banks have been exposed not only to the credit risk of local companies, but also to that of local banks – and, for that matter, also to documentation, administration and fraud risk. With structured commodity finance, local banks can disappear as lenders. The ultimate beneficiary of the loan can take foreign exchange directly from the international bank offshore and repay the loan directly to an offshore escrow account under the control of the international bank (if authorised by the country's regulations).

Paradoxically, the emergence of structured finance has also meant an increasing need for a local correspondent to assist international banks in all matters relating to the commodities held as collateral (due diligence process). For this reason, local banks are now often asked to act as co-arrangers of structured finance transactions, although inspection companies can also play this role. There are also pragmatic motives for including local banks as co-arrangers, such as political clout and financial support in term of performance guarantees or financial participation in the loan, and, perhaps most importantly, their expertise in managing and enforcing the legal security under local laws and customs. This is a very important trend, which is definitely a 'win-win' situation. The best example is Turkey, where local bank participation can significantly enhance credit risk.

Eventually, local banks can be expected to leverage on their traditional client relationship and compete with international banks to arrange structured commodity finance transactions on their own, using any reputable offshore bank to provide for the foreign exchange element. Yet if this situation were to develop significantly, international banks would still retain various competitive advantages: for instance their ability to integrate hedging programmes, and to arrange and place large syndicated and securitised deals.

Impact of Basle II

Structured commodity finance mitigates the risk of default on the underlying loan. This is definitely a benefit for the banks' bottom line, but is this benefit also recognised by bank regulators in setting provisioning requirements? The answer to this question will soon be positive, since the upcoming Basle II Capital Accord will take into account the credit risk mitigation provided by structured commodity finance.

Exhibit 19.1 briefly presents the purpose of provisioning requirements and the main tenets of the new Basle Capital Accords.[5] The particular application to the field of structured commodity finance is discussed in Exhibit 19.2.

The earliest drafts of the new Basle Capital Accord did not seem to propose any favourable treatment for collateral provided by the assignment of commodity inventories or sales receivables. Only credit derivatives qualified as acceptable credit risk mitigants, alongside collateral provided by cash (and acceptable securities) and third-party guarantees. Some market professionals had expressed concern about the implications of Basle II for structured

Exhibit 19.1

Provisioning requirements and the main tenets of the new Basle Capital Accord

The Basle Committee on Banking Supervision is a committee of central banks, bank supervisors and regulators from major industrialised countries that meets every three months at the Bank for International Settlements in Basle. The committee provides broad policy guidelines that each country's supervisors can use to determine supervisory policies.

Provisioning requirements can be defined as guidelines (mandatory or not – this is different from country to country) on the minimum capital that banks must apply to their operations, which is vital to reduce the risk of bank insolvency and the potential cost of a bank failure for depositors. More than a decade has passed since the Basle Committee introduced its 1988 Capital Accord. Recognising that the business of banking, risk management, supervisory approaches and financial markets had undergone significant transformations, in 1999 the committee released a proposal to replace the existing Accord with a more risk-sensitive approach, to be implemented in 2004.

The new framework is intended to improve safety and soundness in the financial system by placing more emphasis on banks' own internal control and management, the supervisory review process and market discipline. The 1988 Accord provided essentially one single option for measuring the appropriate capital of internationally active banks. The new framework provides a flexible structure in which banks will adopt approaches that best fit their level of sophistication and their risk profile, and will consist of three mutually reinforcing pillars:

1. minimum capital requirement;
2. supervisory review process; and
3. market discipline.

The first pillar sets out minimum capital requirements. The new framework maintains both the current definition of capital and the minimum requirement of 8 per cent of capital to risk-weighted assets. The bank's capital adequacy is measured as the ratio of: (1) total capital and (2) the sum of credit risk, market risk and operational risk. A risk weight of 100 per cent means that an exposure is included in the calculation of risk-weighted assets at its full value, which translates into a capital charge equal to 8 per cent of that value. Similarly, a risk weight of 20 per cent results in a capital charge of 1.6 per cent. As before half of the bank's measured capital should be held in Tier 1 form (shareholders' equity and retained earnings). The credit risk measurement methods are more elaborate than those in the current Accord. The new framework also proposes for the first time a measure for operational risk (expected to constitute on average approximately 20 per cent of the overall capital requirements under the new framework), while the market risk measure remains unchanged.

For the measurement of credit risk, two principal options are being proposed. The first is the standardised approach and the second the internal rating-based (IRB) approach, itself further split between a foundation and an advanced approach.

- The standardised approach is conceptually the same as in the present Accord, but is more risk-sensitive, as it proposes more risk categories and related weighting. The simple 'bucket' approach of the existing Accord had indeed given banks an incentive to move high-quality assets off the balance sheet, thus reducing the average quality of bank loan portfolios. As before, the bank allocates a risk weight to each of its assets and off-balance sheet positions and produces a sum of risk-weighted asset values. For corporate lending, the new risk weights are to be refined by reference to a rating provided by an external credit assessment institution (such as a rating agency). Risk categories also differ for 'specialised lending' (which includes commodity-based financing).
- Under the IRB approach (foundation and advanced), banks will be allowed to use their internal rating systems to allocate risk weighting, subject to strict methodological and disclosure standards.

(continued)

Exhibit 19.1 *(continued)*

Provisioning requirements and the main tenets of the new Basle Capital Accord

The new framework also introduces more risk-sensitive approaches to credit risk mitigation through the treatment of collateral, guarantees, credit derivatives and netting, as well as asset securitisation.

1. Credit risk mitigation

- *Collateral.* A collateral transaction is one in which (i) banks have a credit exposure or potential credit exposure to another party by virtue of cash or financial instruments lent or posted as collateral, or an OTC derivatives contract; and (ii) the exposure or potential exposure is hedged in whole or in part by collateral posted by the counterparty. Minimum conditions to qualify as collateral are legal certainty (perfection of security interest, legal opinion, proper documentation, etc), low correlation with exposure and robust risk management process. Commodities can be eligible as collateral for specialised lending. 'Haircuts' will be applied to the market value of collateral in order to protect against price volatilities.
- *Guarantees and credit derivatives.* Minimum conditions common for guarantees and credit derivatives are a robust risk management process and that they be direct, explicit, irrevocable and unconditional. There are also separate operational requirements for guarantees and credit derivatives. Credit protection will be recognised when given by either (a) sovereign entities, PSEs and banks with a lower risk weight than the obligor or (b) corporations (including insurance companies) including parental guarantees rated A or better.

2. Asset securitisation

The committee defines traditional securitisation as the legal or economic transfer of assets or obligations to a third party that issues asset-backed securities (ABS) that are claims against specific asset pools. Synthetic securitisation refers to structured transactions in which banks use credit derivatives to transfer the credit risk of a specified pool of assets to third parties, such as insurance companies, other banks and unregulated entities. In order for an originating bank to remove a pool of securitised assets from its balance sheet for the purposes of calculating risk-based capital the bank must transfer the assets legally or economically via a true sale – for example, by novation, assignment, declaration of trust or subparticipation to produce a 'clean break'.

The committee expects to neither raise nor lower the aggregate regulatory capital, inclusive of operational risk, for internationally active banks using the standardised approach.

Source: BIS.

finance: 'It is still under discussion as to how most international structured finance business will fare in this new system. Given the underlying intentions of Basle II, however, the omens cannot be good . . . transactions grow more and more complex. It is increasingly the case that it takes more than one financing technique to complete any business opportunity. Basle II bites at the very principles of structured finance'.[6] Moreover, under Basle II, most borrowers in the commodity sector of emerging countries would now fall in the highest risk category defined by the new Accord: 'The weighting of capital applied to emerging market assets on a simple level makes the assumption of default almost before the ink is dry on the loan agreement'.[7]

One consequence of this new top risk category may be a surge in financing structures in which commodities are sold outright rather than used as collateral to a loan. This would be the case, for instance, with structured prepayments (unless limited recourse) and factoring. Likewise, one could expect a further expansion of the securitised forms of structured commodity finance.

Fortunately, in October 2001, the Basle Committee for the first time proposed to treat structured commodity finance transactions differently from other corporate loans, including

Exhibit 19.2

Application of Basle II to commodity finance transactions

Commodity finance is defined as short-term financing for the acquisition of readily marketable commodities that are to be resold and the proceeds applied to loan repayment.

If the lender is able to determine the three key variables of probability of default (PD), loss given default (LGD) or exposure at default (EAD) in respect to its specialised commodity finance portfolio, commodity finance loans will be treated like any other 'Advanced IRB' corporate loan and be entitled to the appropriate risk weighting. Banks that can determine only the PD and LGD still have a great scope for reduced regulatory capital than under alternative approaches in respect of specialised commodity finance portfolios.

If a bank is able to calculate PD but unable to quantify the more complex LGD, the bank would be required to adopt the 'Foundation IRB' and apply the standard corporate LGD rate of 45 per cent for short- and medium-term commodity finance loans. This rate is subject to further reductions to the extent the exposure is covered by cash or qualified financial collateral, by physical commodities (minimum over-collateralisation of 140 per cent) and by eligible receivables (minimum over-collateralisation of 135 per cent), and meets structuring requirements and operational criteria.

The critical variable for Foundation and Advanced IRB banks is LGD, because this is the sole means of reversing the negative impact of a high PD for a BB or lesser-rated borrower (virtually all commodity borrowers in emerging countries). The technical guidance instructions provide, under the heading 'Operational Requirements', minimum requirements that a bank must apply in order to recognise collateral for the purposes of LGD calculations, both in its internal written policies and procedures, and as covenants and other conditions present in loans agreements. Specific requirements are established in the area of documentation, legal enforceability (physical collateral and receivables), risk management (receivables), collateral valuation (physical collateral), collateral liquidation (physical collateral), collateral inspection (physical collateral), insurance (physical collateral), priority claims and environment liability (physical collateral). Physical commodity or receivables collateral that does not meet the standards of eligibility would not be permitted to be taken into account for calculating LGD under the IRB approach.

For banks that are unable to calculate any of PD, LGD or EAD across their commodity finance portfolio the 'Basic Approach' should be used to determine whether the loan should be classified as 'strong', 'good', 'satisfactory', 'weak' or 'default'. These so-called 'Supervisory Rating Grades' correspond to mandatory risk weightings of 50 per cent to 75 per cent for loans rated 'strong', 75 per cent to 100 per cent for 'good', 150 per cent for 'satisfactory', 350 per cent for 'weak' and 625 per cent for 'default'. Considering that the weighting for non-rated corporate borrowers under the non-IRB approach is 100 per cent, there is clearly a large disincentive for IRB banks to enter into specialised commodity finance transactions with a risk rating lower than 'good'. Under the Basic Approach, individual structured commodity finance transactions are rated on the following criteria: (1) level of loan over-collateralisation; (2) country risk level and mitigation of country risk; (3) market liquidity of the commodity collateral; (4) financial strength of the off-taker including key ratios, track record and logistical capabilities for the particular commodity, trading controls, hedging policies and reliability of financial disclosure; (5) collateral control measures embedded in the financing facility; (6) the form of legal security; (7) the lender's ability to gain prompt access to the commodities and sales proceeds; and (8) insurance against loss or damage.

Source: Nicholas Budd (see note 8).

them under the 'specialised lending' category. In the future, provided that criteria are respected in terms of structure, collateral management and documentation, Basle II will enable the commodity sector to achieve competitive funding costs, as described in Exhibit 19.2.[8]

As explained by Nicholas Budd of law firm Denton Wilde Sapte, no development in commodity finance: 'has the potential to change the practice of cross-border commodity financing as dramatically as the Basle II Accord with its direct, immediate and relentless impact on the borrowing costs charged to commodity trading companies which are operating in a low-margin and highly competitive environment'.[9] This observation was echoed by

Diane Boogard of Fortis Bank: 'Trade finance instruments were hardly differentiated in capital weighting under the old BIS rules. More sophisticated models will be used to reallocate the capital of banks over newly defined risk categories . . . . The higher risks will become relatively more expensive. We therefore believe that structured commodity finance will provide good solutions to potential shrinking liquidity in emerging markets'.[10]

Nevertheless, in practice some forms of structured commodity finance are already attracting favourable provisioning requirements under the existing Basle Accord and could be expected to continue to do so under the new Accord. Typically negotiated for large transactions between loan arrangers and bank regulators, favourable treatment can be obtained for structured loans that are essentially trade-related and can be repaid within 360 days if need be, thus escaping potential external debt rescheduling agreements. Favourable provisioning requirements can even be obtained when the structure allows for the financing to extend into the medium term, provided that certain conditions are met regarding the possibility for participating banks to opt out. For example, the benchmark three-year prepayment deal arranged for Sonangol (Angola) in 1995 by UBS and BPOI attracted favourable provisioning requirements from the Bank of England. Likewise, the deal arranged back in 1989 for Sonangol by the same team of arrangers, but then on the back of the assignment of export receivables, was deemed not provisionable by most European bank regulators. This is because (as was explained in Part II) this three-year credit was provisioned on the basis that it was in reality a one-year credit. The receivables assigned during each year were so large in amount that if the loan were accelerated the cash flow would have been sufficient to repay the entire loan within 360 days following acceleration.

Integration of banks' commodities, trade and export finance operations

In the mid-1990s the offering by banks of structured finance products to support the trade and investment needs of their clients was typically split between various departments. For example, the London-based subsidiary of a large South African bank provided structured trade and commodity finance products under two divisions: (i) corporate and investment banking; and (ii) trade finance. The first division was in turn divided into three units: (a) a large 'specialised finance' unit, which developed 'imaginative and comprehensive solutions to business requirements' (medium- and long-term asset financing, infrastructure project financing and advice, structured debt, plus origination, distribution and trading of corporate securities); (b) an emerging markets finance unit (export credit finance, trade finance, project finance); and (c) an international banking unit (short-term trade finance products, letters of credit facilities, specialised international finance in the form of structured transactions, commodity finance, bid bonds and export syndication finance). The second division provided exclusively trade finance products (short-term trade finance, but also receivables finance, inventory finance and factoring), several of which were complex enough to qualify as structured finance. In short, the knowledge of structured trade and commodity finance at this South African bank was completely disseminated, at the expense of a consistent offering and risk management strategy. In many large banks, matters were further complicated by horizontal divisions across industries (oil and gas, metals and mining, forestry, paper and packaging, and so on).

In the past few years, however, many banks have integrated their structured commodity finance activities with their traditional trade finance departments, their commodity financing departments and/or their export credit departments. This is taking place for a variety of reasons. One factor has been the increasing willingness on the part of large OECD-based trading companies to offer prepayment terms for the goods supplied by emerging countries' borrowers, forcing banks to reassess their competitive strategy. As noted by one trade finance specialist: 'From the banker's perspective this is ideal, as it offers the chance to provide additional financing through parties that they know well, to those, generally in the emerging markets, who they do not. The enhancement of the "relationship return" can then permit an ongoing relationship at the base trade facility level. Many financial institutions now combine their commodity finance and structured trade finance teams in one operation to benefit from these synergies'.[12] WestLB, for example, at the end of 2001 opened a new structured commodity finance desk within its London-based international trade and commodity finance division (ITCF).

At the same time, the volume of traditional domestically led export credits in the operations of European banks has declined, to the benefit of trade finance with international companies and structured finance techniques. This is also affecting the organisation of banks. BNP Paribas, for example, has been developing an international network of 'trade centres' bringing short-term and longer-term trade-related products together under the same roof. Additionally, BNPP provides under its global energy and commodities group four broad categories of operations – namely commodity trade finance, structured financing, corporate activities and derivatives and futures – running from five geographical platforms worldwide. An even wider consolidation took place at ING Bank, which put together its activities in the field of trade and commodity finance, structured commodity finance, and structured export finance into a newly created international trade and export finance division (ITEF).

In the Awards for Excellence published by *Trade Finance* magazine in June 2003, SG and WestLB were ranked best structured commodity finance banks. In 2002, ING was ranked first, followed by WestLB. Other banks recognised for their expertise in this field were ABN Amro, Standard Bank London, RZB and BNP Paribas.

SCF capital market debt

In recent years more and more structured commodity finance deals have wound up in the capital markets, enabling commodity sector borrowers in emerging markets to finally tap this source of funds.

Attractive privately placements

Before the advent of structured commodity finance, the bulk of notes or bonds issued by the commodity sector originated from large companies based in industrialised countries. In general, these securities were not tied in to a particular trade or project financing need, although it was not uncommon for some features of the issue to be linked to the volume or price of the commodities produced. For instance, as far back as June 1986 the then Standard Oil issued a zero-coupon domestic bond that entitled investors to a bonus equal to 200 times the amount by which the oil price exceeded US$25 a barrel.

Just before the recent cycle of emerging market crises that began in South-East Asia in the summer of 1997, there was also a sizeable number of bond issues by Latin American oil companies. Many such bond issues were offered publicly. For example, in August 1997 the Argentinean oil company YPF took advantage of its new investment grade rating (BBB-) and publicly issued a US$300 million 10-year bond that carried a 7.75 per cent coupon and was priced at 162 basis points (bp) over US Treasuries. The issue price was at that time the tightest spread achieved by a Latin American corporate based in a non-investment grade country. A few bond issues were privately placed, for example the ¥25 billion, six-year bond issued the same year by Brazilian oil company Petrobras, with a 4.10 per cent coupon and priced at 210bp over the yen 'Libor' rate. The yen loan proceeds and debt service obligations were swapped into US dollars with a bank counterparty, so that the borrower did not have a currency or interest rate risk.

Recent emerging market financial crises have spurred the development of bond issues securitised by inventory or export receivables. These securitised bond issues have largely taken place through private placements, as opposed to public offers. Privately placed debt can actually incorporate unusual terms and conditions and be custom-tailored for companies with special problems or opportunities. Renegotiating the debt contract in response to unexpected developments is also relatively easy under a private placement. Private placements are also more conducive to smaller issues. All these characteristics have thus made private placement the favoured route for securitised capital market issues by commodity sector borrowers. Although institutional investors sometimes have restrictions regarding countries in which they can invest, these restrictions can usually be circumvented with structures relying on offshore SPVs, as was the case in the privately placed Mobil Nigeria securitisation mentioned previously.

As opposed to privately placed debt, publicly offered bond issues are highly standardised products and indeed investors rarely check the fine print in bond agreements. However, this 'hands off' attitude may change with the recent thrust to end the status of bond holders as de facto privileged creditors during external crises. Eventually, structured commodity finance deals should also support more frequent public bond offerings.

Wider range of financing opportunities

Companies also tend to turn to the capital markets as they grow, and the commodity sector is no exception. For example, referring to the RusAl conglomerate, a spokesperson for Natexis commodity finance in Paris noted that: 'RusAl said from the very beginning that its long-term financial strategy included access to international capital markets and ultimately an IPO. The first step was progressively to secure financing independently of international offtakers, and form relationships with international banks as well as Russian ones .... The second step is the development in parallel to debt finance of hybrid structures, which could include asset-backed notes. After that comes the possibility of bonds and an IPO'.[12] On the other hand, it is virtually impossible for most companies outside an OECD country to obtain an investment grade credit rating without convincing credit enhancement. Securitised issues may therefore be the only way for an emerging market issuer to obtain an investment grade rating. The above-mentioned Mobil Nigeria securitisation, for instance, attracted a Baa3 rating from Moody's. Nevertheless, even on the back of inventory or export receivables, at the present time and for the foreseeable future capital market solutions are realistic only for the top-tier emerging market borrowers.

Second-tier borrowers willing to attract capital market investors would have to offer really tightly structured deals to make them attractive. Lamon Rutten of UNCTAD believes that this is possible: 'There are many possibilities to apply [securitisations based on warehouse receipt financing enhanced by a third-party credit guarantee] in developing countries. For example, billions of US dollar of fertiliser stocks are currently not used to underwrite financings; there are also large stocks of seasonal commodities (eg, sugar and cotton) and food reserves. Collateral managers could take control over such stocks, and they (or a bank with which they work) could issue paper backed by physical inventory of these stocks'.[13]

Longer-term financing

In any case, capital market issues remain more expensive than comparable bank financing. Yet they can provide the longer-term financing that commercial banks, because of provisioning requirements, are unable to extend on their own to borrowers located in high-risk countries, as the maturity of structured commodity finance bank loans is still typically limited to, say, three to four years, and relies mainly on rollover mechanisms that would not be necessary with capital market debt. Encouraging the further development of structured financing techniques in the capital market is actually essential to counterbalance the detrimental impact that the Basle II provisioning requirements are likely to have on the availability of bank loans (of any maturity) to commodity sector borrowers in emerging countries.

Note in particular a possible route offered by capital market funds. Trading companies, such as Cargill, now regularly repackage some of their pre-export finance deals and sell them to investors, especially through hedge funds.

---

1 For a detailed discussion of 'push' and 'pull' factors influencing the demand for structured commodity finance, see 'Under-explored potential of SCF' by Lamon Rutten, *Trade Finance,* April 2002.

2 *A Primer On New Techniques Used by the Sophisticated Financial Fraudster, With Special Reference To Commodity Market Instruments* by Lamon Rutten, UNCTAD, 2003.

3 *Structured Trade and Commodity Finance In Emerging Markets: What Can Go Wrong and How To Avoid It* by John McNamara, Woodhead Publishing Limited, 2001.

4 'Performance risk deals' by John McNamara, *Trade Finance,* April 2002.

5 For more information refer to www.bis.org/publ/bcbsca.htm listing publications and press releases.

6 'Whither or wither' by Stephen Kemp (formerly first vice president and head of business development at KBC Bank), *Trade Finance,* April 2002.

7 Ibid.

8 Material in this exhibit is extracted from 'Treatment of structural and operational risk in commodity finance transactions under Basle II' by Nicholas Budd of Denton Wilde Sapte, *Trade and Forfaiting Review,* 2003.

9 Ibid.

10 'Pathfinders' by Alex Cox, *Trade Finance,* October 2001.

11 'Whither or wither' by Stephen Kemp, *Trade Finance,* April 2002.

12 'Consolidation pays off' by Simon Pirani, *Trade Finance,* March 2002.

13 'The under-explored potential of SCF', *Trade Finance,* April 2002.

Chapter 20

Equity

This chapter discusses equity financing and its relevance for the commodities sector. The discussion starts with a summary of the general characteristics and forms of equity available to the commodities sector, and continues with an overview of private and public equity finance opportunities.

Types of equity

Commodities sector companies use equity financing when they rely on internal funds, make equity or rights issues, or reduce dividend payments.

Internal funds

The most immediate source of financing for a company is internal funds.[1] For instance, in the commodities sector, the Argentinean company CAPSA relied partially on available internal funds to finance its secondary oil recovery programme in the mid-1990s.

Reliance on internal funds may also be a necessity if current market conditions are not favourable for an immediate debt or equity issue. In Argentina again, in the two years that followed the economic crisis that began in early 2001 foreign equity investors and lenders all but disappeared, and the local banking sector was in ruins. Argentinean companies were forced to rely on internally generated funds for the bulk of their financing needs, resulting of course in dramatic cuts in investment in all sectors of the economy. Internal funds can also become the only source of financing available to fund projects deemed too risky by third-party creditors.

Note that, following the example of the United States, many countries now permit companies to use internal funds to repurchase their own shares in order to sustain their share price or return money to shareholders other than through dividends. In 1998, Ghana's Ashanti Goldfields bought back shares on a massive scale at a cost of over US$20 million in order to restore the share price to what the company considered to be its true value.

New equity issues

In many emerging countries, rights issues are the most common method for public companies to issue equity, while preferred stock issues are a rarity. Again in the oil sector, an exception was the secondary offering of preferred shares worth US$534.9 million made in the mid-1990s by Petrobras. The issue comprised two billion preferred shares and ADS each representing 100 preferred shares. Brazilian investors (pension funds, banks, etc) took a fifth of the issue. Priced at a 3.3 per cent discount to the price of the shares traded on Bovespa (the Brazilian stock exchange), the preferred share offering was placed at what was up to then one of the smallest discounts for a Brazilian equity offering.

Convertible bonds are very popular among large commodity sector companies. For instance, analysing a database of convertible bonds[2] one can observe that between 1993 and 1996 there were in total 42 convertible bonds issued by natural resources companies, two-thirds of which came from the mining, metal and ores sector (for example gold, but also tungsten or titanium). The main countries of origination were South Korea, the United States and Japan. Half of the issues were denominated in US dollars, followed by Swiss francs, yen, French francs, Dutch guilders and even Russian roubles. In US dollar equivalents at the time of issue amounts ranged between US$7.9 million (for South Korea's DongYang Tinplate Industry Co) and US$347.0 million (for Russia's Lukoil). Maturities ranged between four years and 14 years.

Public companies in the commodities sector

As a company expands, internal resources and debt are not sufficient to finance the company's development. To raise large amounts as equity, a company is likely to seek to attract a wider range of investors by listing its shares on a stock exchange.

Wider range of financing alternatives

In the commodity sector, listed companies used to be either subsidiaries of multinational companies, or former large state-owned companies or commodity boards that were subsequently privatised (discussed below).

Companies decide to publicly list their shares on a stock exchange for a variety of reasons. The current decade is seeing private companies seek a listing to raise equity for their operations, giving them a wider choice in terms of future access to the capital market for both their debt and equity financing needs. This should mean less reliance on bank loans in general and on structured commodity bank loans in particular.

The extent to which the commodities sector has taken advantage of the opportunities offered by public equity varies enormously across the world. In Latin America and in Asia most commodities and mining producers are now listed on stock exchanges, while a quick analysis of the commodities companies listed on African stock exchanges in the late 1990s showed listed companies operating in a wide range of natural resources and agro-commodity sectors, although most of these companies still had a sizeable government or foreign (non-African) investor shareholding. This situation has since evolved, supported in part by the expansion of South African companies northwards. In the private sector, most public offerings of equity took place in the oil and mining sectors, in particular in Nigeria and South Africa.

Large companies operating in the commodities sector of emerging countries can raise larger amounts of equity by listing their shares directly on international stock exchanges. For instance, in the natural resources sector Russian oil and gas sector companies have widely used American depositary receipts (ADRs) to raise public equity in the United States, starting in December 1995 with Lukoil and followed in 1996 by Gazprom with a US$430 million public share offering. Likewise, in the 1990s many South African companies operating in the commodities sector (mainly natural resources) moved their domicile to London and sought a primary listing on the London Stock Exchange. Others listed their shares on the stock exchanges of Belgium, France, Germany, the United States or Switzerland. Listing shares on more than one exchange places companies in a better position to raise both debt and equity in the future. Similarly, South African companies expanding their operations northwards have tended to organise a secondary listing of their shares in the countries in which they operate, mainly Botswana, Namibia and Zimbabwe. The widest geographical spread is probably achieved by diamond producer De Beers, whose shares are listed on more than half a dozen stock exchanges outside South Africa. Dual listings of emerging countries' companies tend to have a detrimental effect on the smaller stock exchange in which the shares are listed, as international investors prefer to trade on the more sophisticated stock exchanges with higher liquidity and faster settlement. In this regard, the dual listing of Ashanti Goldfields is more problematic for the Ghana Stock Exchange than that of Randgold Resources for the Johannesburg Stock Exchange.

Privatisations

In the late 1980s (Latin America and South-East Asia) and the 1990s (Africa and central Europe), most of the initial public offerings (IPOs) that took place in emerging countries resulted from state divestiture or outright privatisation. In emerging countries, the pace of privatisation has been rapid throughout all economic sectors. In Africa again, some of the largest IPOs in fact occurred with the privatisation of former marketing boards or state-owned companies having a monopoly in the production or trade of a particular commodity. One of the first, largest and most visible privatisations was that of Ashanti Goldfields (Ghana) in 1994. In South Africa, most agricultural boards were phased out in 1997. After Ashanti, the long-awaited sale of Zambia's ZCCM in 1999 marked another milestone in the African mining sector. Still on the African continent, new privatisations are announced (although less often carried out) almost every month in the commodities sector. Even in Ghana and Côte d'Ivoire, which have long held out against privatisation, external pressure is leading to a drastic overhaul of the role of the state in cocoa production and marketing. Clearly resisting privatisation have been the national oil companies, although these companies are generally investing and financing project development in joint ventures with private international oil companies.[3]

How do privatisations serve the financing needs of the commodities sector? For a start, privatisations are not meant to raise new equity for the company, but to provide cash to the government. Yet some new equity is generally raised at the time of privatisation and, in any case, newly privatised and listed companies are in a better position to raise funds in the future. As summarised a few years ago by Valentine Chitalu, chief executive of the Zambia Privatisation Agency (ZPA):

> The most significant and lasting benefits will not be the cash received. Rather it will be the capital investments the new owners make into privatised companies, the jobs taken forward and the jobs created over the next few years, the liabilities assumed, the transformation of inefficient subsidised companies into growing profitable and competitive companies that generate expanding tax revenues – rather than deficits which consume revenues.

Advising governments, especially in the early stages of privatisation programmes, and investing in, or financing, privatised companies became one of the main activities of the IFC and other donor-supported organisations. However, in many emerging countries – and in most industrialised countries – privatisations have also been extremely controversial, not only because the privatisation process can be biased by vested interests, but also because privatisation represents a complete turnaround from the ideologies that shaped the liberation struggles of emerging countries. Criticism of privatisations have typically focused on four concerns.

1. *Privatisations replace state monopolies by private monopolies.* For example, when Uganda's Coffee Marketing Board Ltd was put up for sale, it had a processing capacity of 2.5 million bags a year against 1.6 million bags for the country's other 320 processors. The risk of creating a private monopoly can be mitigated in many ways, for instance by the appointment of a regulatory authority (setting performance targets, limitations on profits, and so on), or by breaking down a monopoly into several concessions before privatising.
2. *The sale of large companies to foreigners would amount to a new colonisation.* Empirical studies show the level of participation of foreign investors varies, ranging between more than half for recorded privatisations in eastern Europe and central Asia, where local capital was insufficient, to less than 10 per cent in southern Asia, where foreign participation was restricted. Some countries outright exclude foreign investors from primary public share offerings.
3. *Privatisations increase unemployment and threaten the stability of governments.* In the short term, privatisation goes hand-in-hand with restructuring, and this generally means laying people off. For example, the ZCCM privatisation sale to Anglo American was expected to eliminate more than 7,000 jobs. This could be acceptable if governments properly cushioned the short-term social harm brought about by privatisations, which, experience demonstrates, they generally have not done.
4. *Privatisations would mean losing control of key sectors of the economy.* Yet the *raison d'être* of privatisations is that the private sector should be better than the government at running companies. Nevertheless, some governments have insisted on retaining a controlling or critical interest (for example, in Ghana through partial 'divestitures'), which markedly reduced the attractiveness of privatisations to private investors.

In any case, short of conducting outright and immediate privatisations of the remaining commodity marketing boards and national petroleum or mining companies, emerging market governments should continue to steadily liberalise their markets, allowing more participants to get involved at the various stages of the cycle of commodity production in their country.

The impact of privatisation on the offer of structured commodity finance has been mixed. On the one hand, the disappearance of sovereign counterparties and related government guarantees has forced loan arrangers to devise more creative structures to mitigate performance and payment risk. On the other hand, the immediate lack of sizeable counterparties with a reliable track record probably temporarily reduced overall access to foreign exchange financing by the commodities sector.

Equity investors in the commodities sector

To simplify matters, the first part of this section is divided between strategic investors and financial investors. Companies based in emerging countries can also hope to attract equity investment from donor-supported investment funds.

Strategic investors

Strategic investors are typically operating in the same sector as the target company, and their equity investment may be aimed at complementing their offer of products and services in geographical regions or market niches or products that they do not cover. Certain companies may also be willing to invest equity in a company with which they have a new or established commercial relationship (such as a supplier) to show their long-term commitment. A strategic investor can also be the operating company of a new project. In the commodities sector certain project finance structures propose that the future operating company invests some equity in the new project, either as cash or, more frequently, as partial or full payment for its services or against its purchase of certain capital goods. For example, a preliminary proposal for the financing of Ghana's Tano gas-fuelled power project included a US utilities company providing the turbines in exchange for a share in the equity of the project. A commodity buyer may also buy a minority or controlling stake in a company producing a rare commodity in order to influence its production and commercial strategy.

Depending on circumstances, strategic investors can either become minority shareholders or take control of the company in which they invest. However, as many of the synergies and benefits of closer business relations can often be met without relinquishing control, companies and project sponsors should think twice before giving too much power to strategic investors.

Financial investors

The overwhelming objective of financial investors of private equity is to make money with their investment, not so much on the back of dividend payments but through the capital gains they hope to realise when they eventually sell their shares, usually when the company goes public.

Venture capital

Venture capital is the name generally given to equity investment in young private companies. Regardless of whether or not they have a majority of directors, venture capital companies are seldom silent partners. Their judgements and contacts can often prove useful to a relatively inexperienced management team. Venture capital is an appropriate source of financing for start-up companies with a big upside potential.

In the area of commodities, venture capital could be available to finance projects that have the potential to become extremely profitable. Companies that hold a potentially lucrative mining or exploration licence should therefore consider raising venture capital and subsequently listing their shares in a future round of financing. A myriad of junior mining companies are, for instance, listed on the Vancouver Stock Exchange (VSE) in Canada in order to finance investment in natural resource projects worldwide. One of these mining companies was actually the infamous Bre-X Minerals Busang gold deposit in Indonesia, which subsequently proved a sham and caused a drop in the value of other medium-sized mining companies, independently of their own commercial or financial situation.[4]

Venture capital would probably be less available to finance agro-projects, except perhaps where significant growth prospects can be expected (for example, with horticultural products). Moreover, an overseas listing is rarely used to finance start-up agricultural projects and therefore the development of venture capital for agro-projects is also restricted by the limited capacity of local stock exchanges.

Private equity financing for projects in the commodities sector of emerging countries is best sourced from local banks and other types of investors, or from donor-supported funds.

Banks

Merchant banks can invest equity in promising companies or as part of complex financing transactions that require equity, for example an acquisition financing. In emerging countries, some local banks have put equity into companies operating in the commodities sector.

Banks can also be equity investors in certain forms of structured finance, for example tax-driven financial leases. In many continental European countries, banks have also traditionally held large chunks of the equity of the main listed companies, through which they exercise a varying degree of control.

Investment funds

Investment funds differ from venture capital in that they normally have a much more 'hands off' style. However, having suffered in the Asian crisis of 1997–98 from the lack of influence that their minority ownership gave them, investment funds are now insisting on more participation in important decisions of the companies in which they have a stake.

Most investment funds invest only a small amount in private equity, typically a maximum of 15–20 per cent. This happens usually if the target company is about to be privatised or is expected to go public within two or three years. Thus, if a company is not listed on a stock exchange, its chances of attracting investment fund money are slimmer. A few investment funds, however, invest exclusively in private equity, some of which target energy or natural resources projects. Closed-end funds have no obligation to redeem shares until a set or contingent date in the future and as such are more appropriate for equity or debt investment in the small or thinly traded companies that constitute opportunities in the commodities sectors of emerging countries.

International funds

With regard to funds targeting emerging countries, maybe up to one-third of senior management's time is spent travelling, meeting companies, politicians, governors of central banks, local brokers, accountants, lawyers and so on. Fund managers also develop detailed proprietary databases that form the backbone of their strategy, be it top-down (that is, choosing the economic sector before the specific investment) or bottom-up (ie, picking up undervalued firms), or a combination of both. In any case, investment funds will invest in companies if the fund manager feels confident that it has obtained timely and reliable information about the company and the business environment. Companies unable or unwilling to fully open their books would therefore most often not be acceptable targets.

In high-risk environments, funds have the disadvantage of being potentially quick to sell if the wind changes. Massive sales by foreign fund managers greatly contributed to the dramatic fall in share prices on South-East Asian stock markets at the end of 1997 and subsequent currency crises in the region. In Africa, where foreign investors account for a much smaller share, their actions are visible and sometimes send strong signals to the market: for instance, when fund managers started to sell their holdings in the Zimbabwe Stock Exchange from the summer of 1997 onwards.

The number of investment funds is huge and they can track a particular index or specialise in every niche market that could be attractive to investors. There are high-yield funds, hedge funds, new technology funds, privatisation funds, small cap funds, global bond funds, etc, but there are very few investment funds targeting the commodities sector. A few years ago, out of the hundreds of funds listed on the *Financial Times's* FT Managed Funds Service, 20 or so were targeting commodities and natural resources. These funds can now be counted on the fingers of one hand, although several are now dedicated to equity investment in the energy sector. Some of the old commodities funds were actually taking positions on commodities futures markets, which did not bring any new money to the commodities sector and could also have had a destabilising effect on commodity prices.

Short of being supported by specialised funds, investment in companies operating in the commodities sector can also take place through emerging market funds selecting such companies as part of their investment portfolio. For instance, the prospectus of Baring's Simba Fund, a pan-African equity fund launched in the mid-1990s, stressed the fund's intention to 'diversify into low-cost volume exporters', anticipating that the growth in Asia's economies would benefit Africa's primary sectors – ie, mining, agriculture and tourism. The now defunct Simba Fund, like many other emerging market funds targeting Africa, thus invested an average of 10–15 per cent in the mining and agricultural sectors. Funds investing in countries with more diversified economies would obviously not be so much skewed in favour of commodities. In any case, with the exception of hedge funds, investment funds rarely bring new money, as they typically buy shares of listed companies from the market.

Local investment funds

Taking advantage of market liberalisation, local venture capitalists have also set up in several emerging countries Their time horizon is typically longer than that of 'traditional' venture capitalists. In general, local investment funds would gladly trade the hope of a rapid public issue for that of a profitable private sale, a high income stream many years in the future, or synergies with their own line of business. For example, an active local investment fund operating in West Africa is the Groupe d'Investissements et de Participations (GIP) of Côte d'Ivoire.

In South Africa, many of these new investment companies are part of a wider thrust at black empowerment and typically aim at channelling funds into black-owned businesses or at making investments that benefit the black population in general. Thus new investment in the commodities sector that promotes black empowerment could tap this source of funds.

Some funds are co-sponsored and financed by local financial institutions. This is the case, for instance, with South Africa's NewFarmers, which provides equity, debt and development advice to new farming projects in South Africa (see Exhibit 20.1[5]).

Development-oriented funds

Like NewFarmers, many local investment funds or venture capital companies are also seeking to promote economic development or other social goals, and thus are supported by bilateral or multilateral banks and development finance institutions. A few examples of such development-oriented funds are given below, while direct support from such institutions is discussed in the next chapter.

A few years ago, the African Development Bank (AfDB), for instance, invested US$2 million for a 13.3 per cent stake in the Zambia Venture Capital Fund (ZVCF). ZVCF makes grants and provides debt and equity financing to private sector companies, including small- and medium-sized enterprises, and the newly privatised Zambian companies with growth

Exhibit 20.1

NewFarmers Development Company Ltd (South Africa)

NewFarmers is South Africa's first venture capital investor and catalyst in the agribusiness sector. NewFarmers is an agricultural development fund investing equity in, and making loans to, agricultural projects in South Africa. The fund also aims to contribute to land and agricultural reform in general.

In 1996, NewFarmers raised R40 million through a private placement. About half of the private placement was taken by existing investors, which included several of the country's leading financial institutions, fruit and wine growers, and exporters. An additional equity stake of R25 million was to be offered to European development finance institutions. As of the end of 2002 NewFarmers had a paid-in capital of R51.4 million and expected to eventually listed its shares on the Johannesburg Stock Exchange.

NewFarmers' mandate is to 'create opportunities for viable farming enterprises, focusing on developing communities, through project development, loan finance and equity participation'. NewFarmers' involvement in projects is generally alongside other private investors, including, for example, commercial banks and farm owners, management and workers. Public aid can also be part of projects. NewFarmers normally prefers to take minority stakes of between 25 and 49 per cent with investment ranging from R1 million to R5 million.

While NewFarmers was created to benefit small black entrepreneurs, it is not strictly a development institution and each venture must be commercially viable. NewFarmers' own return on equity was anticipated to stabilise at around 20 per cent. In line with NewFarmers' commercial viability requirements, the fund tends to favour export-oriented projects. Initial focus was to be on the deciduous fruit, sub-tropical fruit, citrus, flower, wine and vegetable sectors. As explained by the managing director of the fund: 'These sectors are labour-intensive, but they are technically sophisticated. They lend themselves to further processing and thus are able to add value to the primary products. This in turn creates the opportunity for increasing the producer's overall profitability'.

One of the first projects of NewFarmers was the Onderburg project to expand sugar cane planting and banana production. The existing farm was to be purchased from the owner by a new partnership formed between his family trust, the existing management team, farm workers and NewFarmers. Total financing was R21 million of equity, broken down to around R12.4 million equity and R8.6 million loans (50 per cent NewFarmers, 50 per cent commercial banks).

Sources: NewFarmers; author's own research.

potential. Apart from the AfDB, the main sponsors and investors of ZVCF were the CDC Group (formerly the Commonwealth Development Corporation, CDC), the European Investment Bank (EIB), and the German (DEG), Dutch (FMO) and Swedish (SIDA or Swedfund) development finance institutions. Likewise, from 1990 to 1994, the United States Agency for International Development (USAID) ran an Africa Venture Capital Project (AVCP) whose objective was to provide equity and loan capital to small- and medium-sized companies in Africa. Small venture capital funds were actually started by USAID in Ghana, Tanzania and Uganda. CDC and the IFC also started, or contributed to the early stages of, a large number of venture capital funds operating around the world.

There are many 'hybrid' funds supporting new projects in the commodities sector by combining the strengths of public and private investors. For example, a few years ago the IFC established, in a joint venture with India's Creditcapital Venture Fund, the India Oil and Gas Finance Facility, which is geared towards small- and medium-sized projects in India's oil and gas sector. Likewise, a US$30 million fund was launched to invest in the African mining sector (excluding oil and gas) supported by CDC, Lion Selection group (Australia), Comafin (a CDC group investment fund for Africa), and two South African banking groups, Investec and Rand Merchant Bank.

[1] The 'pecking order' theory argues that companies prefer to rely on internal funds and, if these are not sufficient, prefer raising debt over equity. Factors playing against equity include higher issuance costs, wider disclosure requirements, fear of sending negative signals to the market and reluctance to dilute ownership.

[2] Source: Bondware.

[3] For more information about the African oil sector refer to the annual African Oil Trade and Finance conferences organised by UNCTAD, and to conferences organised by Europe Energy Environment Limited and CWC Associates.

[4] See the presentation by Pieter Wesselink, head of emerging markets finance, Investec Bank, at the Third Annual Global Forum: Structured Commodity and Trade Finance, organised by IBC in Amsterdam, December 1997.

[5] *Africa Financing Review,* March 1999.

Chapter 21

Non-commercial sources of financing and support

This chapter discusses financing available from institutions whose prime objective is not profit but development, even though some of them are increasingly operating on a commercial basis. The discussion covers multilateral and regional development banks, development finance institutions, and other forms of official development assistance.

Multilateral development banks and financial institutions

The World Bank group, as well as other multilateral and regional banks and financial institutions, provides loan and equity financing, as well as insurance and guarantees (discussed in Part III), advice and other forms of support to governments and/or companies in emerging countries.

The largest multilateral development banks are the affiliates of the World Bank group. Other multilateral banks operate on a regional basis. Development banks are concerned with economic development and poverty alleviation (now explicitly part of their mission), and as such are more involved in building physical and institutional capacity than in fostering particular sectors of the economy.

It is beyond the scope of this book to investigate the range of activities conducted by every multilateral and regional bank to determine to what extent they have been involved in the commodity sector. However, a brief overview of their operations, as well as selected examples, should be useful in assessing their potential involvement in financing the trade and investment finance needs of the commodity sector.

The World Bank group

The main affiliates of the World Bank group are the International Bank for Reconstruction and Development (IBRD), commonly referred to as the World Bank; the International Finance Corporation (IFC), which operates exclusively in the private sector; and the International Development Association (IDA), which covers the poorest countries.

In its own words: 'The World Bank group is one of the world's largest sources of development assistance. In fiscal year 2002, the institution provided more than US$19.5 billion in loans to its client countries. It works in more than 100 developing economies with the primary focus of helping the poorest people and the poorest countries'.[1]

International Bank for Reconstruction and Development (IBRD) and International Development Association (IDA)

There are two types of bank lending. The first type is for developing countries that are able to pay near-market interest rates (IBRD countries). The second type of loan goes to the poorest countries (IDA countries), which are usually not creditworthy in the international financial markets and are unable to pay near-market interest rates on the money they borrow.

At US$11.5 billion, new lending by IBRD in the fiscal year ending June 2002 was US$1 billion higher than the previous year. Public administration was by far the leading sector for IBRD lending, receiving US$3.6 billion (almost a third of the total), reflecting the bank's focus on assisting its clients to improve development strategies, implement reforms and build institutional capacities. IBRD lending to agriculture, fishing and forestry, and to the energy and mining sectors, represented only 5 per cent and 6 per cent respectively.

International Finance Corporation (IFC)

The IFC 'promotes sustainable private sector investment in developing countries as a way to reduce poverty and improve people's lives. IFC operates on a commercial basis. It invests exclusively in for-profit projects and charges market rates for its products and services, which cover three broad areas: financial products; advisory services; and resource mobilisation'.[2]

- *Financial products.* The IFC's traditional and largest activity is to finance private sector projects in developing countries. The IFC provides loans, equity finance and quasi-equity. It also offers financial risk management products and intermediary finance.
- *Advisory services.* The IFC provides advice and technical assistance to private businesses and governments in developing countries. These services cover a broad spectrum, including advice on privatisation, business-related public policy and industry-specific issues.
- *Resource mobilisation.* The IFC helps companies in developing countries tap into international capital markets. The cornerstone of the mobilisation effort is the loan participation programme, which arranges syndicated loans from banks. The IFC also mobilises financing from international financial institutions through investment funds, underwriting, securitisation, private placement and other innovative approaches. By acting as a catalyst, the IFC leverages its limited resources to a maximum.

Although the IFC lends on market terms, it does not compete with, but rather complements, private capital. The IFC invests in projects that meet its investment criteria, but which cannot get financing and/or technical expertise elsewhere on reasonable terms. The IFC's presence is beneficial to a project from a financial as well as a technical and political standpoint. Foreign investors seek the IFC's participation because of its extensive hands-on knowledge of how to do business in developing countries and because of its excellent relationships with developing country governments. The IFC's status as an independent international organisation reassures both foreign investors and host countries, and it can provide added comfort by helping companies and sponsors to negotiate with host governments.

For the fiscal year ended June 2002 the IFC committed US$3.1 billion of new money, with 40 per cent going to the financial sector, reflecting the IFC's use of financial institutions as intermediaries (to finance small and medium-sized companies) and investment in collective investment vehicles.[3] New commitments were 5.9 per cent in the food and beverages sector, 1.4 per cent in the agriculture and forestry sector, and 3.5 per cent in the oil, gas, mining and chemicals sector.

Two of the IFC's specialised departments are relevant to the commodity sector: (a) oil, gas, mining and chemicals; and (b) agribusiness. To improve the effectiveness and reach of its activities in the mining sector, the World Bank group actually combined IBRD/IDA and IFC operations in the sector within a global oil, gas, mining and chemicals department. The new department aims to bring closer together work on the public sector policy side and the private sector investment support side, to achieve synergies and provide a simpler and more direct contact point for government, private sector and civil society clients.

Oil, gas, mining and chemicals (OGMC)

In its own words: 'The World Bank group envisions a mining sector that, by attracting responsible private investments, creates a foundation for economic and social well-being and environmental sustainability. In the mining sector, the World Bank group provides/facilitates three types of projects.

1. Equity investment in and loans to mining companies, including loans syndicated from commercial banks under the IFC's syndications loan umbrella.
2. Loans and grants to governments financing the development and implementation of government policies that support private sector development.
3. Various risk management instruments (IBRD/IDA/MIGA)'.

An example of a project approved in this sector in the early 2000s was the US$2 million equity investment by the IFC into a new project for Kalahari Diamonds Ltd (KDL) through its Godi (Proprietary) Ltd subsidiary in Botswana. KDL's ownership was expected to be 40 per cent institutional investors (including the IFC), 40 per cent institutions involved in diamond cutting, polishing and retailing, and 20 per cent BHP Billiton Group (the project sponsor). In another project, signed in December 2002, the IFC will lend up to US$20 million to finance the US$72 million development of the Galata offshore gas field in Bulgaria.

Agribusiness

The IFC supports projects involving primary agricultural production, aquaculture and fishing, as well as marketing (for example, silos, cold and controlled atmosphere storage facilities, and wholesale markets), food processing and distribution. The IFC's objective is to support the development of efficient agribusiness systems from producers to consumers in developing countries. As a general rule, preference is given to investment projects that have the largest demonstrated benefits to the overall efficiency and competitiveness of the supply chain, and make the highest overall contribution to economic development.

In fiscal year 2002 the IFC presented 17 projects for approval in the agribusiness sector. In particular, the IFC is involved in a US$60 million project with Vicentin, Argentina's second leading family-owned oilseed processor and exporter company. The proposed IFC investment is a US$30 million 'A' loan for its own account and up to US$30 million via a syndicated 'B' loan that will enable Vicentin to continue soybean and sunflower seed purchases. This particular facility was structured as a short-term, pre-export finance, export receivables-backed facility, renewable annually for a maximum of three years. The IFC's participation in this project will provide capital not accessible today from the markets for Argentina, enhance the operational and financial sustainability of a major domestic agro-exporter, and also ensure the participation of foreign investors through a 'B' loan. This is an important development, representing the involvement of the IFC (and also the IBRD and the EBRD) in short-term secured lending operations. In the case of Argentina, the transaction is in the nature of disaster relief, because of a total lack of liquidity in the domestic banking system. However, there are other, more straightforward examples, such as the IFC's oil export loan guarantee programme in West Africa and the EBRD's warehouse receipt finance facility. This means that the multilateral institutions, in spite of their charter limitations, are going in for short-term commodity-related finance deals as a quick way to get liquidity into client countries. This is an important new development that could have a major impact on during the next few years.

Another significant project in terms of value added provided by the IFC was the US$5.8 million project approved in June 2002 for Eberege Tea Factory Ltd in Kenya, in which the IFC invested US$1.8 million for its own account. Sponsored by the Kenya Tea Development Agency (KTDA), a private company that provides management services to local smallholder tea factories, the project will finance the construction of a new tea factory to process green-leaf tea, primarily for export. The IFC will provide long-term foreign currency finance, which is not otherwise available in Kenya.

The IFC's loans and equity investments can also be combined with World Bank guarantees. This was the case, for example, with the US$223 million Azito Power project (Côte d'Ivoire's second independent power project), in which the IFC provided US$10 million in equity and US$62 million in loans, and where the private investments were in part covered by an IDA partial risk guarantee.

The World Bank group is also involved in specific initiatives for the commodities sector, in particular through the International Task Force (ITF) on commodity price risk management. Some of the operations sponsored by the ITF's Commodity Risk Management Group (CRMG) involve a finance element and thus border on structured commodity finance. For example, in 2002 CRMG began a pilot study with the Coffee Board of India and a bank in the State of Karnataka to deliver risk management instruments in conjunction with credit.[4]

Regional development banks

Multilateral development banks operating on a regional basis include the European Bank for Reconstruction and Development (EBRD), the Asian Development Bank (ADB), the African Development Bank (AfDB) and the Inter-American Development Bank (IDB).

The European Bank for Reconstruction and Development (EBRD)

The EBRD was established in 1991 'when communism was crumbling in central and eastern Europe, and ex-soviet countries needed support to nurture a new private sector in a democratic environment. Today the EBRD uses the tools of investment to help build market economies and democracies in 27 countries from central Europe to central Asia'.[5] The EBRD invests mainly in private companies, usually together with commercial partners, providing project financing for banks, industries and businesses, both new ventures and existing projects. It also supports privatisation, restructuring of state-owned firms, improvement of municipal services and other policies that bolster the business environment.

Agribusiness has become one of the major sectors for the EBRD, with cumulative commitments of over €2.56 billion invested in 153 transactions in 21 countries. However, the EBRD has strategically concentrated its efforts downstream of agricultural production, mostly in agro-processing, marketing and distribution. Notable in the agribusiness sector, for example, was the US$15 million loan approved in 2001 for a warehouse receipt programme for Cargill Ukraine.

The EBRD also provides financing for oil (covering the whole product cycle), gas, coal-mining, and mining of precious and non-precious metals. In the natural resources sector one of the EBRD's recent flagship deals was a €96 million financing to Rosneft-Sakhalinmorneftegaz (R-SMNG), a subsidiary of Russian government-owned Rosneft. The EBRD's long-term loan will support R-SMNG's investment programme on Sakhalin island. In particular, the financing will allow the company to continue production drilling at Odoptu-More field and to implement an environmental action plan, which includes provision for improvements in equipment and training for oil spill response and emergency response. It will also serve its working capital needs and enhance the company's liquidity by restructuring its short-term debt.

The African Development Bank (AfDB)

In its own words: 'The African Development Bank group, in its capacity of premier financial development institution of Africa, is dedicated to combating poverty and improving the lives of people on the continent, and engaged in the task of mobilising resources towards the economic and social progress of its regional member countries (RMCs)'.[6] The bank's principal functions are: (i) to make loans and equity investments for the economic and social advancement of the RMCs; (ii) to provide technical assistance for the preparation and execution of development projects and programmes; (iii) to promote investment of public and private capital for development purposes; and (iv) to respond to requests for assistance in coordinating development policies and plans of RMCs. The ADB group includes the AfDB, the African Development Fund and the Nigeria Trust Fund.

The AfDB's involvement in soft commodities has been mainly through projects targeted at rural development in general. In the natural resources sector a few oil, gas and mining projects were approved in 2001, including, for example, a US$12.5 million loan to Liptake Mining Company (SML) to finance the Samira Hill project in Niger, involving the construction of a gold mine and a processing plant. SML SA is a limited liability company governed by the laws of Niger and established in December 1999 between the government of Niger (20 per cent) and the African GeoMin Mining Development Corporation, AGMDC (80 per cent), controlled by ONA of Morocco and Etruscan Resources Inc. of Canada.

The Asian Development Bank (ADB)

The ADB is a multilateral development finance institution dedicated primarily to reducing poverty in Asia and the Pacific region.[7] In 2002, the ADB approved 89 loans and four equity investments valued at US$5.7 billion, 324 technical assistance projects valued at US$178.7 million, and four guarantees amounting to US$885 million.

As regards agricultural commodities, the ADB is primarily involved in rural financing and technical assistance. For instance, in 2002 it approved the US$40 million financing of a government-supported tea and fruit development project in Vietnam, providing a credit line for field development, nursery operations and small- and medium-scale processing of these crops. There does not seem to be much ADB involvement in the natural resources sector.

The Inter-American Development Bank (IDB)

The IDB's[8] objectives are to finance the development of the borrowing member countries; to supplement private investment when private capital is not available on reasonable terms and conditions; and to provide technical assistance for the preparation, financing and imple-

Exhibit 21.1

The African Export–Import Bank (Afreximbank)

Afreximbank was created in 1993 under the auspices of the AfDB to facilitate, promote and expand intra-African and extra-African trade. To this end, the bank's functions include:

(i) extending direct credit to eligible African exporters in the form of pre- and post-shipment export finance;

(ii) extending indirect short-term credit (up to 12 months) and medium-term credit (over one year up to seven years) by way of lines of credit (LOCP) to eligible trade finance intermediaries;

(iii) promoting and financing intra-African trade and non-traditional African exports;

(iv) financing export-generative African imports of equipment, spare parts and raw materials;

(v) providing risk-bearing facilities, such as the issuance and confirmation of letters of credit, guarantees and bill-discounting facilities;

(vi) providing insurance services, covering commercial and non-commercial risks associated with African exports; and

(vii) providing support to payment arrangements in Africa and financing South–North trade.

In practice, Afreximbank essentially supports the commodity sector of Africa. For example, LOCP have been useful to assist newly established private commodity trading companies that are slowly replacing the state-owned monopolies. Afreximbank can also channel financing through various other facilities, including the direct financing programme (DFP), the syndication programme (SP) and the project-related financing programme (PFP). The PFP has a very particular role, in that it is provides medium-term financing (maximum seven years) that would otherwise be difficult to obtain on a strictly commercial bank basis, even on the basis of structured finance. In the area of medium-term financing Afreximbank offers additional facilities under a special risk programme (SRP) – namely country risk guarantees, export credit insurance, price and exchange rate guarantees, joint bill discounting/financing, and countertrade-linked guarantee facilities. In many cases, Afreximbank is able to accept local currency assets (for example, pledges of Treasury bills or government bonds) as collateral for the provision of loan guarantees expressed in hard currency (backed by its own strong credit rating). Afreximbank also provides bid bonds and performance guarantees.

Through its forfaiting programme, Afreximbank offers without-recourse discounting facilities for bills of exchange, promissory notes, irrevocable letters of credit and receivables – in the case of obligations from governments, large companies and subsidiaries of certain multinationals, even without guarantees by an acceptable bank. These facilities are available for most African countries, for maturities ranging from 180 days to around seven years. Furthermore, the country risk guarantees proposed by Afreximbank are extremely useful for financing new projects. The preferred creditor status of Afreximbank also means that its guaranteeing of a loan enables lenders to obviate the heavy provisioning they would otherwise have to make for medium-term loans to African companies. As far as joint bill discounting is concerned, it has enabled Afreximbank to share the payment risk of African banks through funded participations in certain trade finance deals.

In short, Afreximbank has designed and operated many facilities that are extremely attractive to the commodity sector. Some of these facilities enable the bank to participate in transactions arranged by commercial banks and, since these transactions are increasingly structured, it can be argued that Afreximbank has supported the development of structured commodity finance. Increasingly, Afreximbank is itself leading in the structuring of financings in non-traditional sectors and countries. Also, Afreximbank is making a deliberate effort to educate domestic banks throughout the continent on structured financing techniques. At the same time, the activities of Afreximbank in the area of medium-term financing are probably very attractive on a stand-alone basis for a company operating in the commodity sector, provided, of course, that the proposed transaction supports trade with or within Africa.

Sources: Afreximbank; author's own research.

mentation of development plans and projects. Annual lending was US$7.9 billion in 2001. The IDB's operations cover the entire spectrum of economic and social development. In addition to the bank, the IDB group consists of the Inter-American Investment Corporation (IIC), dedicated to small- and medium-sized private companies, and the Multilateral Investment Fund, also geared to the private sector.

In the agricultural sector, the IDB recently approved a US$14.4 million loan to support small- and medium-scale farmers in low-income areas. The programme's goal is to raise competitiveness through techniques, such as conservation agriculture and organic farming, that will allow producers to take advantage of market opportunities and improve their management of natural resources. The only IDB involvement in the mining, oil and gas sector has seemed to be through its private sector arm and is in any case marginal. One notable exception was the US$132 million financing (a US$75 million 'A' loan and US$57 million 'B' loan) approved to Transredes SA to support a capital investment plan for its natural gas pipeline operations in Bolivia.

Other regional banks

Development finance is also provided by smaller regional development banks, such as, in Africa, the PTA Bank,[9] the Development Bank of Southern Africa or the African Export–Import Bank (Afreximbank). Based in Cairo (Egypt), Afreximbank is particularly useful in financing the commodity sector. Its activities are summarised in Exhibit 21.1.[10]

A few other multilateral development institutions are based in industrialised countries and yet support a wide range of projects in developing countries – for example, the European Investment Bank (EIB). In the farming/fishery/forestry sector, in 2001 the EIB approved a US$3.5 million loan to finance the construction of facilities for the production of geraniums in Kenya. The EIB does not have a natural resources sector but a few gas-related projects in its energy sector, such as a US$20 million loan for the extension of a natural gas distribution and transmission network in Portugal.

Development finance institutions

To assist in the determination or implementation of bilateral official development assistance (ODA) most donor countries have set up development finance institutions (DFIs). The largest bilateral DFIs include Belgium's Société Belge d'Investissement (SBI-BMI); France's Groupe Agence Française de Développement (AFD) and its private arm Proparco; the United Kingdom's CDC Group, now functioning virtually as a private commercial company; Denmark's Industrialisation Fund for Developing Countries (IFU); Germany's Deutsche Investitions-und-Entwicklungsgesellschaft (DEG); The Netherlands' Nederlandse Financierings Maatschappij voor Ontwikkelingslanden (FMO); Finland's FinnFund; Spain's Compania Espanola de Financiacion del Desarollo (Cofides); Italy's Societa Italiana per le Imprese Miste all'Estero (SIMEST); Sweden's SwedFund (SIDA); the US Agency for International Development (USAID); Portugal's Banco de Fomento e Exterior; the Japan International Cooperation Agency (JICA); and the Overseas Economic Cooperation Fund (OECF).

Not all bilateral DFIs operate in the same way. A few have specific or preferred geographical criteria, such as CDC in former British Commonwealth countries and AFD in France's former colonies, but the majority of DFIs are active worldwide. The financing offered by DFIs is normally in the form of both debt and equity. Although most DFIs are now seeking to operate on a commercial basis, the debt financing is generally cheap. Consequently, the financing package may be an attractive alternative to structured commodity finance transactions arranged by commercial banks. DFIs are increasingly, and sometimes exclusively, focusing on the private sector.

Bilateral development finance institutions can provide attractive long-term financing to the commodity sector, provided that the underlying project has a clear benefit for the economic development of the country. A company seeking equity or debt financing from DFIs should also be prepared to relinquish some managerial or ownership control.

Other forms of government support

Government financial support can take the form of concessional lending, grants, or direct or indirect subsidies, as well as insurance and guarantees (discussed in Part III). Governments can also support certain sectors of the economy by sustaining ad hoc projects and programmes, in particular through United Nations agencies.

Direct and indirect financial support

Local and regional government aid is widely available for the commodity sector of industrialised countries, both in the field of natural resources (for example, government subsidies to coal mines in northern Europe or the recent US tariff against steel imports) and for agricultural commodities. The EU, for instance, hands out cash to olive oil producers in most parts of Italy. On a bigger scale, subsidies available as part of the Common Agricultural Policy continue to consume about half of the budget of the EU and are being increasingly criticised – especially in view of the planned enlargement of the EU. Paradoxically, there does not seem to be the same level of support from governments of emerging countries, where privatisation and liberalisation of the producing and trading activities of companies operating in the commodity sector have been actively encouraged by the Bretton Woods institutions.

Governments should always be careful in granting direct or indirect financial support to specific sectors of the economy, as badly designed and managed schemes can have perverse effects on the local, regional and international economy. In general, government support should be limited to specific areas, such as young or strategic industries. Therefore, companies should not count on, and be vulnerable to, sudden changes in aid policies or regulations, or be tempted to influence illegally the granting of such aid. In any case, government support in emerging markets is typically for capacity-building or new development-oriented projects, more rarely to finance recurring trade transactions or fixed capital investment.

UN agencies

UN agencies can support the commodity sector both directly (eg, through loans, grants, proprietary projects and programmes) and indirectly (eg, by giving advice, influencing government policies, and so on). First on the list is the United Nations Conference on Trade and Development (UNCTAD). Two other main UN agencies are also involved with the commodity sector by virtue of their focus on the agricultural sector: the Food and Agriculture Organisation (FAO) and the International Fund for Agricultural Development (IFAD).

United Nations Conference on Trade and Development (UNCTAD)

Based in Geneva, UNCTAD has evolved as the leading international organisation assisting commodity-dependent countries to enhance their capacity to use structured finance as well as modern commodity price risk management tools. The work of UNCTAD in this respect involves policy advice, training and technical cooperation activities, and is geared to both the private and the public sectors for both agricultural and natural resources commodities.

Much of the recent work of UNCTAD has focused on warehouse receipt finance and more complex forms of structured finance. With respect to warehouse receipts, UNCTAD has focused on the requirements for introducing tradable warehouse receipts and on the mechanisms through which these receipts can be used to facilitate finance. This has included the development of organised market-places (physical or through an electronic network) where warehouse receipts can be traded. UNCTAD is also a forum where discussion of the latest techniques and applications of structured finance tools can take place, in particular through its expert meetings and regular conferences.

UNCTAD has also specialised in the legal and regulatory requirements necessary to take full advantage of these techniques, such as clear ownership rules, bankruptcy laws and export licensing regulations. In this regard, UNCTAD has been actively encouraging governments to promote the necessary reforms and has also warned all parties against the risks of fraud in structured commodity finance.

Common Fund for Commodities

At the initiative of UNCTAD, the Common Fund for Commodities[11] was established in 1989 as an intergovernmental financial institution. Currently the Common Fund has 106 member countries, plus the EU, the African Union (AU) and the Common Market for Eastern and Southern Africa (Comesa). The rationale of the Common Fund's mandate is 'to enhance the socio-economic development of commodity producers and contribute to the development of society as a whole'. The Common Fund is specifically mandated to assist emerging countries with commodity price risk management, and it is also involved in warehouse receipt and commodity finance development projects in Russia and sub-Saharan Africa. For example, in 2001 the Common Fund launched, and provided the initial funding (grant) for, a three-year programme to provide financing to small coffee and cotton exporters in certain eastern and southern African countries on the back of inventories held in selected warehouses. This collective programme allows high-risk borrowers to obtain small loans (US$5–10 million) which otherwise could not be structured economically.

The Food and Agriculture Organisation (FAO)

Created in 1945 to raise levels of nutrition and standards of living, to improve agricultural productivity, and to better the condition of rural populations, the FAO intervenes mainly through a mixture of direct development assistance, collection, analysis and dissemination of information, and advice to governments. A particular focus of the FAO is to improve access to finance by rural populations. Its guiding principles in this area are to promote realistic interest rates, to encourage mobilisation of local savings, and to facilitate the development and efficient operation of a variety of financial intermediaries – including those in the informal sector. In particular, the FAO provides a forum for coordination between rural financial institutions in emerging countries and organisations and agencies in industrialised countries. The FAO also supports the formation of regional agricultural credit associations, the members of which are specialised agricultural banks, central banks, commercial banks, cooperative banks and other institutions involved in rural finance.

International Fund for Agricultural Development (IFAD)

The IFAD seeks to improve the productivity of on- and off-farm activities for the benefit of the rural poor (poor farmers, herders, fishermen, craftsmen and, across all groups, poor rural women). Its domain of intervention is not as wide as that of the FAO, since generally the IFAD is only involved in the identification, design and funding of projects. The IFAD is authorised to supervise the implementation of a limited number of exceptional projects. A notable example of a recent operation relevant to the commodity sector is the US$12.5 million smallholder flood plains development programme in Malawi. The project involved a combination of irrigation development, better crop production techniques, training on the importance of protecting the water attachment areas for irrigation and credit to enable farmers to finance their on-farm investments.

In short, most of the support provided by the FAO and the IFAD to the agricultural commodity sector is in the form of proprietary projects.

Evaluation of non-commercial financiers

Multilateral and smaller regional development banks can provide attractive financing (debt and equity), as well as insurance and guarantees, to borrowers in emerging countries. Their involvement is generally through co-financing, which stretches their resources over a broader portfolio of projects, while giving co-lenders or co-investors additional assurances of the quality of projects and the prospect of reduced sovereign risk attributable to their presence. In addition, multilateral institutions are increasingly responsive to the needs of their private partners.

However, multilaterals do impose more restrictions than commercial lenders. For instance, in supporting the Chad–Cameroon pipeline, the IFC was deeply involved in issues of good governance and the impact of the project on the environment. It may be argued that this was the main rationale for the involvement of the World Bank group in that project. Each project is supported by a thorough environmental document, and attracts a specific rating on environmental and social issues (child labour, resettlement of population and so forth). Raising a loan from multilaterals takes time. It also depends on the state of relations between the country and the Bretton Woods institutions.

The involvement of the World Bank and regional development banks in the commodity sector is important in terms of rural development and capacity-building for emerging countries. For its part, the IFC is an active lender and equity investor in greenfield projects, predominantly in the natural resources sector. The IFC has also shown its availability to support trade and working capital financing needs, adding value through long-term financing and commitments to countries facing difficulties in attracting commercial financing (eg, Argentina). Another reliable provider of trade finance has been Afreximbank (see Exhibit 21.1), whose particular mandate is actually geared at promoting trade within the Africa region.

As mentioned in Part III, structured finance techniques have been adopted by export credit agencies, as their traditional guarantee structures have proved more elusive due to the withdrawal of governments from commercial transactions and the emerging countries' bank failures of the late 1990s. The Italian export credit agency SACE, for example, has a separate division dealing exclusively with structured transactions through which it can provide cover to countries otherwise not acceptable. Multilateral banks, especially those involved in the private sector such as the IFC or the EBRD, also extensively use structured commodity finance techniques. Likewise, the PTA Bank has specialised in the provision of inventory financing to small commodity sector borrowers.

In fact, many commercial banks complain that multilaterals have become too commercial, in effect competing with commercial banks in the same markets for the same deals – and increasingly with similar use of structured finance risk mitigating methods. Multilaterals, of course, deny the accusation, but examples abound to prove that they are often involved in transactions that could probably fly with commercial investors and lenders alone. For example, in 1996 the IFC supported a US$61 million financing for the expansion of Chile's Fundicion Refimet's copper smelter. A few months earlier, a US$1.75 billion 10-year financing was closed for a much bigger mining project in Chile (the Collahuasi copper and gold mine) without any multilateral loan or guarantee.

In countries where private international inflows are still limited – for example in most of sub-Saharan Africa – multilateral banks and financial institutions still retain a decisive role. They also become vital for all emerging countries and economies in transition during a financial crisis. Increasingly, and especially in the commodities sector, multilaterals are also paying special attention to the natural environment, which commercial lenders may not fully commit to if left on their own.

---

[1] *Source:* www.worldbank.org.

[2] *Source:* www.ifc.org.

[3] Standard & Poor's report on the IFC, November 2002.

[4] *The ITF Quarterly*, Vol. 4, 30 January 2003.

[5] www.ebrd.com.

[6] www.afdb.org.

[7] www.adb.org.

[8] www.idb.org.

[9] www.ptabank.org.

[10] www.imf.org/external/np/sec/decdo/aeib.htm.

[11] www.common-fund.org.

Chapter 22

Geographical spread

Although various forms of structured commodity finance have mushroomed in specific regions or countries, such as export receivables-backed financing in the CIS countries or prepayment in Angola, this financial product is steadily expanding to every corner of the world, adjusting to the local commercial, financial and regulatory situation. As noted by one market specialist:

> Collateral management [structured commodity finance] has become successful in the former eastern bloc countries, the CIS and Africa. It is also gaining more awareness and acceptance in Asia. It is not surprising that collateral management is mainly practised in emerging markets and countries suffering certain degrees of political instability. In many of these countries traditional forms of trade financing are not readily available and a considerable number of companies face liquidity problems.[1]

Through mainly anecdotal evidence the following sections discuss the use of structured commodity finance techniques in different regions of the world.

Russia and other former CIS countries

After Russia's external finance crisis in August 1998, Russian borrowers jumped onto the structured finance bandwagon. Compared with other regions, however, Russian borrowers often paid a high interest rate to raise foreign exchange loans, even on the back of structured transactions. This was due to the fact that banks asked for a premium to compensate for the higher risk resulting from sometimes, unclear corporate ownership and management structure. Nevertheless, amounts raised were generally very large and maturities rapidly extended into the medium term.

The bulk of structured loans at this stage went to large oil producers. Later, banks ventured into other sectors, in particular gas and aluminium, and to second-tier oil producers, as pricing on structured loans to the local oil majors had become too tight. In 2002, for example, Natexis syndicated a three-year US$30 million loan to Ritek, a small Russian oil exploration and production company controlled by Lukoil. Priced at a hefty Libor plus 4.7 per cent, the deal was collateralised on export proceeds and enabled the financing of capital investment to develop new oilfields. Other medium-sized borrowers in the oil and gas sectors of CIS countries can expect to obtain much-needed foreign exchange financing thanks to similar structures.

For their part, large Russian borrowers have increasingly resorted to the capital markets, starting with export receivables-backed securitisation. Subsequently, many Russian issuers went for unsecured bond issues, which were very highly priced. For example, in 2001 Rosneft issued a US$150 million five-year bond priced to yield 13 per cent; the next year steel producer Magnitogorsk Metallurgical Combine (MMK) issued a three-year bond at a 10.10 per cent yield. Lead Russian names can still raise financing more cheaply from the bank markets on the back of export receivables structures, with a price difference in 2002 of perhaps 300 basis points, but bonds are more attractive for larger-scale financing needs, say in excess of US$300 million. They also have the advantage of paving the way with institutional investors for equity issues.

East Asia

There seem to be fewer examples of structured commodity finance deals arranged for borrowers in East Asia than in other parts of the world. Throughout the region, large producers in semi-industrialised countries have long raised bank loans or financing in the capital markets on a straight basis, while ECAs still tend to operate on the back of their traditional security structures.

In less developed countries of the region, the use of structured commodity finance techniques is also limited, in particular due to restrictive local regulations. As observed by one legal adviser: 'In Indonesia, for example, it is very difficult, if not impossible, to enforce security locally. Even if you can, the time delays you are looking at are years rather than months. This means that offshore security is the key to concluding deals in these cases, whether it be oil in tanks for instance, or more frequently assignment of receivables in offshore collection accounts'.[2] There is thus a potential for structured commodity finance to pick up in these countries, as in other parts of the world, once the proper conditions are in place.

Middle East

Many Middle Eastern countries are awash with cash and thus do not need foreign exchange financing. For instance, many contracts arranged for capital investment in the oil and gas industries of the Arabian Peninsula are still paid for in cash.

One country that has tapped the international bank markets on a serious scale is Iran, due primarily to the country's efforts at industrial diversification and expansion of its petroleum and petrochemical sectors. Most loans to Iran have been made in the form of multi-sourcing export credits arranged by a limited number of European banks, with particularly strong support from France's Coface and Italy's SACE. These deals were structured as buyers' credit granted through five nominated Iranian banks (Bank Mellat, Bank Melli, Bank Saderat, Bank Sepah and Bank Tejarat) and secured by a sovereign guarantee to finance imports of capital goods and services. In 2002, leading French banks Société Générale, Crédit Agricole Indosuez and BNP Paribas had in place a general framework agreement (GFA) with credit lines of US$1 billion. In May 2001, BNP Paribas signed with Bank Mellat a €182.2 million multi-sourcing export credit to finance the development by the Technip-Coflexip group of an ethylene unit at the ninth Olefin complex in Badar Asaluye for Pars Petrochemical Company, a wholly owned subsidiary of the National Petrochemical Company. This particular export credit was supported by a traditional sovereign guarantee and is one of a myriad of export financing deals arranged in just a few years for Iranian borrowers.

However, the Iranian market too has experienced a notable shift towards structured finance. This is partly in response to the dwindling interest on the part of continental

European ECAs in taking additional straight Iranian risk. As observed by a spokesman from Deutsche Bank in Frankfurt: 'There is a real competition because demand is more than bank capacity at the moment. The tendency is now for different forms of financing to take place, with classic export finance structures, backed by the ministry of finance, levelling out. The new sources of finance are structured export finance arrangements backed by export receivables. We also anticipate that project finance will come along in Iran shortly'.[3] In 2002, for example, Crédit Agricole Indosuez arranged a three-year US$500 million pre-export finance facility for the National Iranian Oil Company (NIOC). The beneficiary was the central bank, and the deal was secured by export contracts between NIOC and one major offtaker. However, some market participants are concerned about the fall in transaction pricing that results from a move to more structured forms of financing. In respect of the NIOC deal, for example, one banker observed that pricing was 'far too low for a three-year deal in Iran, despite NIOC's excellent record'.

In the area of finance, one of the most notable developments in the Middle East over recent decades has been the surge of Islamic banking. This has spurred the development of sophisticated financial engineering throughout the region, most particularly for project financing in Saudi Arabia and other Gulf states. The principles of Islamic banking and their relationship with structured commodity finance are discussed in the next chapter.

Latin America

After a slow start, due in part to the widespread availability of funds from US banks until the emerging market crises of the mid-1990s, structured commodity finance has boomed in Latin America. Nicholas Budd of Denton Wilde Sapte (Paris) observed in this regard that 'the most significant region today for structured commodity finance work in terms of active transactions is Latin America, and in particular Brazil'. However, he also added: 'I suspect that in 10 years' time Latin American exporters will be funded through credit-enhanced money market instruments and securitisation programmes, and the more sophisticated security techniques will be used more widely in Asia and Africa'.[4]

Less developed countries in Latin America where structured commodity finance could further develop centre on the Caribbean nations.

Africa

Structured commodity finance was pioneered in eastern and southern Africa in the mid-1980s. Today, however, with the exception of benchmark deals such as the recurrent Sonangol (Angola) and Cocobod (Ghana) transactions (and to a lesser extent loans made to newcomers such as SNPC, Republic of Congo), borrowers in Africa are not milking all the opportunities provided by structured commodity finance techniques. Amounts raised have been small, reflecting in part the changing production systems in the aftermath of massive privatisation and deregulation of the commodity sector. However, as observed by Jean-Louis Salas, deputy head of energy and commodities, African and the Middle East, at BNP Paribas in Paris: 'A number of countries such as Zambia, South Africa and Angola have opened up to structured financing. In the case of Angola, there are improvements in terms of the management capacity and the ability to deal with the legal and financial issues involved, and the perception of risk has improved'.[5]

1 'The collateral advantage', *Trade Finance,* November 2001.

2 Philip Badge, partner at Linklaters in Singapore, quoted in 'Lawyers win again', *Trade Finance,* February 2002.

3 'Iran expands credit lines' by Jonathan Bell, *Trade Finance,* May 2002.

4 'Lawyers win again', *Trade Finance,* February 2002.

5 'Cover story: Priorities are being reassessed at the IMF and the World Bank', *Trade Finance,* December 2001.

Chapter 23

Islamic banking

While Islamic banking originated in the Middle East, it has rapidly expanded to other parts of the world, such as Asia (Pakistan, Malaysia and Indonesia) and, more recently, Nigeria. Islamic banks or bank divisions are also based in the United States and in Europe to cater to the needs of Muslim clients worldwide.

General principles

Exhibit 23.1 describes the rules governing Islamic banking and its principal instruments. Next there is a brief discussion of applications to the commodity sector and areas where structured finance techniques can be consistent with Islamic banking philosophy.[1]

As it stresses the form that a financing takes, and not its economic function, Islamic finance is well-suited to financial engineering. If a certain objective cannot be reached by method A, it is perfectly legitimate to look for other ways. Islamic banks can use their own capital (including through syndications) or act like an investment bank and place a financing with Islamic (institutional) investors.

Use in commodity financing

Leading international law firms specialising in trade finance now typically have Islamic finance teams familiar with the legal documentation and tax implications of such contracts – for example, King & Spalding, Allen & Overy, Norton Rose and Clifford Chance. Likewise, Middle Eastern banks all have fully fledged Islamic banking capabilities, while many international western banks have developed specialised Islamic banking subsidiaries or divisions. This is the case, for instance, with HSBC Amanah Finance. Other western banks offering products that meet Islamic banking requirements include (in a non-exhaustive list) ABN Amro, ANZ, Barclays, BNP Paribas and Citibank.

Islamic banks or divisions generally have their own *sharia* boards consisting of reputable Islamic scholars (*ulama*) with expertise in economics or finance. These boards establish guidelines and review proposed transaction structures in detail, to determine whether they conform to Islamic precepts and can be permitted (*halal*). Other authorities in the area of Islamic banking include the Fiqh Academy of the Organisation of Islamic Conference, the Accounting and Auditing Organisation for Islamic Financial Institutions, and the Bahrain Monetary Authority. In April 2002 the International Islamic Financial Market (IIFM) was established in Bahrain following a joint effort between the central banks/monetary agencies of Bahrain, Brunei Darussalam, Indonesia, Malaysia, Sudan and the Islamic Development Bank (Jeddah), to create an environment to encourage active trading of *sharia*-compatible instruments among Muslim countries, and among both Islamic and non-Islamic financial institutions.

Exhibit 23.1

Islamic banking

Rooted in the Arab nationalism of the 1960s, and supported thereafter by a return to the orthodoxy of Islam in many Muslim communities worldwide, Islamic banking has become a large source of financing for a wide range of transactions. Based on Islamic jurisprudence (*Fiqh*), Islamic banking has moved from a theoretical concept to embrace today more than 200 banks and financial institutions operating in over 40 countries with an equivalent balance sheet total of about US$200 billion. Islamic banking is nowadays strongly driven by the pressure of 'Islamic funds' looking for 'clean' investments.

The most prominent feature of Islamic finance is that it does not permit the charging or payment of explicit interest rates, but this is by no means the only feature. Islam encourages people to use money in legitimate, profit-oriented ventures, but it discourages making money through '*riba*', a term that does not have a precise equivalent in English but includes such activities as usury or the explicit earning of interest. Islam recognises capital as a factor of production, as well as the time value of money. However, it does not accept that through the provision of capital one can make a prior or predetermined claim on a productive activity. The rules governing Islamic banking can be broadly summed up as follows:

- Any predetermined payment over and above the actual amount of principal is prohibited, including associated or indirect benefits.
- The lender must share in the profits or losses arising out of the enterprise for which the money was lent. Islam thus encourages the notion of higher risks and higher returns.
- Making money from money is not acceptable. In Islam, money represents purchasing power, which cannot be used to make more purchasing power (money) without undergoing the intermediate step of being used for the purchase of goods and services.
- Unnecessary risk (known as *gharar*), gambling and ignorance (*jahl*) are prohibited, but unavoidable risk, which is a normal part of any trade or investment activity, is acceptable. Options and futures are thus considered as un-Islamic. Some Islamic funds have nevertheless been actively trading on the London Metal Exchange, while countries such as Egypt, Iran and Kuwait do use futures and swaps. This is probably acceptable for hedging, as opposed to speculating, purposes. A number of transactions are also treated as exceptions to the principle of *gharar*.
- Investments should only support practices or products that are not forbidden, or even discouraged, by Islam.

In Islamic finance, the relation between financier and client is one between a seller and a buyer, or an agent and a principal, or an investor and an entrepreneur. It is not the lender–borrower relationship of western banking. Islamic banks around the world have devised many creative and profitable financial products based on the risk-sharing, profit-sharing principles of Islamic banking. Some of the financial techniques of Islamic banking applicable to the commodity sector are as follows:

- *Murabaha*. This involves the sale of a commodity at a price that includes a stated profit known to both the seller and the buyer. Under *murabaha* the Islamic bank would purchase the commodities in its own name and then sell them to the end-buyer at an agreed mark-up. The buyer would typically pay for the purchase through deferred payments. This technique is widely used to finance the trading of commodities. Because the bank takes title to the commodities, which entails a certain risk, its profit is seen as legitimate. *Murabaha* is one of the most common form of Islamic banking, mainly because is does not require the intimate knowledge of a client's business that other forms require.
- *Mudaraba*. This implies a contract between two parties whereby one party, called the *rabbal-mal* (beneficial owner or sleeping partner), would entrust money to the other party, called the *mudarib* (managing trustee or labour partner). For example, an Islamic bank would lend money to a company to finance an investment in return for a specific percentage of profits derived from such investment for a designated period. This share of the profits would provide principal repayment plus a profit. If the investment loses money, the bank, its depositors and the borrower would all jointly absorb the losses, thereby putting into practice the pivotal Islamic principle that the providers and users of capital should share risks and rewards.

(continued)

Exhibit 23.1 *(continued)*

Islamic Banking

- *Musharaka (musharaqah).* This is a partnership, normally of limited duration, formed to carry out a specific project (including the expansion of an existing investment). It is therefore similar to a western-style joint venture. *Musharaka* could be considered one of the purest forms of Islamic finance, since it strictly conforms to the underlying principle of sharing in, and benefiting from, risk. Profits are divided on a predetermined basis and any losses shared in proportion to the capital contribution.
- *Muqarada.* This allows a bank to float what are effectively Islamic bonds to finance a specific project. Investors who buy *muqarada* bonds take a share of the profits of the project being financed, but also share the risk of unexpectedly low profits, or even losses. They have no say in the management of the project and act as preferred (non-voting) shareholders.
- *Ijara wa iktina. Ijara* and *ijara wa iktina* are similar to, respectively, a lease and a hire-purchase arrangement whereby the lease agreement is combined with an undertaking by the client to purchase the leased goods at any time during the term of the lease, at an agreed price. The lessor/owner bears all the costs of the legally binding basic maintenance and replacement of durable parts. This technique requires that the leased items be used productively and in ways permitted by Islamic law.
- *Salam sale.* With *salam*, a buyer would pay in advance for a commodity deliverable on a specific date and at an agreed price. *Salam* is an exception to the rules governing the sale of a commodity under the *sharia*, which stipulates that the commodity being sold must already exist and be owned by, and in the physical possession of, the seller.
- *Istisna.* This is similar to *salam* but applies to goods that need to be manufactured (made-to-order items). Payment can normally be made at various stages of the process and the time for delivery of the product may not be fixed in advance.

Islamic banks also offer a full spectrum of fee-paid services, such as letters of credit and guarantees.

Sources: Al Rahji Banking and Investment Corp.; Islamic Development Bank; the Institute of Islamic Banking and Insurance; author's own research.

Exhibit 23.2

Simplified overview of the uses of Islamic financing instruments for trade and project financing purposes

Islamic financing form	*Trade finance*	*Project finance*
Murabaha	Buyer's credit (including import finance) for consumer, intermediary and capital goods	Mortgages and deferred payment obligations can be used as the under lying for securitisations
Mudaraba	Little used for trade purposes	Non-recourse project finance
Musharaka	Pre-export finance (including applications similar to back-to-back L/Cs) and financing of toll-processing	Equity investments
Muqarada	Buying *murabaha* trade paper	Buying Islamic bonds, or *ijara* paper
Ijara		Leasing
Salam	Campaign (production) credit and pre-export finance	
Istisna	Packing credit; some forms of working capital finance	Limited recourse project finance, eg, for pipelines, ships, plants machinery, independent power projects, etc

Source: UNCTAD.

Like traditional finance, Islamic finance can be applied to trade and project finance (see Exhibit 23.2). However, there are a number of restrictions, not only with respect to the commodities that can be financed (for example, gold and silver are excluded because they are seen as forms of money), but also with respect to the types of instruments that can be financed (for example, debt trading is by and large forbidden – even if the original debt is *halal,* it cannot be sold except for its face value; this means that practices such as forfaiting are not allowed). Barter trade is also not allowed. The main forms of trade finance are *murabaha* contract (similar to buyers' credit), *salam* (similar to a pre-financing) and certain uses of *istisna,* which allow banks to provide pre-export finance for goods for which firm orders have been established. Other forms can also be adapted for trade finance. As to project finance, *ijara* is an Islamic equivalent of leasing. Banks can act as *musharaka* equity partners or provide 'non-recourse' finance to an investor under *mudaraba,* receiving its principal and a share of the profits only if the investment project was successful. *Istisna* can also be used for project finance. Finally, banks can arrange the issuance of bonds for project financing purposes and place these bonds with Islamic investors under *muqarada.* Islamic banking techniques are increasingly being used to finance project finance operations, either in their entirety or alongside conventional financing. In Bahrain, for example, a US$1.7 billion project to consolidate the position of Aluminium Bahrain (ALBA) as one of the world's largest aluminium producers (bringing the ALBA plant's capacity to over 800,000 tonnes) included an Islamic finance tranche of US$250 million.

The following list details the various ways in which Islamic banking can fund the commodity sector and discusses briefly how these techniques can be reconciled with the principles of structured commodity finance.

- In the popular *murabaha* technique (which accounts for almost 80 per cent of all financing provided by Islamic institutions), the Islamic bank would take a principal's position by buying the commodity from a third party and re-selling it to its client with a mark-up (generally explicitly linked to prevailing interest rates), usually payable on a deferred basis. The mark-up is a function of the time between the date when the bank buys the commodity and the date when the buyer pays the bank. There is a serious problem with payment delays in *murabaha,* because it is impossible to charge extra interest on late payments. To overcome this problem, Pakistani banks have resorted to what is called mark-down, in effect giving time-limited rebates as an incentive for early payments. Alternatively, an extra mark-up can be included for delays. To ensure the validity of the *murabaha* sale, the commodity must come into the ownership and possession (physical or constructive) of the bank, so that it may assume all the related risks (although the commodity is of course shipped straight to the final buyer and the bank just retains the corresponding documents). The bank can include a disclaimer in the contract or limit its own liability by the indemnities received from the seller. This form of Islamic financing can accommodate sale through letters of credit as well as open account or cash against documents. In the event of default by its client, the bank has recourse to the commodity financed. In this regard, *murabaha* could be compared to inventory financing, provided of course that the bank retains title or adequate security in the commodity until it is paid in full. Alternatively, once ownership of the commodity is passed on to its client, the bank can take a security interest in onward sales by its client of the same or processed commodities as in receivables financing structures.

Otherwise, the bank would remain exposed to the risk of its client defaulting on its deferred payments. The Islamic bank can also ask for a local bank to provide a standby letter of credit as guarantee. While this technique is used mainly for short-term trade financing, the deferred payment element allows it to extend into the medium term. *Murabaha* can also be arranged on a revolving basis, as was the case, for instance, with a medium-sized syndicated revolving *murabaha* transaction arranged by the Islamic Investment Banking Unit of the United Bank of Kuwait (London) for a Saudi Arabian company to finance the purchase of raw materials. Deferred payments can also form the basis of securitisations. Finally, note the *istijrar* technique, recently introduced in Pakistan, which can be considered as a more complex variant of *murabaha.* Whereas in *murabaha* the bank's return is a simple percentage (mark-up), in *istijrar* the bank's return depends on the prices of the goods between delivery of the goods to the buyer and the maturity date of the *istijrar.*

- Non-recourse or limited-recourse forms of structured commodity finance, in which the bank has to bear some underlying performance risk, are particularly in line with Islamic banking philosophy. This is the case, for instance, with *mudaraba* when used to provide non-recourse project financing. In the field of trade finance, the *mudaraba* technique could be used for import financing. For instance, an Islamic bank would entrust money to a commodity buyer to finance the import and onward sale of commodities, and share in the profits (or losses). In this particular form of limited-recourse financing the bank would be exposed to some of the underlying performance risk. Such transactions, however, would be regarded as a form of structured commodity finance only to the extent that it is properly secured on the physical commodities, which per se Islamic banking does not prohibit. In fact, collateral-based structures based on the *rahn-adl* principle, for instance, are now widely used in secured Islamic financings throughout the Middle East. *Mudaraba* can also be applied in a syndicated loan agreement whereby participants in the loan give capital to the arranger to be used for a specified purpose.
- *Musharaka,* sometimes considered the purest form of Islamic finance, is similar to a western-style joint venture. *Musharaka* financing is risky for banks because they rely on the 'partner' to manage the business properly and banks therefore take a large portion of the profits. Banks therefore prefer to enter into *musharaka* transactions with large companies. For example, in 1991 Sarawak Shell raised several hundred million US dollars in *musharaka* finance for an oil-drilling operation. In practice, however, such international partners can be difficult to find and *musharaka* is therefore mostly used for very limited purposes, such as the procurement of goods and their onward sale, with or without processing. One application is comparable to a back-to-back letter of credit (L/C). The Islamic bank and an exporter would form a *musharaka* to pre-finance the commodities to be exported and paid by a foreign L/C opened in its favour. The exporter would undertake to comply with the terms of the L/C and to indemnify the Islamic bank for any losses that may arise if it fails to do so. Once payments under the L/C have been received, the *musharaka* would be extinguished. Alternatively, *musharaka* can also be used for financing imports: the Islamic bank would open an L/C in favour of the exporter and appoint the importer as its agent, with deferred payment terms for the importer. *Musharaka* is used as an underlying for securitisations for large projects.
- Other than in genuine projects, under *muqarada* funds of a group of investors could be pooled for investments in *murabaha* trade deals or in *ijara* financings.

- Investors in the commodity sector can also benefit from leases structured alongside the *ijara* form of Islamic banking. In 2001, legal firm Allen & Overy assisted a Malaysian company on a US$250 million palm-oil transaction involving a US$150 million issuance through First Global Sukuk Inc., a Labuan-incorporated SPV. The deal featured the issuance of *sukuk* evidencing an undivided ownership interest in a series of leases over various palm-oil plantations located in Malaysia. Payment on the leases was the primary source of payments to sukukholders. This was the first asset-backed Islamic financing featuring both *ijara* and *sukuk* principles, the first Islamic form of securitisation in Asia, and the first primary listing of Islamic securities. This listing paved the way for the subsequent listing of other *sharia*-compliant instruments on the Labuan stock exchange and the development of the Islamic financial market. However, although the structure of the above deal was complex, it would not fall into the structured commodity finance category in the absence of an adequate credit enhancement element for investors. In terms of security, apart from retaining ownership the Islamic bank can build in additional security through the payment by the lessee of an amount to be mutually agreed upon by the parties as a security deposit. To ensure timely payment, liquidated damages can also included in the *ijara* contract, specifying extra payments that need to be made for any day of delay. The bank would also require strong undertakings in the lease contract to give incentives to the lessee to properly manage and maintain the assets, especially since (unlike in a traditional lease) the lessee cannot be asked to continue paying under the lease if the property has been destroyed, or otherwise loses its economic value. Although the bank can require the lessee to purchase the leased property, this can be done only at a fair market value, which means that in practice the bank remains exposed to a substantial risk. Note that the bank can issue *ijara* bonds for placement with Islamic investors, as a way to refinance itself.
- Perhaps the technique more directly consistent with the tenets of structured commodity finance is the *salam* sale, whereby the bank is exposed to the performance risk of its client, as opposed to its payment risk. This is comparable to the structured prepayment (or forward sale) of commodities that do not exist yet but are to be produced (grown, mined, pumped and so on) and delivered at a later date. An advance would be made to the commodity owner against an agreement by the latter to deliver the commodities over a certain period. The basic purpose of this technique is to meet the needs of small-scale farmers who need money until harvest; it is thus particularly applicable to seasonal agricultural purchases, to buy seeds or any other input required by the commodity owner, including general working capital expenses. *Salam* is beneficial to the seller, who receives the price in advance, and to the buyer, as generally the price in *salam* is lower than the price in spot sales. However, there are strict conditions governing the validity of a *salam,* in particular (i) the price must be paid in full at the time of effecting the sale; and (ii) quality and quantity must be specified exactly – in effect, as noted by one market specialist: 'Precious stones cannot be sold on the basis of *salam,* because every piece of precious stones is normally different from the other either in its quality or in its size or weight and their exact specification is not generally possible';[2] (iii) the sale cannot be restricted to a particular identified commodity that may no longer be available at the time of delivery; (iv) the quantity of the commodity must be specified exactly; and (v) the exact date of delivery must be stipulated. Note that, except for the last condition, which may be difficult to strictly abide to, the conditions for the validity of *salam* would also improve the security structure of a prepayment transaction.

Salam can be used for direct forward contracts between buyer and seller. Banks would generally use two parallel *salam* to avoid having to take possession of the commodity. In terms of security structure, although the bank does not have ownership of the commodities until delivery has taken place, it is allowed to require security from the seller, for instance in the form of a guarantee or mortgage. Moreover, in case of a delivery default, the borrower may be asked to deliver the same commodity by purchasing it from the market, or to reimburse the advance.

- Finally, note the *istisna* technique, whereby a bank (or any buyer) can order a specified quantity and quality of a manufactured good, deliverable in the future on or before an agreed date. Payment can be made in one lump sum or in instalments (corresponding to work in progress), and at any time up to or after the time of delivery. The manufacturer can use these payments for acquisition and processing of raw material, and general working-capital expenses, as well as marketing of finished goods. Tenors typically extend into the medium term. An *istisna* contract can be used, for example, for alumina or sugar tolling. As with a *salam* sale, banks often use back-to-back (parallel) transactions. In terms of security, the bank can request a performance bond from the manufacturer and some sort of payment guarantee from the end-buyer (such as a standby L/C). If required by the supplier of raw materials, payments can also be supported by letters of credit. The bank could also combine an *istisna* for the construction phase with an *ijara* (lease) contract to enable the operating company to pay in instalments after delivery of the assets. This combination was used, for example, in a 1998 deal for a US$77million project financing for the Bakri Group to construct two chemical tankers, to be chartered by Saudi Basic Industries Corporation. The first tranche of the financing consisted of disbursements under an *istisna,* to be replaced by an *ijara wa iktina* on delivery.

With Islamic banking, banks need to earn their profit not simply because they make money available, but because they take a production- or trade-related risk. Islamic banking and structured commodity finance have a common purpose: to make a particular commercial transaction possible thanks to sophisticated financial engineering. The need to do so stems, in the first case, from the necessity to make the transaction legal *vis-à-vis sharia* law and, in the second case, from the necessity to bring certain credit-enhancement elements to lenders. There is nothing in the tenets of structured commodity finance that should a priori prevent its techniques from being consistent with the requirements of Islamic banking. Similarly, with the right credit-enhancement elements, most forms of Islamic banking could qualify as structured commodity finance. On the other hand, according to the precepts of Islamic banking, the Islamic bank is entitled to a portion of the profits of a particular transaction only to the extent that it assumes risk. If the bank takes no risks, it can only charge for its administrative costs. Thus the elusive watertight structured commodity finance transaction that would eliminate all risks could not be reconciled with the principles underlying Islamic banking.

---

1 Some material in this section is based on extracts from UNCTAD's training course on Islamic finance.

2 http://www.alrajhibank.com.sa/instruments-salam.htm, http://www.isdb.org, http://www.islamic-banking.com.

Chapter 24

Applications: conclusions

The range of applications of structured commodity finance techniques is undoubtedly expanding. Over recent years these techniques have served nearly all commodities produced or extracted on all continents, and they are now capable of providing finance to all participants in the commodity chain. In particular, tighter and more creative structures have led structured commodity finance into the medium term (now a common feature), and have enabled second-tier producers to obtain hard-currency financing on attractive terms and conditions. These techniques are also increasingly being used by regional development banks.

It can also reasonably be assumed that structured commodity finance techniques have been used more than is currently known. As noted by Malcolm Watson, deputy general manager of KBC's trade finance unit: 'Many structured trade deals remain hidden because of the banks' need to retain their competitive strategies.' Borrowers also do not like to confess to the granting of security to their lenders, while in many cases insurance cover cannot be publicly divulged. Also, as noted by David Miller of the structured finance syndication group of KBC: 'The players in the structured trade and structured commodity finance market are very innovative, and at times banks are reluctant to divulge structures to the market in order to maintain their structuring edge'.[1]

One conclusion we can draw from looking at the application of structured commodity finance deals over recent years is that they clearly do pave the way for eventual access to the capital markets for debt and equity issues. As observed by John McNamara in respect of prime Russian borrowers: 'Increasingly, the banks are actually lending to a corporate, and using the security structure as a fall back position, rather than expecting to get paid out of the export proceeds. [It is] only a matter of time before bond issues become the principal source of debt finance for big Russian borrowers'.[2] For their part, smaller and younger companies in the commodities sector should probably consider the private equity and concessional lending alternatives discussed in Chapters 20 and 21 before turning to the techniques of structured commodity finance that require a consistent track record.

Gauging the impact on structured commodity finance of the Enron and WorldCom scandals, and creative accounting in general, is difficult. On the one hand, structures that are essentially serving tax or accounting benefits will certainly be looked at with more caution in the future. On the other, structures built around commodity ownership and flows, which essentially serve as risk mitigants, should not be negatively affected by the current thrust in the market for clean deals. On the contrary, the true commercial transactions underlying structured commodity finance might even give lenders more comfort about the numbers reported in the borrower's financial statements.

Finally, the economic slowdown that began in the early 2000s has led to a flight to quality, which has meant tighter structures for high-risk borrowers or projects and even more opportunities for structured commodity finance deals. As noted by one market professional: 'During 2001, we have seen an increased focus on transaction fundamentals: credit quality, shareholder quality, hard currency generation, political and credit risk mitigation, supplier quality'.[3] However, emerging markets are cyclical and structures can be expected to loosen up. Likewise, high commodity prices at the beginning of 2003 have meant lower financing needs in general for the commodity sector. This could result in a shift to smaller or higher-risk borrowers by structured finance banks eager for business opportunities.

---

1 'Keeping the deals flowing' by Jonathan Bell, *Trade Finance*, November 2001.

2 'Onward and upwards' by Simon Pirani, *Trade Finance*, April 2002.

3 Jonathan Joseph-Horne, associate director, distribution and risk advisory at Barclays Capital in London, quoted in 'Syndicated loans' by Jonathan Bell, *Trade Finance*, December 2001.

Part V

Final notes

Chapter 25

Final notes

Banks rarely take credit risk without requiring some security, even if only a positive covenant to maintain existing activities. When borrowers based in emerging countries seek to finance operations in the commodity sector, the security required by lenders tends to be quite onerous – for example, a mortgage on fixed assets or partial cash collateral – unless, of course, the financing is arranged on a structured basis.

As observed by Lamon Rutten of UNCTAD: 'Many of the more innovative financings of the last decade were based on the recognition of a receivable where, earlier, financiers had not identified any'.[1] The techniques of structured commodity finance discussed in Parts II and III rely on a security structure that is both acceptable to lenders and less restrictive for borrowers. Lenders trade off the payment risk of borrowers for their performance risk, which is more controllable and more immune to country risk. For borrowers, the security structure is essentially a mere formalisation of existing commercial flows and relations, and thus is not excessively painful.

Structured transactions are designed on an ad hoc basis and require the identification of every risk involved in the proposed transaction, and their mitigation through third-party credit enhancement (buyers' payment in offshore escrow accounts, performance bond, commodity price risk hedge and so on). The result is that high-risk borrowers can obtain financing on better terms and conditions than under comparable alternatives. By linking the financial obligations of the borrower to its commercial activities and the risks thereof, structured commodity finance treats the company as whole. This holistic approach is notably supported by a due diligence process that sometimes resembles a strengths, weaknesses, opportunities and threats (SWOT) analysis typically used in the area of strategy and psychology, rather than in a traditional financial statements analysis.

There are few prerequisites for the use of such techniques, except perhaps a reliable performance track record on the part of the borrower, but the due diligence is time-consuming and thus expensive. Also, as calculated by Geoffrey Wynne, a partner in law firm Denton Wilde Sapte, the success rate of structured commodity finance deals is only about one in four.[2] Even with a good structure, timely repayment still requires a tight monitoring of the underlying elements of the transaction, and relies on the goodwill and honesty of the borrower and the other parties involved.

In terms of its applications, structured commodity finance is an effective tool for providing attractive short- and medium-term bank financing to medium-sized commodity exporters in high-risk countries. Its techniques are increasingly extending to other lenders (for example, multilateral banks, capital market debt and trading companies) and now support a large range of financing needs, as the separation line between trade, commodities, export and project financing is thinning. Moreover, by fostering tighter control of commercial operations, good corporate governance and transparent borrowing practices, while strengthening direct relationships with foreign banks, structured commodity finance has paved the way for capital market issues by companies operating in the commodities sector of emerging countries.

This gradual emancipation from traditional lending is particularly useful for longer-term financing because of the provisioning requirements faced by banks. This will remain the case until the new Basle II Accord is implemented by all primary banks around the globe – scheduled to start in 2004 – as it finally provides for favourable treatment of the credit enhancement element provided by the basic techniques of structured commodity finance. To encourage bank regulators and supervisors to effectively take into account these techniques as credit risk mitigants, more academic research is definitely needed to determine the impact of structured commodity finance on the various aspects of default risk. Such research should be strongly encouraged, while recognising its inherent difficulties due to the lack of standardisation of structured commodity finance transactions.

Structured commodity finance should be actively supported by donors, given their steady withdrawal from commercial financing to focus on poverty alleviation in emerging countries. Structured commodity finance has indeed proved its ability to provide financing of last resort in times of economic, financial or political crises, in particular in the aftermath of the terrorist attacks of September 2001 and in the concurrent worldwide economic slowdown. In that sense, structured commodity finance is counter-cyclical. Its techniques also enable lenders to enter the production cycle earlier and thus add more value to the commodity sectors of emerging countries. Moreover, structured commodity finance makes it possible to arbitrage between low international interest rates and high local ones, to the benefit of emerging country borrowers.

Donors should emulate initiatives taken by UNCTAD, whose relentless efforts to provide advice and set up pilot programmes have enabled the spread of structured finance techniques in every corner of the world. There should also be more support for the construction of infrastructure projects relevant to performance-based financings, such as inland roads, port facilities and warehouses. Of course, donors should also reconsider obligations attached to multilateral lending that might impede structured deals, such as negative pledge covenants.

To conclude on a simpler note, it is to be hoped that companies operating in the commodity sector will be convinced of the benefits and will add structured commodity finance to the range of their possible financing alternatives. While a particular financing need may be better met with other forms of financing, the due diligence required to assess the opportunity for, and design of, a structured finance transaction has invaluable and lasting benefits for a company, notably to know itself better.

---

[1] 'The under-explored potential of SCF' by Lamon Rutten, *Trade Finance,* April 2002.

[2] 'The law and the profit', *Trade Finance,* April 2000.